The Pragmatics of Propositional Attitude Reports

Current Research in the Semantics/Pragmatics Interface

Series Editors:
K.M. Jaszczolt, University of Cambridge, UK
K. Turner, University of Brighton, UK

Related books

GEURTS	*Presuppositions and Pronouns (CRiSPI vol. 3)*
JASZCZOLT & TURNER	*Contrastive Semantics and Pragmatics (2-Volume Set)*
JASZCZOLT	*Discourse, Beliefs and Intentions (CRiSPI vol. 2)*
KOERNER & ASHER	*Concise History of the Language Sciences*
LAMARQUE	*Concise Encyclopedia of Philosophy of Language*
MEY	*Concise Encyclopedia of Pragmatics*
TURNER	*The Semantics/Pragmatics Interface from Different Points of View (CRiSPI vol. 1)*

Related journals

Journal of Pragmatics
Editor: Jacob Mey

Language & Communication
Editors: Roy Harris and Talbot J. Taylor

Language Sciences
Editor: Nigel Love

Lingua
Editors: John Anderson and Neil Smith

Free specimen copies of journals available on request

For further information on the CRiSPI series and for details of how to submit a proposal go to:
www.elsevier.nl/locate/series/crispi

THE PRAGMATICS OF PROPOSITIONAL ATTITUDE REPORTS

Edited by **K.M. Jaszczolt**
University of Cambridge, UK

2000
ELSEVIER

Oxford – Amsterdam – Lausanne – New York – Shannon – Singapore – Tokyo

ELSEVIER SCIENCE Ltd
The Boulevard, Langford Lane
Kidlington, Oxford OX5 1GB, UK

First edition 2000

British Library Cataloguing in Publication Data
A catalogue record from the British Library has been applied for.

Library of Congress Cataloging in Publication Data

ISBN: 0 08 0436358

∞ The paper used in this publication meets the requirements of ANSI/NISO Z39.48-1992 (Permanence of Paper).
Printed in The Netherlands.

Current Research in the Semantics/Pragmatics Interface (CRiSPI)

The aim of this series is to focus upon the relationship between semantic and pragmatic theories for a variety of natural language constructions. The boundary between semantics and pragmatics can be drawn in many various ways, the relative benefits of each gave rise to a vivid theoretical dispute in the literature in the last two decades. As a side-effect, this variety has given rise to a certain amount of confusion and lack of purpose in the extant publications on the topic.

This series provides a forum where the confusion within existing literature can be removed and the issues raised by different positions can be discussed with a renewed sense of purpose. The editors intend the contributions to this series to take further strides towards clarity and cautious consensus.

List of Contributors

Bach, K., *San Francisco State University* (Chs. 6, 7).
Bezuidenhout, A., *University of South Carolina* (Ch. 8).
Clapp, L., *Illinois Wesleyan University* (Ch. 4).
Cresswell, M.J., *Victoria University of Wellington* (Ch. 5).
Jaszczolt, K.M., *University of Cambridge* (Chs. 1, 9).
Ludlow, P., *State University of New York, Stony Brook* (Ch. 3).
Schiffer, S., *New York University* (Ch. 2).
Smith, D.W., *University of California, Irvine* (Ch. 10).

Contents

CHAPTER 1

Introduction
Belief Reports and Pragmatic Theory: The State of the Art

K.M. Jaszczolt

Contents

PRAGMATICS OF PROPOSITIONAL ATTITUDE REPORTS
Current Research in the Semantics/Pragmatics Interface, Vol. 4
Edited by K.M. Jaszczolt

1. Propositional content and substitutivity

Reporting on people's beliefs gives rise to many problems for philosophers, linguists, and average language users. First, the reporter may not be in a position to assess the extent of the believer's knowledge about the object of the belief and hence be unable to decide how to phrase the report. *A fortiori*, the reporter may misconstrue the evidence. For example, when the believer says (1), the reporter has to assess whether the believer knows what he is talking about or rather repeats a half-digested proposition (see Sperber (1985, 1996) on semi-propositional beliefs).

(1) Red giants become white dwarfs.

A belief can easily be ascribed in the presence of evidence that the believer knows who he is talking about, but it can also be ascribed in spite of the reporter's doubt as to this familiarity, and even in spite of the evidence that the believer does not know what/who he is talking about. Belief ascription can also be based on non-linguistic evidence, e.g., (2) can be reported about somebody arriving at a Spanish holiday resort with winter coats in his luggage.

(2) He believes that it is cold in southern Spain.

Finally, the believer may be referentially mistaken and use an incorrect name or description of the individual. For instance, the believer may announce (3), having Bernard J. Smith in mind.

(3) Bernard J. Ortcutt is an honest citizen.

The reporter has to assess the validity of all this contextual information before constructing her report in order to make the report communicative in a conversation.

Traditionally, propositional attitude sentences have been regarded as ambiguous between the transparent and the opaque reading. Sentence (4) acquires two semantic interpretations that correspond to the wide and narrow scope of the existential quantifier, as in (4a) and (4b).

(4) Max believes that the king of France is bald.

(4a) $\exists x\ (\mathrm{KoF}(x)\ \&\ \forall y\ (\mathrm{KoF}(y) \supset y = x)\ \&\ \mathrm{Bel_M}\ \mathrm{Bald}\ (x))$

(4b) $\mathrm{Bel_M}\ \exists x\ (\mathrm{KoF}(x)\ \&\ \forall y\ (\mathrm{KoF}(y) \supset y = x)\ \&\ \mathrm{Bald}\ (x))$

By using (4a), the reporter ascribes to Max a belief about a particular, known individual (*de re*) and by using (4b) she states that Max believes in the existence of such an individual (*de dicto*). However, there is more to this ambiguity than the logical forms capture. If Max is referentially mistaken, the reporter may use (4c), substituting the correct description (or name) for the object of the belief.

(4c) $\exists x\ (\mathrm{KoS}(x)\ \&\ \forall y\ (\mathrm{KoS}(y) \supset y = x)\ \&\ \mathrm{Bel_M\ Bald}(x))$

$\mathrm{Bel_M}$ stands for 'Max believes that', 'KoF' for 'the king of France' and 'KoS' for 'the king of Sweden' (see also Neale, 1990; Larson and Segal, 1995; Russell, 1905, 1919). Leaving the development of this tri-partite distinction aside, we can observe that the strict ambiguity does not hold. A prediction can be drawn that the two readings of belief reports, *de re* and *de dicto*, do not correspond directly to the two scopes taken by the existential quantifier. There is more to the distinction than the logical forms of (4) reveal. The interpretations of (4) are, to a certain extent, pragmatic, and this pragmatic information has to be acknowledged in the adequate theory of propositional attitudes. Perhaps the *de re/de dicto* distinction is itself pragmatic, just as Donnellan's (1966) referential/attributive distinction of definite descriptions proved to be a duality of their use and so, at most, a pragmatic ambiguity (see Jaszczolt, forthcoming).

Semantic problems with attitude ascription begin with the content of the expression used to refer in non-extensional contexts. In order to preserve compositional semantics, it has been suggested, among others, that one has to establish under what mode of presentation (sense, guise, way of givenness) the object referred to is known to the believer. For instance, (3) may or may not be regarded as equal to (5) in its semantic (or wider informational) content, depending on the mode of presentation.

(5) The man in the brown hat is an honest citizen.

The speaker of (3) may not consent to believing (5) because he may not know the individual under the guise expressed in (5). So, the core problem with belief ascription amounts to what we take reference to be in non-extensional contexts, and in particular to the use of the notion of reference in the semantics of propositional attitude sentences of the form in (6).

(6) *A* believes that *B* ϕs.

Substitutivity of coreferential expressions does not hold in these contexts, at least according to common-sense judgement. This failure of the principle of substitutivity suggests that we have to either abandon compositional semantics or incorporate contextual information in our semantic theory. Various solutions have been suggested. First, the role of reference in intensional contexts is taken by sense (Frege, 1892, 1918-19). Next, the *that*-clause can be said to refer to a sentence rather than a proposition (see Bach (1997, this volume) for a discussion). Quine (1956) postulated degrees of intensions for quantifying into such contexts. More recently, there have been various proposals that use the idea of mode of presentation and contextually determined type of mode of presentation, stemming out of the hidden-indexical theory (Schiffer, 1977, 1987, 1992, 1996, this volume; see also Ludlow, 1995, 1996), developed also in the idea of Crimmins and Perry's (1989) and Crimmins's (1992) 'notion', which is an unarticulated constituent of the proposition (see also Bach, 1993, this volume; Reimer, 1995). There is also ample literature that focuses on constructive criticism of these dominant solutions (Clapp, 1995, this volume; Salmon, 1986; Donnellan, 1990; Soames, 1987; Recanati, 1993, 1996). For example, the neo-Russellian approaches (e.g., Salmon, 1986; Soames, 1987, 1995) deny the contribution of the mode of presentation to the semantics of attitude reports: the semantic content of a sentence is a singular proposition (see also Bach, 1997, this volume). In addition, Richard (1990, 1995) suggests the indexicality of the verb 'believe', making the verb contextually sensitive. Larson and Ludlow (1993) and Ludlow (this volume) propose 'interpreted logical forms' or composites of linguistic forms and extralinguistic objects. Finally, for indirect speech with the predicate 'say' there is Davidson's (1968-9) paratactic account where a demonstrative refers to an utterance (for a discussion see Cresswell, this volume). But some form of the mode of presentation, however finely-grained it eventually turns out to be, seems to be acknowledged by all parties to the debate, either on the semantic or the pragmatic level. The question that remains to be answered is the degree of contribution of the mode of presentation to the proposition expressed (see, e.g., Bezuidenhout, 1996, this volume vs. Recanati, 1993, 1996).

2. Semantics and pragmatics of propositional attitude reports

Propositional attitudes, represented most prominently by belief reports, have been the object of inner-theoretical disputes for several decades. It is only recently that these theories are beginning to form a coherent and diaphanous paradigm. This has been engendered by the current discussion on contextualism and the various forms and strengths contextualism can take. To put it crudely, more and more responsibility for the puzzles with belief ascription has been shifted from semantics to pragmatics, only to return, in one form or other, to the semantics as 'extras' that contribute to the semantic representation of the proposition. The tendency can be observed both in philosophy and in linguistics and is in line with the ongoing trend to see the study of language use as an important component of the study of sentence meaning. This tendency is not completely new; it can be traced to Strawson (1950), some scattered remarks in Grice (1978, see Levinson, 1988, 1995) and even to continental phenomenologists (Brentano, 1874; Husserl, 1900-01) whose ideas permeated through Frege (1892, 1918-19) to the plethora of British analytical accounts of sense (or the more personalised mode of presentation) and its contribution to the proposition (see Dummett, 1991; Jaszczolt, 1996, 1997).

In addition to the philosophical approaches listed here, linguistic considerations produced a number of solutions concerning the form in which pragmatic information can play a role in the semantic content of an utterance. Gricean original views have evolved into several trends such as the neo-Gricean approach (Levinson, 1988, 1995; Horn, 1988, 1989), broadly, relevance-theoretic (Sperber and

Wilson, 1986; Carston, 1988; Kempson, 1986) and its more radical partner of *impliciture* as implicit constituents of what is said (Bach, 1987a, 1994a, 1994b, this volume), as well as the semanticization of the output of some inferences in Discourse Representation Theory (Kamp, 1990, in progress; Kamp and Reyle, 1993; Jaszczolt, 1998, forthcoming). This progress from inner-theoretic concerns about intensional contexts and truth-preserving substitutivity to a more global concern with the role of context in semantic theory requires a new type of paradigm which emphasises the compatibility of these concerns and their common aim. This collection has been prepared with this objective in mind. First, it presents the extent to which semantic representation requires supplementing by pragmatics; next, it offers several suggestions on how this interface is supposed to work.

It is in the debate over the way the proposition is taken by the holder of the attitude that the practical and theoretical problems with attitude ascription meet. The exact informational (and semantic) contribution of the believer's knowledge of the referent to the proposition expressed is a condensed formulation of the main preoccupation of propositional-attitude theorists. Naturally, the standpoints vary from endorsing singular propositions through denying that the proposition expressed specifies the content of the belief (see Bach, this volume), to allocating semantic status to some aspects of this knowledge. For example, for this purpose, Schiffer proposed a hidden-indexical theory which is based on the premise that believing is a three-place relation among the believer, the structured proposition, and the mode of presentation under which x believes p. The mode of presentation of the proposition is determined by the modes of presentation of the objects and properties and their position in the structure of the sentence, in agreement with Frege and the principle of compositionality. Sentence (7) acquires the logical form as in (8), where Φ^*m is a type of mode of presentation, i.e. a property of modes of presentation determined by the context (Schiffer, 1992, p. 503, this volume; see also defence by Ludlow, 1995, 1996, this volume).

(7) Ralph believes that Fido is a dog.

(8) $(\exists m)\,(\Phi^*m \;\&\; \mathrm{B}(\mathrm{Ralph}, \langle \mathrm{Fido, doghood} \rangle, m))$

Postulating a device such as types of modes of presentation is only the tip of an iceberg. It has to be determined next what information falls under Φ^*m, whether there are any formal constraints on the context-dependence of Φ^*m, and in what sense is Φ^*m semantic and in what pragmatic.

A more global rephrasing of the problem takes the form of the contextualism/anti-contextualism debate. Contextualism allows for the contextual information to contribute to the propositional form of an utterance. Anti-contextualism regards contextual information as implicatures that function in addition to the propositional form in the process of utterance interpretation (see Recanati, 1994). Now, the assignment of reference in attitude ascription, and the resolution of reference in the interpretation of belief reports, may require this contextual information. The core of the issue is whether this information is also required for the truth-conditional representation of propositional attitude sentences. One dominant standpoint seems to be that the truth-conditional representation requires some context-dependent resolution of reference in belief reports, although it does not require fully spelled-out modes of presentation. Modes of presentation are overly fine-grained for semantic purposes. Naturally, this representation requires indexical resolution, lexical and syntactic disambiguation, and, generally, may require other completion and expansion of the proposition expressed (see Bach, 1987a; Levinson, 1988; Recanati, 1981, 1993, 1996).

All in all, this collection aims at answering two questions that follow from this state-of-the-art:

(i) What is the type and extent of pragmatic information that contributes to specifying what the speaker believes?

and

(ii) What is the relation between the pragmatic information and the semantic (propositional) representation of attitude expressions?

Answers to these questions are attempted in all the contributions to this collection, on the level of truth-conditional semantics, linguistic semantics (Carston, 1988, 1998), and macropragmatics (Mey, 1993), including intentions and goals of actions. Since Grice's seminal work on implicature, it has been widely acknowledged that there are two types of semantics: linguistic semantics which is an output of grammar, and truth-conditional semantics which incorporates some degree of pragmatic analysis of utterances (Grice, 1989; Levinson, 1988; Sperber and Wilson, 1995, p. 256; Carston, 1988, p. 178). It is this degree that is subject to debate.

Various problems engendered by attitude ascription cannot be clearly separated. This collection corroborates the claim that the semantics/pragmatics interface in propositional attitude research has to be approached from these three levels in order to result in a comprehensive picture. The aspects of pragmatic information that contribute to the propositional form have to be exhausted in order to render an adequate, coherent and diaphanous overview.

Now, if attitude contexts are at all ambiguous, they are either semantically or pragmatically ambiguous. Semantic ambiguity is the duality of logical form strengthened by a requirement of the logical independence of these forms (Kempson, 1979), whereas pragmatic ambiguity is a built-in ambiguity of use. Both approaches are discussed in this collection. However, the ambiguity itself can be denied altogether. It is viable to hold that there is one semantic representation which is either general, underspecified (here the literature is ample, see, e.g., Atlas, 1989; Carston, 1988; van Deemter and Peters, 1996) or takes the form of the default interpretation (Levinson, 1995; Jaszczolt, 1992, 1993, 1997, 1998, 1999, forthcoming).

As Levinson (1995, p. 109–110) claims, there is a level of utterance-type meaning, default interpretation, which should be placed between sentence meaning and speaker's intentions. General expectations concerning the world give rise to default inferences (Levinson, 1995, p. 93). The contextually appropriate interpretation is arrived at through the process of pragmatic inference from the underspecified semantic form or the default semantic representation respectively.

The postulate of speaker's background knowledge (see, e.g., Smith, this volume) comes in handy at this point. Modes of presentation, for example, are not always known to the hearer and not always relevant. However, some aspects of the way in which the referent is known to the speaker may prove to function as constituents of the proposition expressed. Now, to quote Richard,

> "What counts as faithful representation varies from context to context with our interests and expectations. Context places certain restrictions on what can represent what." Richard (1990, p. 3).

Intentions belong to these relevant contextual factors. Richard leaves the problem without proposing a theory of intentions. This is where other parties to the debate come in (Bach, 1984, 1987a, 1987b, 1992; Smith, 1989, this volume; Jaszczolt, 1997, this volume), developing, in various not unrelated ways, the idea of communicative-informative intention. This is one of the macropragmatic aspects discussed above.

3. Summary of the papers

All the contributions have been invited especially for this collection and, save for one exception, have not been previously published. Kent Bach's 'Do Belief Reports Report Beliefs?' appeared in *Pacific Philosophical Quarterly* 78 (1997) and is reprinted here with permission from Blackwell Publishers. It is included because it originated as a contribution to this volume and constitutes a sequel to his other contribution, 'A Puzzle about Belief Reports'.

The content of the volume is as follows. Stephen Schiffer discusses modes of presentation and types of modes of presentation in the hidden-indexical theory and compares the problems of this theory with those facing Recanati's proposal of the availability hypothesis and quasi-singular propositions. In particular, he points out the logical-form problem, the difficulty with applying the theory to propositional speech acts and with attributing intentions to speakers that would pertain to however coarsely defined modes of presentation. He stresses the advantages of Recanati's approach (which he calls the indexical theory) over the hidden-indexical one. Peter Ludlow defends the applicability of so-called Interpreted Logical Forms to the Paderewski-type puzzle, i.e. to the instances where sentences of the form 'A believes that B ϕs' and 'A believes that B doesn't ϕ' are both true descriptions of A's beliefs. The theory assumes that semantic values are attached to the components of the *that*-clause. The advantage of this move is joining together the linguistic expression and its semantic value so as to avoid postulating intensional objects. By rejecting claims to psychological reality of ILFs, Ludlow establishes the status of the theories of ILFs as explanatory of how the reporter copes with the acquired information about the holder of the belief, for the benefit of the hearer. This processing of the original belief is taken to involve a tacit theory of belief, a tacit theory of the goals of belief ascription, and a tacit theory of the logistics of belief ascription. Lenny Clapp argues against sentential compositionality and proposes instead a so-called discourse holistic approach to attitude ascription. He founds it on his criticism of the use of the concept of 'ways of thinking' of an individual and stresses the role of the discourse environment, which he illustrates in the framework of Discourse Representation Theory. Max Cresswell sheds some new light on Davidson's paratactic account of *that*-clauses. He analyses the relation of 'samesaying' and poses a question as to whether samesaying is determined by the semantic theories of the language(s) involved in the original expression and its report in *oratio obliqua*. The problem leads to an attempt to classify the phenomenon of samesaying as semantic or pragmatic. If it is semantic, then a serious difficulty ensues for Davidson's account. He discusses Davidson's claim that samesaying is an unanalysed notion rather than part of the theory of meaning for a language and concludes that samesaying is a pragmatic phenomenon. Kent Bach sets off to reject the idea that *that*-clauses specify the content of a belief, which he calls a Specification Assumption. Instead, the *that*-clause in a belief report merely characterizes something a person believes. As a result, a belief report can be true even if the holder of the belief does not believe the proposition expressed by the *that*-clause. The problem, however, is to specify the relation between the proposition expressed by the *that*-clause and the various beliefs to which it corresponds. In the follow-up to this paper, Bach further develops the thesis that belief reports merely describe (or characterize) rather than report (or specify) beliefs. He points out the weaknesses of some dominant accounts of attitude contexts and develops a descriptivist view introduced in the previous paper according to which what we believe is not a proposition expressed by a *that*-clause. What exactly the belief would have to be for the report to be true can only be said having taken context into consideration. Belief sentences are said to be semantically incomplete: their truth conditions are context-dependent. Hence, the substitution of coreferential expressions can sometimes make a difference to the truth conditions, while on other occasions it does not. Similarly, one and the same referring expression may be completed differently in different contexts, which explains the illusion of contradictory beliefs. Anne Bezuidenhout focuses on the pragmatic aspects of attitude reports, i.e. on the components of meaning that are not semantically encoded. She endorses the relevance-theoretic approach of Sperber and Wilson and utilizes their ideas of (1) the interpretive resemblance between the content of a belief and the proposition expressed by the *that*-clause, and (2) the conceptual-procedural distinction, in order to account for the pragmatics of attitude reports. She suggests that *that*-clauses encode procedural information, i.e. they encode procedures, instructions as to how the expression is to be processed. She proposes to deal with the problem of different modes of presentation of a referent through the concept of pragmatic adjustment such as loosening, enrichment and transfer. Finally, she compares and contrasts this account with Recanati's proposal of some cognitive processes involved in entertaining attitude reports. Kasia Jaszczolt distinguishes three readings of belief reports which she calls *de re*, *de dicto*$_1$ and *de dicto proper* and argues for the default status of the *de re* interpretation. This reading is supported by the Default Semantics that allows for the contribution of intentions (and in particular the referential intention) to the semantic representation. The default reading, as well as the departures from the default, are independently supported by the intentionality of mental states. She proposes a mild, default-based version of contextualism whereby the departures from the default interpretation are guided by the context and in particular by the 'degree' to which the referential intention is present. The three readings make up a scale of degrees of intentionality which can also be interpreted as degrees of fineness of grain of the referent's mode of presentation. Last but not least, David Woodruff Smith discusses the role of a background of basic beliefs and practices that underlie our intentional activities, including reports on attitudes. He emphasizes the role of intentionality of mental acts for the analysis of propositional attitudes, as well as speech acts of reporting on them and sentences expressing these acts. Since attitude reports are the public-language renderings of our private attitudes, the semantics and pragmatics of attitude reports are, by analogy, founded on phenomenological reflection. The background that contributes to the speaker's meaning turns out to include assumptions about our psychology and culture, and even varying degrees of metaphysical commitments. All these constituents of the background have to be accounted for in the pragmatics of propositional attitude reports.

The papers have one common objective, which is the division of labour between semantics and pragmatics in accounting for propositional attitude reports. The different angles and levels of analysis from which the problem is approached by the contributors constitute the main strength of the collection. Although no clearly superior theory or paradigm emerges, the volume makes public some new ideas on the form and degree of contribution of pragmatic processes to the meaning of propositional attitude reports. Grice once observed about presupposition:

> "In recent years, linguists have made it increasingly difficult for philosophers to continue to keep their eyes glued to a handful of stock examples of (alleged) presupposition, such as the king of France's baldness and the inquiry whether you have left off beating your wife." Grice (1981, p. 195).

A similar phenomenon is happening with propositional attitude research, as far as the type and scope of relevant problems are concerned. Progress in pragmatic research necessitates redrawing the boundaries between semantics and pragmatics in propositional attitude research. This volume gives evidence of this progress.

References

Atlas, J.D. (1989), *Philosophy Without Ambiguity: A Logico-Linguistic Essay*, Clarendon Press, Oxford.

Bach, K. (1984), *Default reasoning: Jumping to conclusions and knowing when to think twice*, Pacific Philosophical Quarterly **65**, 37–58.

Bach, K. (1987a), *Thought and Reference*, Clarendon Press, Oxford.

Bach, K. (1987b), *On communicative intentions: A reply to Recanati*, Mind and Language **2**, 141–154.

Bach, K. (1992), *Intentions and demonstrations*, Analysis **52**, 140–146.

Bach, K. (1993), *Sometimes a great notion: A critical notice of Mark Crimmins' Talk About Beliefs*, Mind & Language **8**, 431–441.

Bach, K. (1994a), *Conversational impliciture*, Mind & Language **9**, 124–162.

Bach, K. (1994b), *Semantic slack*, Foundations of Speech Act Theory, S.L. Tsohatzidis, ed., Routledge, London, 267–291.

Bach, K. (1997), *Do belief reports report beliefs?* Pacific Philosophical Quarterly **78**, 215–241. Reprinted in this volume.

Bezuidenhout, A. (1996), *Pragmatics and singular reference*, Mind and Language **11**, 133–159.

Brentano, F. (1874), *Psychologie vom empirischen Standpunkt*, Duncker u. Humblot, Leipzig. Reprinted in 1924, Felix Meiner, Leipzig, 2nd edn.

Carston, R. (1988), *Implicature, explicature, and truth-theoretic semantics*, Mental Representations: The Interface Between Language and Reality, R.M. Kempson, ed., CUP, Cambridge, 155–181.

Carston, R. (1998), *Postscript (1995) to Carston 1988*, Pragmatics: Critical Concepts, Vol. 4, A. Kasher, ed., Routledge, London, 464–479.

Clapp, L. (1995), *How to be direct and innocent: A criticism of Crimmins and Perry's theory of attitude ascriptions*, Linguistics & Philosophy **18**, 529–565.

Crimmins, M. (1992), *Talk About Beliefs*, The MIT Press, Cambridge, MA.

Crimmins, M. and Perry, J. (1989), *The prince and the phone booth: Reporting puzzling beliefs*, Journal of Philosophy **86**, 685–711.

Davidson, D. (1968-9), *On saying that*, Synthese **19**, 130–146.

Donnellan, K.S. (1966), *Reference and definite descriptions*, Philosophical Review **75**, 281–304.

Donnellan, K.S. (1990), *Belief and the identity of reference*, Propositional Attitudes: The Role of Content in Logic, Language, and Mind, C.A. Anderson and J. Owens, eds, CSLI, Stanford, 201–214.

Dummett, M. (1991), *Thought and perception: The views of two philosophical innovators*, Frege and Other Philosophers, Clarendon Press, Oxford, 263–288.

Frege, G. (1892), *Über Sinn und Bedeutung*, Zeitschrift f. Philosophie u. Philosophische Kritik **100**, 25–50.

Frege, G. (1918-19), *Der Gedanke*, Beiträge zur Philosophie des Deutschen Idealismus **1**. Reprinted in Frege, G. (1966), *Logische Untersuchungen*, Vandenhoeck u. Ruprecht, Göttingen, 30–53.

Grice, H.P. (1978), *Further notes on logic and conversation*, Syntax and Semantics, Vol. 9, P. Cole, ed., Academic Press, New York. Reprinted in Grice (1989), 41–57.

Grice, H.P. (1981), *Presupposition and conversational implicature*, Radical Pragmatics, P. Cole, ed., Academic Press, New York, 183–198. Reprinted in Grice (1989), 269–282.

Grice, H.P. (1989), *Studies in the Way of Words*, Harvard University Press, Cambridge, MA.

Horn, L.R. (1988), *Pragmatic theory*, Linguistics: the Cambridge Survey, Vol. 1, F.J. Newmeyer, ed., CUP, Cambridge, 113–145.

Horn, L.R. (1989), *A Natural History of Negation*, University of Chicago Press, Chicago.

Husserl, E. (1900-01), *Logische Untersuchungen*, Vol. 2, Max Niemeyer, Halle. Reprinted in 1984 after the 2nd edition (1913–21), Martinus Nijhoff, The Hague.

Jaszczolt, K.M. (1992), *Belief sentences and the semantics of propositional attitudes*, D.Phil. dissertation, University of Oxford.

Jaszczolt, K.M. (1993), *De re/de dicto: A semantics of belief sentences*, Papers and Studies in Contrastive Linguistics **28**, 39–64.

Jaszczolt, K.M. (1996), *Reported speech, vehicles of thought, and the horizon*, Lingua e Stile **31**, 113–133.

Jaszczolt, K.M. (1997), *The 'default de re' principle for the interpretation of belief utterances*, Journal of Pragmatics **28**, 315–336.

Jaszczolt, K.M. (1998), *Discourse about beliefs*, Theoretical Linguistics **24**, 1–28.

Jaszczolt, K.M. (1999), *Default semantics, pragmatics, and intentions*, The Semantics/Pragmatics Interface from Different Points of View, K. Turner, ed., Elsevier Science, Oxford, 199–232.

Jaszczolt, K.M. (forthcoming), *Discourse, Beliefs, and Intentions: Semantic Defaults and Propositional Attitude Ascription*, Elsevier Science, Oxford.

Kamp, H. (1990), *Prolegomena to a structural account of belief and other attitudes*, Propositional Attitudes: The Role of Content in Logic, Language, and Mind, C.A. Anderson and J. Owens, eds, CSLI, Stanford, 27–90.

Kamp, H. (in progress), *Some elements of a DRT-based theory of the representation of mental states and verbal communication.*

Kamp, H. and Reyle, U. (1993), *From Discourse to Logic*, Kluwer, Dordrecht.

Kempson, R.M. (1979), *Presupposition, opacity, and ambiguity*, Syntax and Semantics, Vol. 11, C.-K. Oh and D.A. Dinneen, eds, Academic Press, New York, 283–297.

Kempson, R.M. (1986), *Ambiguity and the semantics – pragmatics distinction*, Meaning and Interpretation, C. Travis, ed., B. Blackwell, Oxford, 77–103.

Larson, R.K. and Ludlow, P. (1993), *Interpreted logical forms*, Synthese **95**, 305–355.

Larson, R. and Segal, G. (1995), *Knowledge of Meaning: An Introduction to Semantic Theory*, The MIT Press, Cambridge, MA.

Levinson, S.C. (1988), *Generalized conversational implicature and the semantics/pragmatics interface*, Unpublished paper.

Levinson, S.C. (1995), *Three levels of meaning*, Grammar and Meaning: Essays in Honour of Sir John Lyons, F.R. Palmer, ed., CUP, Cambridge, 90–115.

Ludlow, P. (1995), *Logical form and the hidden-indexical theory: A reply to Schiffer*, Journal of Philosophy **92**, 102–107.

Ludlow, P. (1996), *The adicity of 'believes' and the hidden indexical theory*, Analysis **56**, 97–101.

Mey, J.L. (1993), *Pragmatics: An Introduction*, Blackwell, Oxford.

Neale, S. (1990), *Descriptions*, The MIT Press, Cambridge, MA.

Quine, W.V.O. (1956), *Quantifiers and propositional attitudes*, Journal of Philosophy **53**. Reprinted in A. Marras, ed. (1972), *Intentionality, Mind and Language*, University of Illinois Press, Urbana, 402–414.

Recanati, F. (1981), *On Kripke on Donnellan*, Possibilities and Limitations of Pragmatics, H. Parret, M. Sbisà and J. Verschueren, eds, J. Benjamins, Amsterdam, 593–630.

Recanati, F. (1993), *Direct Reference: From Language to Thought*, B. Blackwell, Oxford.

Recanati, F. (1994), *Contextualism and anti-contextualism in the philosophy of language*, Foundations of Speech Act Theory, S.L. Tsohatzidis, ed., Routledge, London, 156–166.

Recanati, F. (1996), *Domains of discourse*, Linguistics & Philosophy **19**, 445–475.

Reimer, M. (1995), *A defense of de re belief reports*, Mind & Language **10**, 446–463.

Richard, M. (1990), *Propositional Attitudes*, CUP, Cambridge.

Richard, M. (1995), *Defective contexts, accommodation, and normalization*, Canadian Journal of Philosophy **25**, 551–570.

Russell, B. (1905), *On denoting*, Reprinted in B. Russell (1956), *Logic and Knowledge: Essays 1901–1950*, Allen and Unwin, London, 49–56.

Russell, B. (1919), *Descriptions*, From: *Introduction to Mathematical Philosophy*, Allen and Unwin, London, 167–180. Reprinted in A.P. Martinich, ed. (1985), *The Philosophy of Language*, OUP, Oxford, 213–219.

Salmon, N. (1986), *Frege's Puzzle*, The MIT Press, Cambridge, MA.

Schiffer, S. (1977), *Naming and knowing*, Midwest Studies in Philosophy **2**, 28–41.

Schiffer, S. (1987), *Remnants of Meaning*, The MIT Press, Cambridge, MA.

Schiffer, S. (1992), *Belief ascription*, Journal of Philosophy **89**, 499–521.

Schiffer, S. (1996), *The hidden-indexical theory's logical-form problem: A rejoinder*, Analysis **56**, 92–97.

Smith, D.W. (1989), *The Circle of Acquaintance: Perception, Consciousness, and Empathy*, Kluwer, Dordrecht.

Soames, S. (1987), *Direct reference, propositional attitudes, and semantic content*, Philosophical Topics **15**, 47–87. Reprinted in N. Salmon and S. Soames, eds, *Propositions and Attitudes*, OUP, Oxford, 197–239.

Soames, S. (1995), *Beyond singular propositions?* Canadian Journal of Philosophy **25**, 515–549.

Sperber, D. (1985), *On Anthropological Knowledge*, CUP, Cambridge.

Sperber, D. (1996), *Explaining Culture: A Naturalistic Approach*, Blackwell, Oxford.

Sperber, D. and Wilson, D. (1986), *Relevance: Communication and Cognition*, Blackwell, Oxford.

Sperber, D. and Wilson, D. (1995), *Relevance: Communication and Cognition*, 2nd ed., Blackwell, Oxford.

Strawson, P.F. (1950), *On referring*, Mind **59**. Reprinted in P.F. Strawson (1971), *Logico-Linguistic Papers*, Methuen, London, 1–27.

van Deemter, K. and Peters, S., eds (1996), *Semantic Ambiguity and Underspecification*, CSLI, Stanford.

CHAPTER 2

Propositional Attitudes in Direct-Reference Semantics

Stephen Schiffer

Contents

PRAGMATICS OF PROPOSITIONAL ATTITUDE REPORTS
Current Research in the Semantics/Pragmatics Interface, Vol. 4
Edited by K.M. Jaszczolt

1. Introduction: the problem space

Direct-reference semantics is arguably the presently dominant program in the philosophy of language. It has two parts, one for singular terms and one for general terms, and to a first approximation these can be stated thus:

Singular terms: Certain kinds of singular terms – including at least proper names and single-word pronouns and demonstratives – typically function as *directly-referential singular terms*. A token of a singular term *directly refers* to a thing just in case it introduces that thing into the proposition expressed by the utterance containing the token.

General terms: Every general term, we might say, *directly-expresses* the property it ascribes.[1] A token of a general term *directly expresses* a property just in case it introduces that property into the proposition expressed by the utterance containing the token.

Direct-reference semantics, as just characterized, faces an obvious challenge: How can it account for the truth-values of such belief reports as the following?

Lois Lane believes that Superman flies.
Lois doesn't believe that Clark Kent flies.

Ralph believes that no woodchuck is a groundhog.
Ralph doesn't believe that no woodchuck is a woodchuck.

The problem should be clear. We want to be able to recognize that all four reports are true, but how can this be if the propositions referred to by the four that-clauses contain Superman, Clark Kent, and the properties of being a woodchuck and a groundhog? For Superman = Clark Kent and the property of being a woodchuck = the property of being a groundhog.

One extreme direct-reference response to this problem is to deny that the displayed sentences *can* all be true, and to try to defuse the counterintuitiveness of this move by appeal to Gricean implicature (see, e.g., Salmon, 1986). But I believe it's now generally recognized that there are insuperable difficulties in getting Grice to do the needed work.[2] In any case, I don't have much sympathy for the extreme line and will say nothing more about it here.

Twenty three years ago (Schiffer, 1977; see also Schiffer, 1978, 1992, 1995), I proposed a different way out for the direct-reference theorist, one that recognizes

[1] Grelling's paradox shows that not every general term can be construed as expressing a property. For consider the evidently true sentence 'Doghood is non-self-instantiating', which is true iff the property of being a dog isn't itself a dog. If we allow that there is a property of being non-self-instantiating, then we'll be landed with a property that is self-instantiating iff it is not self-instantiating, which is absurd. I shall not here discuss whether this is a problem for direct-reference semantics.

[2] See Schiffer (1987). Nathan Salmon replies in (Salmon, 1989).

that the displayed reports *can* all be true, notwithstanding that the first two that-clauses refer to the same proposition, as do the second two. It's a view I call the *hidden-indexical theory*, and it's recently been independently advanced by other philosophers, most notably Mark Crimmins and John Perry (Crimmins and Perry, 1989; Crimmins, 1992). But my own relationship to the hidden-indexical theory is equivocal. While I've argued that it's the best account of the semantics of belief reports compatible with the widely-held assumption that natural languages have compositional semantics, I've also raised problems for the theory. In this paper I continue the discussion of the hidden-indexical theory, but now with special reference to the not-too-dissimilar account of belief reports offered by François Recanati in his recent book (Recanati, 1993).

The rest of this paper proceeds as follows. In the next section, I briefly describe the hidden-indexical theory and its motivation. In Section 3, I give a brief statement of three problems I find with the hidden-indexical theory, and in Section 4 I consider how a certain revision of the hidden-indexical theory in the direction of Recanati's theory would appear to avoid these problems. In the final section I consider a possible problem with the Recanati-inspired revision.

2. The hidden-indexical theory

The theory has in effect two parts: one about the nature of the belief relation, the other about the logical form of belief reports (and it will go without further saying that what applies to belief applies, *mutatis mutandis*, to all propositional attitudes and propositional-attitude reports). As regards the belief relation, the hidden-indexical theory holds that believing – the relation expressed by 'believes' in sentences of the form 'A believes that S' – is a three-place relation, $B(x, p, m)$, holding among a believer x, a mode-of-presentation-less proposition p, and a mode of presentation m under which x believes p. Thus, it's possible for x to believe p under one mode of presentation m while believing not-p under a second mode of presentation m', and while suspending judgment altogether under a third mode of presentation m''. By a "mode-of-presentation-less" proposition I mean, quite roughly, a proposition that contains the objects and properties the belief is about unaccompanied by any modes of presentation of them. Such a proposition might be a mere "singular proposition", like the ordered pair ⟨Fido, doghood⟩, but it could also be a set-theoretic construction of the proposition that some dogs bark.

So much for the relation's second term. Its third term is a mode of presentation under which the believer believes the proposition believed. This propositional mode of presentation is determined by modes of presentation of the objects and properties the proposition is about. Here it's not supposed that we have some antecedent understanding of what these modes of presentation are. Rather, our understanding of the notion of a mode of presentation is *functional*: a mode of presentation of an *object or property* is whatever can play a role in determining a propositional mode of presentation, and a *propositional* mode of presentation is whatever can play the role defined by the mode-of-presentation place in the belief relation. Thus, it remains to be determined what sorts of things in fact play the mode-of-presentation role – that is to say, it remains to be determined what modes of presentation *are*. Although I won't have space to go into the matter, my own view is that the direct-reference theorist would do best to hold that modes of presentation are conceptual roles of mental representations.

The second part of the hidden-indexical theory, its account of the logical form of particular occurrences of belief-ascribing sentences, is its crux. As applied to the sentence

(1) Ralph believes that no woodchuck is a groundhog,

the theory holds that the logical form of an utterance of this sentence may be represented as

$\exists m[\Phi^* m$ & B (Ralph, the proposition that no woodchuck is a groundhog, m)],

where Φ^* is an implicitly-referred-to and contextually-determined *type* of propositional mode of presentation, where by this I mean a *property* of modes of presentation of propositions. It's assumed that the proposition that no woodchuck is a groundhog = the proposition that no woodchuck is a woodchuck. This type of mode of presentation will be made up, as it were, of contextually-relevant types of modes of presentation of the constituents of the proposition that no woodchuck is a groundhog. There will be a type of mode of presentation for the first occurrence of the property of being a woodchuck/groundhog, a type of mode of presentation for the second occurrence of that property, and types of modes of presentation for the other constituents of the proposition.

This theory is aptly called the *hidden*-indexical theory because the reference to the mode-of-presentation type isn't carried by any expression in the belief ascription. In this sense, it's like the reference to a place at which it's raining which occurs in an utterance of 'It's raining'. And the theory is aptly called the hidden-*indexical* theory, because the mode-of-presentation type to which reference is made in the utterance of a belief sentence can vary from one utterance of the sentence to another.

Now that we know what the theory is, let's look briefly at what motivates it. It would actually be a good idea to begin with what the motivation *isn't*. I had wanted a discussion of this in view of Chapter 19 of Recanati's book (1993) "Comparison with Other Accounts", but again there simply isn't space. Two brief remarks will have to suffice. First, *I* don't begin by assuming *any* account of the semantics of the sentences contained in that-clauses. So when I approach the semantics of belief reports I most emphatically am not assuming that that-clauses have got to refer to singular propositions or to any other kind of mode-of-presentation-less proposition. For more on this, see §IV of (Schiffer, 1992). Second, I'm unimpressed by

Davidsonian appeals to "semantic innocence", and thus semantic innocence has nothing to do with the motivation for my version of the hidden-indexical theory.

The motivation I do find for the hidden-indexical theory is straightforward. To begin, there are reasons for taking that-clauses in sentences of the form '*A* believes that *S*' to be referential singular terms.[3] Then there are reasons for taking their referents to be propositions of some stripe or other, where by this I mean abstract, mind- and language-independent entities that have truth conditions, and have their truth conditions both essentially and absolutely, i.e. without relativization to anything else, such as a language or population of speakers. The reasons for taking that-clauses to refer to propositions are pretty good, but I can't now take the space to go into them.[4] Instead, I'll concentrate on what can be said to motivate the hidden-indexical theory to someone who is willing to assume that that-clauses refer to propositions of some kind or other.

The point of the theory then is well illustrated by the example already used, an utterance of (1) ('Ralph believes that no woodchuck is a groundhog'). One wants to recognize that an utterance of (l) is true, while at the same time recognizing that an utterance of

(2) Ralph doesn't believe that no woodchuck is a woodchuck

would also be true. This would be impossible if, as the extreme direct-reference theory holds, 'believes' in these sentences expressed a two-place relation and both that-clauses referred to the same proposition, as they would if 'woodchuck' and 'groundhog' in those that-clauses simply referred to the single property they both express.

Now, one famous way of accounting for the truth of these two utterances is Frege's way: take the two that-clauses to have different references. Specifically, take the occurrences of 'woodchuck' and 'groundhog' to introduce into the propositions to which the that-clauses refer distinct modes of presentation of the single property they both express. But it's implausible that this should be required to account for the truth of both utterances. In the first place, the that-clause in (1), 'that no woodchuck is a groundhog', can't be making a context-*in*dependent reference to a mode-of-presentation-containing proposition, for the predicate 'believes that no woodchuck is a groundhog' can be univocally and correctly predicated of people – say, you and Helen Keller – who think of the property of being a woodchuck/groundhog in radically different and non-overlapping ways. And in the second place, no context-*dependent* reference can be required, for a speaker can make a true statement in uttering (1) even though she isn't in a position to refer to any specific mode of presentation that Ralph has for the property of being a woodchuck/groundhog.

[3] For present purposes, I count a that-clause as a "referential singular term" even if it's construed on analogy with a Russellian treatment of extensional occurrences of definite descriptions, the "denotation" of the that-clause being the proposition uniquely characterized by the that-clause.

[4] I do go into them in (Schiffer, 1992) and (Schiffer, 1994).

Although a speaker may not know any relevant *specific* mode of presentation under which Ralph believes that no woodchuck is a groundhog, she may know a relevant *type* of mode of presentation. For example, she may know that Ralph believes that no woodchuck is a groundhog under some propositional mode of presentation that requires thinking of woodchuckhood first under a mode of presentation associated with Ralph's use of 'woodchuck' and then under a mode of presentation associated with Ralph's use of 'groundhog'. Thus, we can see how the hidden-indexical theory captures the attractive features of both the extreme direct-reference theory of belief ascription and the Fregean theory while at the same time avoiding the pitfalls of both theories. With the extreme direct-reference theory, the hidden-indexical theory sees the that-clauses in (1) and (2) as referring to the same mode-of-presentation-less proposition, while, with the Fregean theory, it recognizes that both utterances are true. This is possible because the two utterances involve implicit references to distinct mode-of-presentation types. Presently, however, we'll see that this motivation fails to motivate every aspect of the hidden-indexical theory.

3. Three problems for the hidden-indexical theory

Two of these problems I discuss in (Schiffer, 1992), though I aim now for sharpened restatements, and one I haven't discussed elsewhere.

1. *The logical-form problem.* This problem can be stated as the following simple argument.

(i) If the hidden-indexical theory is correct, then a substitution instance of 'm' in

(3) Ralph believes that Fido is a dog under mode of presentation m.

is (if the resulting sentence is true) the specification of the third argument in an instance of the three-place belief relation.[5]

(ii) But the substitution instance would be no such thing (it would rather be part of an adverbial modifier, or "adjunct").

(iii) Therefore, the hidden-indexical theory is not correct.

This little argument is clearly valid, so it remains to see what can be said for its two premises.

Premise (i) seems clearly true. The hidden-indexical theory entails that believing is a three-place relation, $B(x, p, m)$, holding among a believer x, a proposition p,

[5] As I remarked in (Schiffer, 1992), talk of believing *under a mode of presentation* is an expression of art and it is not clear how the technical expression would be best represented in unadorned ordinary language. If one thinks that believing "under mode of presentation m" is better expressed as believing *in way w*, then the argument should be restated accordingly. What I would say in defense of the argument would remain *mutatis mutandis* the same.

and a mode of presentation m under which x believes p. The ordinary-language way of representing this open sentence would evidently be 'x believes p under (mode of presentation) m', and from this it follows that a singular term replacing 'm' in a true substitution instance of (3) would be the specification of an argument of the three-place relation expressed by the open sentence.

The case for premise (ii) is essentially intuitive with a technical backup. The intuitive point is that (3) clearly does not *look like* it contains a three-place verb with the specification of a third argument. Rather, it looks to be on all fours with a sentence like

(4) Louise hit Ralph under the influence of crack.

which is paradigmatically a sentence in which the singular term 'the influence of crack' is not the specification of the third argument in an instance of the three-place hitting relation (a relation that holds among a hitter, a hittee, and a psychological condition partly responsible for the hit?!) but rather merely part of the *adverbial phrase* 'under the influence of crack'. The technical point, which I presented as "evidence for this [sort of] assimilation",[6] was that this diagnosis was supported by a test of Noam Chomsky's for distinguishing between arguments and adverbs in their ability to extract from 'whether'-clauses.[7] According to this test, the argument status of, say, 'her husband' in

Mary gave the house to her husband.

is revealed in the fact that we can answer 'Her husband' in response to the question

(5) To whom did you wonder whether Mary gave the house?

for one's answer would mean that one wondered whether Mary gave the house to her husband. Also according to the test, the nonargument, adverbial status of 'the influence of crack' in (4) is revealed by the fact that we cannot answer 'The influence of crack' in response to the question

(6) Under what influence did you wonder whether Louise hit Ralph?

where this answer would be elliptical for

I wondered whether Louise hit Ralph under the influence of crack.

If one answered 'The influence of crack' in response to (6) one would rather be reporting on the stoned condition under which one did one's wondering.

Now, when this test is applied to

(7) Under what mode of presentation did you wonder whether Ralph believes that Fido is a dog?

---

6 Schiffer (1992), p. 518.

7 See Chomsky (1986).

we get the same result as with the preceding example: if one answered “Mode of presentation *m*”, one would be reporting on the mode of presentation under which one did one’s wondering.

Peter Ludlow, in a recent comment (Ludlow, 1995), takes issue with the foregoing argumentation. Specifically, he makes two points with which I shall be concerned.[8] First, he doubts the Chomskian test supporting premise (ii). Second, he proposes a different test for distinguishing arguments from adjuncts and argues that according to it premise (ii) is false.

Ludlow’s challenge to the Chomskian criterion is to question the intuitions that sustain it. “Such judgments”, he writes, “are extremely delicate, and it may be unwise to let a theory of the attitudes turn on them”.[9] Specifically, he would claim that his ear does not perceive the alleged difference between (5) (‘To whom did you wonder whether Mary gave the house?’) and (6) (‘Under what influence did you wonder whether Louise hit Ralph?’) – viz., that whereas (5) asks whom you wondered to be the recipient of the house, (6) asks about the influence under which you did your wondering. And Ludlow would further claim that he cannot tell whether (7) (‘Under what mode of presentation did you wonder whether Ralph believes that Fido is a dog?’) “patterns with (5) or (6) (assuming we can even divine a distinction between (5) and (6))”.[10]

I find this deafness puzzling. There is clearly a difference between (5) and (6). (5) is obviously a grammatical and meaningful question, but it cannot be literally asking to whom one did one’s wondering, since wondering is not something one *can* do *to* someone; it can be asking only about whom one wondered to be the recipient of Mary’s largesse. This is confirmed by appeal to examples with other kinds of verbs. The Chomskian test applies to complementizer clauses other than ‘whether’-clauses, such as

To whom did you think that Mary gave the house?

and it is clear that this question has only one relevant reading. By contrast, (6) clearly can be asking about the influence under which one did one’s wondering, and, likewise, (7) clearly can be asking about the mode of presentation under which one did one’s wondering. If there is a reasonable qualm about the Chomskian test it is that it is not out of the question for a philosopher with a finely-tuned hearing aid (one that comes with a theory) to argue that she hears an ambiguity in (6) and (7), so that (6) can be asking either about the influence under which one did one’s wondering or about what one wondered to be the influence under which Louise hit Ralph, and likewise, *mutatis mutandis*, for (7). It was because of this qualm that I presented the Chomskian test merely as evidence for premise (ii). But notice that

---

[8] Ludlow also makes some criticisms with which I will not be concerned. I do, however, respond to them in (Schiffer, 1996), from which much of my present discussion of the logical-form problem is drawn.

[9] Ludlow (1995), p. 106.

[10] Ludlow (1995), p. 106.

even if there is an ambiguity in (6) and (7) – and a corresponding ambiguity in questions like

> Under what influence did you think that Louise hit Ralph?

and

> Under what mode of presentation did you think that Ralph believes that Fido is a dog?

– this could be taken to suggest a revised Chomskian criterion: when there is no ambiguity, we have an argument, otherwise an adjunct. I would agree, however, that more needs to be said on this subtle topic.

Having rejected the Chomskian test, Ludlow proposes a test of Richard Larson's.[11] The "test is whether the kind of phrase in question can be iterated, for it appears that adjuncts can be iterated, but that arguments cannot. So, for example, we have the following contrast.

> *John buttered the toast the brioche the roll.

> John buttered the toast in the kitchen in the corner in the booth."[12]

Then Ludlow implies that (3) patterns with the first sentence, since we have an iteration failure in

> *Ralph believes that Fido is a dog under mode of presentation m under mode of presentation m' under mode of presentation m''.[13]

But the Larson test is not acceptable. In (4) ('Louise hit Ralph under the influence of crack'), 'under the influence of crack' is paradigmatically an adjunct (we are hardly to suppose that hitting is a three-place relation among a hitter, a hittee, and an influence under which the hitter hit the hittee). Yet

> *Louise hit Ralph under the influence of crack under the influence of heroin under the influence of rock music.

fails to pass the iteration test.

So, as far as I can see, the hidden-indexical theory still has a logical-form problem.

---

[11] Larson (1988).

[12] Ludlow (1995), p. 106. I have dropped the designations of the examples.

[13] Ludlow (1995), p. 107. The example Ludlow uses is

> *John believed that Fido barked in way m in way m' in way m''.

2. *The application-to-speech-acts problem.* This problem arises when we attempt to apply the hidden-indexical theory to propositional *speech acts*. For consider *stating*. The hidden-indexical theory tells us this is a three-place relation, $S(x, p, m)$. But how are we to *understand* this relation? We have an intuitive grasp of what is intended by the three-place belief relation, $B(x, p, m)$, but what should our intuitive understanding be of the allegedly three-place stating relation? What is it to *say* something *under a mode of presentation*?

I think what naturally comes to mind is that to state p under m involves performing a speech act with the following two features:

(i) its propositional content – its truth condition – is the proposition p;

(ii) to understand the statement requires entertaining p under m, and requires knowing that that is required for understanding.

The trouble with this natural interpretation of the three-place proposal is that it is quite implausible that understanding a statement requires entertaining a stated proposition under some particular intended mode of presentation. What, for example, would be the intended mode of presentation when I say to you 'Brian Loar now lives in Manhattan'? Not only is there clearly no particular mode of presentation that would be intended; it also seems quite wrong to think that this is a case of an indeterminate statement owing to indeterminacy in the intended mode of presentation. No particular modes of presentation seem even indeterminately intended.

Is there a weaker, less objection prone, way of understanding stating as the three-place $S(x, p, m)$? Perhaps it's enough for $S(x, p, m)$ that x *intend under* m to state p. Intending, it might be suggested, must, like believing, be under some definite mode of presentation, and one can't state p without intending to state p. This secures a mode of presentation for each act of stating without requiring that mode of presentation to belong to what is essential for *understanding* a statement. But there is a problem with this weaker construal. For suppose

Sam intended to state that Dolores loves Paris.

Then Sam has an intention whose propositional content is *that Sam states that Dolores loves Paris*. But that proposition is identical, on the proposal in question, to the proposition *that Sam intended, under some mode of presentation, to state that Dolores loves Paris*, and it is clear we are off on a regress that appears not to be benign.

It isn't at all clear to me how the hidden-indexical theory can plausibly be applied to propositional speech acts.

3. *The meaning-intention problem.* The problem here is that belief reporters seem not to have the meaning intentions the hidden-indexical theory requires of them. For example, pretend that we're having a casual conversation about the French Riviera, when Stella, a nonphilosopher who likes to drop names, says to us,

(8) Jean Luc Godard believes that Brigitte Bardot is selling her villa in St. Tropez and moving to Brooklyn.

If the hidden-indexical theory is correct – at least in the form that I've so far stated it – then there is a certain mode-of-presentation type Φ such that Stella, in uttering (8), is referring to Φ, and this will be by virtue of her meaning

(9) the proposition that there's something x such that x is of the type Φ and Jean Luc Godard believes *that Brigitte Bardot is selling her villa in St. Tropez and moving to Brooklyn* under x.

Here Φ is a particular type of propositional mode of presentation, and it will incorporate particular types of modes of presentation for each of the constituents of the proposition to which (8)'s that-clause refers – Brigitte Bardot, the selling relation, Bardot's villa, the in relation, St. Tropez, conjunction, the moving-to relation, and Brooklyn.

Thus the hidden-indexical theory requires Stella, in her utterance of (8), to mean some substitution instance of (9). The problem is that Stella has no awareness whatever of meaning any such thing. If you ask her what she meant in uttering (8), she'll tell you that what she meant, and all that she meant, was that Jean Luc Godard believed that Brigitte Bardot was selling her villa in St. Tropez and moving to Brooklyn. She won't recognize herself as having made any reference to a mode-of-presentation type, and she won't recognize herself as having meant, or said, anything more than is contained in what she is consciously able to report.

The contrast is striking with what we may take to be a paradigm case of implicit meaning. When Stella says 'It's raining', she's referring to some place at which it's raining. Yet here she'll be perfectly well aware that this is what she's doing. She's apt, for example, to tell you that what she meant, and what she implicitly said, was that it was raining *where she was*.

It might be proposed, as a way of getting the hidden-indexical theory out of the meaning-intention problem, that, while there is no mode-of-presentation type Φ such that Stella is *definitely* referring to Φ, this is of no great consequence to the theory, because Stella may be construed as *vaguely*, or *indeterminately*, referring to each of a vague bunch of contextually-relevant mode-of-presentation types. That is to say, there is no substitution instance of (9) that she definitely means, but there are several that she sort-of, or indeterminately, means. This move to meaning indeterminacy, however, doesn't really help. Stella wouldn't recognize herself as having even vaguely said that there is something that is both Φ and such that Godard believes *that Brigitte Bardot is selling*, etc. The contrast with a paradigmatic case of vague reference is as striking as the contrast mentioned in the preceding paragraph. When Stella says 'It's raining', she will undoubtedly not be making a determinate reference to some definite area of space; her utterance will rather contain an indeterminate, or vague, such reference. Yet here Stella *will* recognize her statement as involving an implicit indeterminate reference to a place (see Schiffer, 1995).

I don't think there can be any serious doubt about Stella's not being at all aware of meaning what the hidden-indexical theory requires her to mean, even when semantic indeterminacy is taken into account. The big question is what this shows. Why not say that while Stella isn't aware of meaning any substitution instance of (9), she nevertheless does mean such a proposition? Why must what a speaker means or says be consciously accessible to her? It's generally accepted nowadays that people have tacit beliefs and intentions. Why not, then, allow that tacit speech acts can supervene on these tacit propositional attitudes?

I wish I had a decisive answer to this question, but I don't. The best I can do is offer the following indecisive but relevant considerations, considerations that favor denying that speakers mean what the hidden-indexical theory requires them to mean.

(a) The hypothesis that what a speaker says and means in her utterance is consciously accessible to her is what Recanati calls the *availability hypothesis*, and he uses it to good effect in separating what really belongs to the semantics of a sentence from what is merely pragmatically implicated in the utterance of that sentence (Recanati, 1993, p. 248). Whatever the force of Recanati's arguments, to that extent they support the view that belief reporters don't mean what the hidden-indexical theory requires them to mean.

(b) One nice thing about the availability hypothesis – and another thing to be said in its favor – is that it seems to get the clear cases right. I find it difficult to think of a clear counterexample to the hypothesis. When we definitely want to say that a speaker said or meant p, then the speaker is aware of saying or meaning p; she can tell us *explicitly* what she meant.

(c) As I argued in (Schiffer, 1995), if we allow that the belief reporters are stating what the hidden-indexical theory says they're stating, then parity of reasoning will lead one to unacceptable conclusions about the semantics of pronouns and demonstratives.

4. A Recanati-inspired revision

Let's say that a *quasi-singular* proposition is a proposition that contains objects and properties *along with modes of presentation of them.* Thus, in addition to the *singular* proposition

$$\langle \text{Fido, doghood} \rangle$$

we also have the *quasi-singular* proposition

$$\langle \langle m_f, \text{Fido} \rangle, \langle m_d, \text{doghood} \rangle \rangle,$$

where m_f and m_d are modes of presentation of Fido and doghood, respectively.[14] Now, Recanati (1993) holds the following about quasi-singular propositions.[15] First, they provide the *complete contents* of the *thoughts* expressed by utterances of sentences containing directly-referential singular terms. Second, the modes of presentation in quasi-singular propositions are *truth-conditionally irrelevant*. Thus, the displayed quasi-singular proposition has exactly the same possible-worlds truth conditions as the displayed singular proposition. Third, that-clauses commonly refer to quasi-singular propositions.

At the same time, Recanati doesn't claim that that-clauses *always* refer to quasi-singular propositions, since he evidently allows that a belief report may involve not a reference to a specific mode of presentation but merely a reference to a certain *type* of mode of presentation. Thus, let's introduce the notion of a *quasi-quasi-singular proposition*. That's like a quasi-singular proposition, except that it contains mode-of-presentation *types* in place of specific modes of presentation. To believe a quasi-quasi-singular proposition is to believe a guasi-singular proposition whose specific modes of presentation are of the types contained in the quasi-quasi-singular proposition. Thus, letting upper-case 'T's range over mode-of-presentation types, we can say, for example, that:

$$B(x, \langle\langle T, \text{Fido}\rangle, \langle T', \text{doghood}\rangle\rangle) \text{ iff}$$
$$\exists m \exists m' (Tm \,\&\, T'm' \,\&\, B(x, \langle\langle m, \text{Fido}\rangle, \langle m', \text{doghood}\rangle\rangle))$$

Evidently, Recanati holds that that-clauses at least sometimes refer to quasi-quasi-singular propositions. But even if *he* doesn't hold this, the revision of the hidden-indexical theory my reading of him suggests is still worth discussing. That revision is as follows.

According to the hidden-indexical theory, believing is a three-place relation and the reference to a mode-of-presentation type required by a belief report locates that mode-of-presentation type *outside* the proposition referred to by the that-clause. It represents, we know, the logical form of an utterance of

(10) Ralph believes that Fido is a dog

as

(11) $\exists m[\Phi^* m \,\&\, B(\text{Ralph}, \langle \text{Fido}, \text{doghood}\rangle, m)]$,

where Φ^* is a contextually-determined and implicitly referred to type of propositional mode of presentation. The Recanati-inspired revision, on the other hand, takes believing to be a *two*-place relation and represents the logical form of an utterance of (10) as

[14] I introduced the notion of a quasi-singular notion in (Schiffer, 1978).

[15] Actually, he ignores the treatment of general terms in that-clauses, so what I'm really attributing to him is the obvious extension of what he says to general terms.

(12) $B(\text{Ralph}, \langle\langle T, \text{Fido}\rangle, \langle T', \text{doghood}\rangle\rangle)$,

where T and T' are contextually-determined and implicitly referred to properties of modes of presentation of Fido and doghood respectively. In a given case, the mode-of-presentation types to which reference is made might well be tantamount to specific modes of presentation. For reasons that will presently become clear, I'll henceforth refer to the Recanati-inspired revision of the hidden-indexical theory simply as the *indexical theory*.

Before turning to how the indexical theory bears on the hidden-indexical theory's three problems, I would like (at the risk of being slightly repetitive) to make explicit exactly what the differences actually are between the hidden-indexical theory, which issues in (11), and its Recanati-inspired revision, which issues in (12).

(i) Obviously, whereas the hidden-indexical theory takes believing to be a triadic relation, the indexical theory takes it to be dyadic.

(ii) Obviously again, whereas the hidden-indexical theory takes that-clauses to refer to *mode-of-presentation-less* propositions, the indexical theory takes them to refer to *quasi-quasi-singular* propositions.

(iii) The hidden-indexical theory requires modes of presentation of propositions, the indexical theory only of the objects and properties our beliefs are about.

(iv) The indexical theory needn't be construed as a *hidden* indexical theory.

As regards the hidden-indexical theory, what was required was a reference to a type of mode of presentation of a *proposition*, and there was nothing in the that-clause which could reasonably be thought to carry *that* reference. But when we turn to the indexical theory, it seems perfectly reasonable to take the references of 'Fido' and 'dog' in (10) as referring, respectively, to the two ordered pairs contained in the quasi-quasi-singular proposition referred to by the entire that-clause. In other words, the belief reporter, in uttering (10) is referring by her utterance of 'Fido' to a complex containing both Fido and a type of mode of presentation of him. This is why I call the Recanati-inspired revision simply an indexical theory. The references to the mode-of-presentation types are indexical – i.e. contextually-determined – but they are not "hidden"; they are carried by the actual words in the that-clause.

Now we are in a good position to see how the indexical theory fares with respect to the three problems that worry the hidden-indexical theory.

1. *The logical-form problem.* The indexical theory clearly has no logical-form problem, for the theory represents the logical form of a sentence of the form '*A* believes that *S*' as what it appears at face value to be: a two-place predicate linking two arguments, one for the believer, one for what she believes.

2. *The application-to-speech-acts problem.* The indexical theory gives an especially satisfying result for this problem. The hidden-indexical theory couldn't plau-

sibly accommodate modes of presentation in its treatment of the allegedly three-place stating relation. But the indexical theory has no comparable problem. For stating is simply a two-place relation between speakers and propositions stated, and modes of presentation don't enter into either the relation or what is stated. But *types* of modes of presentation do, for things stated, according to this theory, are quasi-quasi-singular propositions.

3. *The meaning-intention problem.* The hidden-indexical theory's meaning-intention problem is that the belief reporter has no awareness of meaning what the theory requires her to mean. When asked what she meant in uttering (8), Stella won't even begin to say that she meant that there's something which is Φ and such that Godard believes *that Brigitte Bardot is selling her villa in St. Tropez and moving to Brooklyn* under it, for some implicitly referred to mode-of-presentation type Φ. By way of showing that she doesn't also suffer from this problem, the indexical theorist is apt first to ask what is required for a speaker to be aware of what she means. Then she is apt to propose the following criterion in answer to her question:

(13) x is *aware* of meaning p (in the sense required by Recanati's availability hypothesis) just in case there's a sentence 'S' such that (1) x can say 'I meant that S' and (2) x's utterance of 'that S' *explicitly* refers to p. To a first approximation, an utterance of a that-clause explicitly refers to its referent if its reference is determined by its syntax and the references its terms have in the utterance of the that-clause.

Thus, suppose that in uttering 'It's snowing', I mean that it's snowing in Manhattan. Then I don't show that I satisfy the availability criterion by saying 'I meant that it's snowing', but I *do* by saying 'I meant that it's snowing here', if my utterance of 'here' refers to Manhattan.

It should be clear that the hidden-indexical theory fails to satisfy the availability hypothesis as interpreted in (13). At the same time, the indexical theorist will urge that her theory avoids the meaning-intention problem because, if her theory is correct, then speakers are aware in the sense of (13). For if the indexical theory is correct, then there *is* a sentence 'S' such that Stella can say 'I meant that S' and have 'that S' explicitly refer to the proposition she was asserting in uttering (12). For she can say 'I meant that Godard believes that Bardot is selling her villa in St. Tropez and moving to Brooklyn', and if the indexical theory is right, the that-clause 'that Godard believes that Bardot is selling...' *will* explicitly refer to the proposition she asserted in uttering (12). This is because the that-clause 'that Bardot is selling her villa in St. Tropez and moving to Brooklyn' contained in her self-ascribed meaning report can explicitly refer to the very same quasi-quasi-singular proposition as was referred to by the that-clause in her belief ascription to Godard. And the reference here is explicit, because, as earlier observed, if the indexical theory is correct, there are no hidden indexicals; each word in a that-clause indexically refers to an ordered pair containing a mode-of-presentation type and a thing falling under a mode of presentation of the type.

5. Trouble with the indexical theory?

I find it difficult to make a lot of trouble for the indexical theory. At one time, I thought of urging a new logical-form problem that turned on the indexical theory's being committed to a certain ambiguity in the belief relation owing to the fact, already remarked on, that the theorist needs to hold that believing a quasi-quasi-singular proposition is to be defined in terms of believing a quasi-singular proposition. The commitment to two belief relations is easy to show, but it's harder to answer the theorist's response that this is an "ambiguity" with which he can comfortably live.

The most serious problem with the indexical theory may be that it hasn't really avoided the meaning-intention problem. Our statement of the hidden-indexical theory's meaning-intention problem was sharpened by the awareness criterion (13). By this criterion, speakers would fail to be aware of what they meant if the hidden-indexical theory were true but not if the indexical theory were true. But even if (13) is correct and even if speakers *would* be aware of what they meant *if* the indexical theory *were* true, it can't be concluded that the theory avoids a meaning-intention problem. It may be that there is a meaning-intention problem in supposing that the indexical theory *can* be correct, for relevant availability considerations may be violated in the assumption that that-clauses *can* refer to quasi-quasi-singular propositions. Let me explain.

True, *if* we can take 'that Fido is a dog' in (10) ('Ralph believes that Fido is a dog') to refer to a quasi-quasi-singular proposition, *then* we can be assured of passing the availability-hypothesis test (13). But there are availability considerations relevant to whether we *can* take the words in the that-clause to have the references they must have if the indexical theory is correct.

According to the indexical theory, one uttering (10) is using 'Fido' to refer to Fido along with some type of mode of presentation of him. If this is so, then the speaker ought to have *some* awareness of referring to such a mode-of-presentation type. After all, since the reference is supposed to be demonstrative, it's to be determined by the speaker's referential intentions. Now, if a speaker really refers to a thing with an indexical, then she's typically in a position to say what she's referring to without using that indexical, and this seems to be part of what referential awareness consists in. For example, suppose I want to tell you the color of my new Ferrari and I say 'It's that color', pointing to a hot pink shirt. Two things are noteworthy here: first, I'm clearly conscious of the reference I'm making by my utterance of 'that color', and second, this consciousness is manifested by my ability to report on my reference in a different context where I can't simply repeat the demonstrative 'that color'. So I might say that I was referring to *the color of a certain shirt* or to *a certain shade of pink*, and so on. Yet, I submit, it seems clear that the belief reporter has no such awareness. If asked what she was referring to in her use of 'Fido', she would not give any restatement that indicated her awareness that she was referring to a mode-of-presentation type. This arguably shows that she had no awareness of the demonstrative reference being made by her use of 'Fido', and it would in this way arguably show, via the availability hypothesis, that she was making no such demonstrative reference. Still, there is more than one thing the indexical theorist might try to say in response to this, and until those responses are clearly articulated and assessed, it is unclear how much force should be credited to the version of the meaning-intention problem with which the indexical theory is confronted.

6. Conclusion

The hidden-indexical theory is attractive, but it has certain problems, three of which are described above. Recanati's theory suggests a way of revising the hidden-indexical theory which may help with these problems: take believing to be a two-place relation, and take that-clauses to refer (at least in some uses) to quasi-quasi-singular propositions. This move clearly avoids the logical-form problem; it seems directly to help with the application-to-speech-acts problem, and there's evidently also a way of having it help with the meaning-intention problem. Alas, however, it's also arguable that the Recanati-inspired indexical theory doesn't really solve the meaning-intention problem after all; it seems, to give the point a certain edge, that Recanati's own theory of the semantics of belief reports doesn't satisfy his own availability hypothesis.

Whatever its weaknesses, the indexical theory does appear to be some improvement on the hidden-indexical theory. If I were a direct-reference semanticist, I think I would prefer it. But I'm not a direct-reference semanticist, and what I'm inclined to suspect is that both theories of the logical form of belief reports along with direct-reference semantics need to be displaced in favor of a much more radical approach, one that's very deflationary about the nature of propositions and skeptical of traditional conceptions of compositional semantics. At least I feel that this more radical, deflationary approach is worth serious exploration. I argue for this most recently in (Schiffer, 1994).

Acknowledgment

Thanks to Kent Bach, Mike Harnish, Stephen Neale, and François Recanati.

References

Chomsky, N. (1986), *Barriers*, MIT Press, Cambridge, MA.

Crimmins, M. (1992), *Talk about Beliefs*, The MIT Press, Cambridge, MA.

Crimmins, M. and Perry, J. (1989), *The Prince and the Phone Booth: Reporting puzzling beliefs*, Journal of Philosophy **86**, 685–711.

Larson, R. (1988), *Implicit arguments in situation semantics*, Linguistics and Philosophy **11**, 169–201.

Ludlow, P. (1995), *Logical form and the hidden-indexical theory: A reply to Schiffer*, Journal of Philosophy **92**, 102–107.

Salmon, N. (1986), *Frege's Puzzle*, MIT Press, Cambridge, MA.

Salmon, N. (1989), *Illogical belief*, Philosophical Perspectives **3**, 243–285.

Schiffer, S. (1977), *Naming and knowing*, Midwest Studies in Philosophy, Vol. II: Studies in the Philosophy of Language (February, 1977), 28–41.

Schiffer, S. (1978), *The basis of reference*, Erkenntnis **13**, 171–206.

Schiffer, S. (1987), *The 'Fido' – Fido theory of belief*, Philosophical Perspectives **1**, 455–480.

Schiffer, S. (1992), *Belief ascription*, Journal of Philosophy **89**, 499–521.

Schiffer, S. (1994), *A paradox of meaning*, Noûs **28**, 279–324.

Schiffer, S. (1995), *Descriptions, indexicals, and belief reports: Some dilemmas (but not the ones you expect)*, Mind **104**, 107–131.

Schiffer, S. (1996), *The hidden-indexical theory's logical-form problem: A rejoinder*, Analysis **56**, 92–97.

Recanati, F. (1993), *Direct Reference: From Language to Thought*, Blackwell, Oxford.

CHAPTER 3

Interpreted Logical Forms, Belief Attribution, and the Dynamic Lexicon

Peter Ludlow

Contents

PRAGMATICS OF PROPOSITIONAL ATTITUDE REPORTS
Current Research in the Semantics/Pragmatics Interface, Vol. 4
Edited by K.M. Jaszczolt

A great deal of recent work at the intersection of philosophy and linguistic theory has argued for the use of Interpreted Logical Forms (ILFs) in the analysis of intensional phenomena. So, for example, ILFs have been argued to serve as the objects of propositional attitudes (see Harman (1972), Higginbotham (1986, 1991), Segal (1989), Larson and Ludlow (1993), Larson and Segal (1995)), and there have been proposals for extending ILF theories to the handling of quotational environments (Seymour, 1996),[1] to intensional transitive constructions (den Dikken, Larson and Ludlow, 1996), and to the analysis of tense (Ludlow, 1999). More generally, it has been proposed that ILF theories might provide a crucial link in the eventual naturalization of Frege's puzzle (Segal, 1996).

Despite the productivity of this philosophical/linguistic paradigm, a number of criticisms have been raised against ILF theories. In this paper I will examine one of these – the criticism that ILF theories cannot handle the Padrewski-type cases of Kripke (1979) – and show that the criticism can be dispensed with if we avoid misunderstandings about the nature of the ILF theory and if we understand the dynamic approach to belief attribution that it employs. I will begin with a brief description of the ILF theory, will then take up some of the misunderstandings about the theory, and will then turn to the specific criticism.

1. ILFs

It is a basic semantic fact that substitution of co-extensive expressions preserves truth values in cases like (1), but does not do so in the context of belief reports like (2).

(1) a. Max met [$_{NP}$ Judy Garland]
b. Max met [$_{NP}$ Frances Gumm]

(2) a. Max believed [$_S$ that Judy Garland was a fine actress]
b. #Max believed [$_S$ that Frances Gumm was a fine actress]

What is going on in contexts like (2)? One possibility would be to argue that (2a) expresses a relation between Max and the embedded clause – i.e. that it expresses a relation between Max and a bit of the syntax itself. In this case, the object of belief would be as in (3).

(3) [$_S$ Judy Garland was a fine actress]

That this solution is inadequate can be seen when we turn to cases like (4) and (5).

(4) Max believed [$_S$ that she was a fine actress]

(5) [$_S$ Galileo believed that [$_S$ that moves]]

[1] But see Cappelen, and Ernie LePore (1997) for criticism of ILF approaches to quotation.

In these cases the problem is that the syntax of the that-clause is not sufficient to distinguish belief reports which are of the same form, but which involve pointing to different individuals. To illustrate, the syntactic theory just sketched would hold that (5) expresses a relation between Galileo and the syntactic object given in (6).

(6) [$_S$ that moves]

But then there is no way to distinguish a belief report in which we say, "Galileo said that that moves" (pointing to the Moon) and "Galileo said that that moves" (pointing to Earth). What we need in addition to the syntactic form of the that-clause, apparently, are the semantic values of the components of the that-clause.[2] This is the basic idea behind the ILF theory.

For example, according to the ILF theory, a belief report like (5) expresses a relation to (6) with semantic values assigned to each node of the clause. If we assume that the syntax of (6) is the syntactic phrase marker in (7) (abstracting from detail here),

(7)

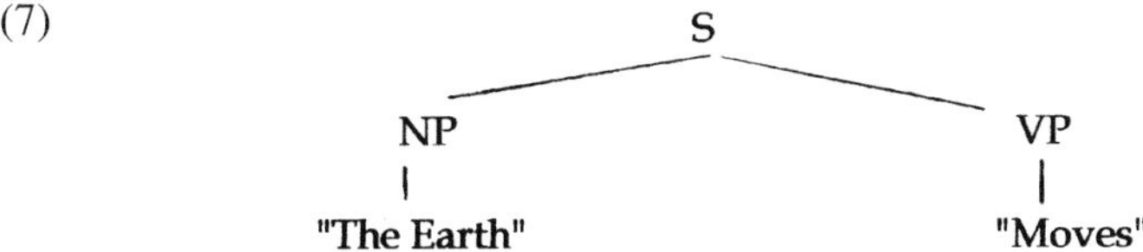

then we might represent the ILF as follows, where each node is paired with its semantic value.

(8)

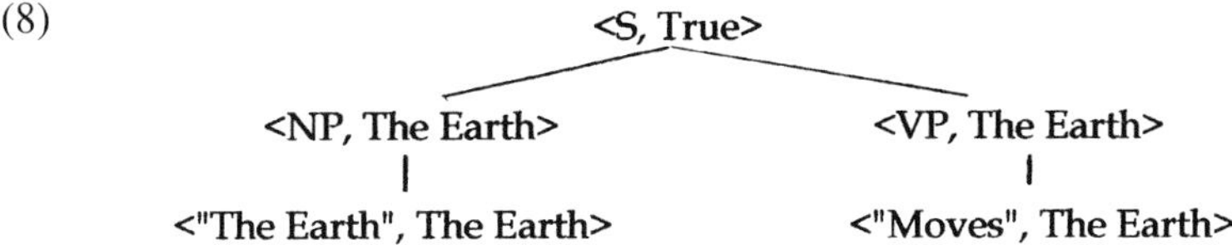

ILFs, in effect, conjoin a semantic value with its linguistic "mode of presentation". Unlike the naive syntactic theory discussed above, ILF theories, by including semantic values, can distinguish both of the beliefs reported as "Galileo said that that moves", because the two different acts of pointing pick out different semantic values (the Moon in one case and Earth in the other). Thus, in the case where I point at the moon, we get the ILF in (9). In the case where I point at Earth, we get the ILF in (10).

2 For an alternative view, see Fiengo and May (1996), who argue that the semantic values are in fact superfluous and that properly augmented syntactic objects should suffice. Due to limitations of space I will have to leave discussion of their view for another day.

(9)

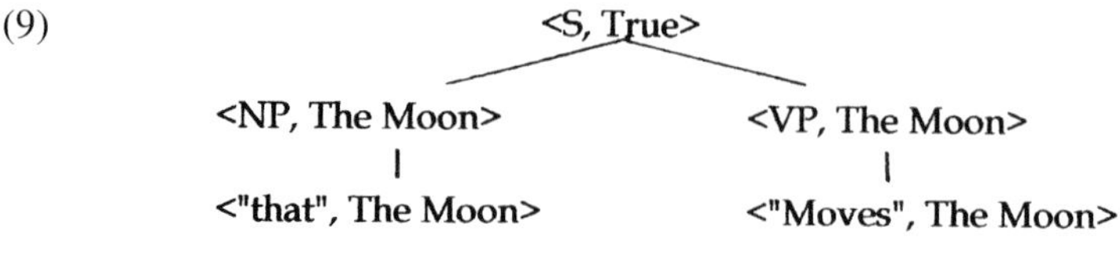

(10)

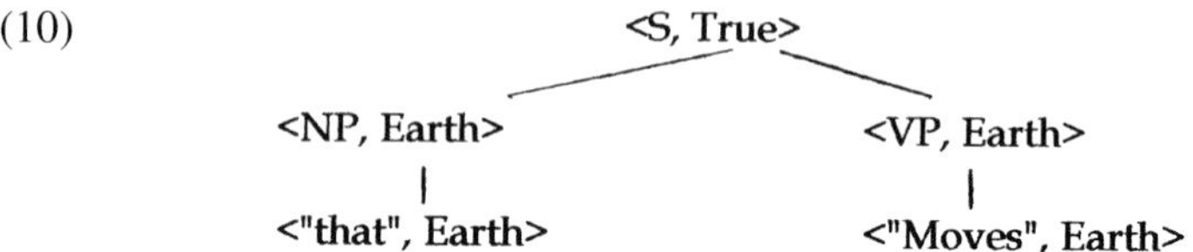

In a nutshell, ILF theories are hybrid theories of the attitudes that incorporate both the semantic values (references) of the expressions used in the that-clause and the expressions themselves. The promise of such theories is that because the ILFs contain linguistic expressions they are fine-grained enough so that we need not invoke Fregean senses, properties, or other kinds of intensional objects. ILFs therefore allow us to give a semantics for the attitudes with purely extensional resources.[3]

2. Misunderstandings about ILFs: Galileo, dogs and babies[4]

If we are speakers of English, we routinely use English to attribute beliefs to individuals like Galileo, as well as to dogs and to other sorts of creatures which do not have a language with English words in them (and which in some cases may not have a language at all). A number of researchers have supposed that an ILF is intended to mirror the structure of some object in the mind/brain of the ascribee, and have argued that if this is the case then the ILF position is implausible; many of the individuals that we ascribe beliefs to have no acquaintance with the English language, and certainly have no representations in their minds/brains that mirror the syntax of English.

As argued in Segal (1989) and Larson and Ludlow (1993) however, this argument rests upon a mistaken assumption about the role that ILFs would play in a theory of belief ascription. I might say, "Fido believes his dish is empty", employ-

[3] Other approaches combine both semantic values (including properties) and lexical material (e.g., Richard (1990) and Kaplan (1990)), but ILF approaches are ordinarily more austere in that they eschew properties. The idea is that if you have the lexical material you can make do without the properties. I say "ordinarily" more austere because there are exceptions. See, for example, Pietroski (1993, 1994, 1996), who allows possible worlds to be built into ILFs.

[4] Portions of this section are drawn from Larson and Ludlow (1993, Section 7) and Ludlow (1999, Chapter 3).

ing an ILF with English words, but I do not thereby suppose that there are English lexical items located somewhere in Fido's language of thought. For that matter, I do not even suppose that what is happening in Fido's language of thought must be "similar" to the ILF that I have constructed.[5] For all I know, Fido may have a language of thought that is radically different from my own and he may even have no language of thought at all.

When I say "Fido believes his dish is empty" I am saying that Fido believes a particular ILF with English expressions in it. Exactly what is going on if "believe" isn't supposed to express a relation between an ILF and something that is going on in Fido's head (and certainly nothing to do with Fido's linguistic practice)? Since we can faithfully ascribe attitudes to creatures without language, it is crucial to see that ILFs aren't intended to describe episodes in the creature's language of thought, but rather are intended to provide information for the benefit of a hearer who wants to construct a theory of the creature's mental life. Put another way, the emphasis should be on the relation between the ascription and the hearer, rather than on the relation between the ascription and the agent to whom the attitude is ascribed.

Larson and Ludlow (1993) make a preliminary sketch of how that could be possible, suggesting that a system underlying our ability to grasp phrases of the form 'x believes y' will involve at least the following three components:[6]

(i) The tacit theory of belief
(ii) The tacit theory of the goals of belief ascription
(iii) The tacit theory of belief ascription logistics

To illustrate, consider a speaker S, who wishes to ascribe an attitude to an agent A for the benefit of a hearer H. Component (i) states the properties that speakers tacitly ascribe to beliefs, including their relations to other components of thought and to action. This component is more commonly recognized under the heading of "folk psychology", which is taken to be the theory of psychology used by individuals to explain the actions of other agents. Philosophical explications of folk psychology have been with us for some time,[7] but full elaboration of the common sense theory of belief will need to make use of the vast psychological research in this area. This research includes the study of the child's concept of mind as in (Astington, Harris and Olson, 1988; Frye and Moore, 1991; Wellman, 1990), related work in anthropology (d'Andrade, 1987), as well as a great deal of work in social

[5] Here apparently I depart from Higginbotham (1986) and Pietroski (1994) who argue that ILFs *are* similar to features of what the agent says or believes.

[6] Larson and Ludlow (1993) speak of this system as being a chapter in pragmatics, but this is a misleading way to describe what is happening. More accurately, there is a deep theory that underlies our comprehension of the meaning of 'believes'. A description of this theory is an *elucidation* (in the sense of Higginbotham (1989)) of the tacit knowledge that an agent must have to be said to know the meaning of 'believes'.

[7] See Audi (1973a, 1973b) for important examples.

psychology (see Tedeschi, Lindskold and Rosenfeld, 1985, Chapters 2 and 4 for a survey).[8]

Component (ii) states the theory a speaker deploys in determining a hearer's interests. In almost every case, the goal of a speaker *S* is to cause a hearer *H* to form a certain theory about the belief structure of an agent *A*. Unless *S* is trying to mislead *H*, *S* will be attempting to assist *H* in forming a theory of *A*'s mental life. What *H* finds helpful will of course depend upon *H*'s interests. As noted in (Larson and Ludlow, 1993) sometimes *H* will want a theory which allows *H* to predict the behavior of *A*. Other times *H* will want a theory of what *A* knows, so that *H* may modify his or her behavior accordingly. For example, *H* may need to know whether to inform *A* of something, ask *A* something, or otherwise act in the knowledge that *A* has the proper information.

Part (iii), the theory of belief ascription logistics, states which expressions must be used in a given context to achieve specific belief ascription goals. For example, depending upon *H*'s interests, it is sometimes the referential component of an ILF and sometimes the syntactic component that will be important to the goals of ascription. In cases where the syntactic component is important, i.e. cases where prediction or explanation of behavior is the goal, Larson and Ludlow argue that the choice of lexical constituents in an ILF involve a two-stage process with respect *S* and *H*. First *S* determines the way in which *H* models *A*'s belief structure (and vice versa). Then *S* tacitly "negotiates" with *H* the expressions to be used in speaking of the components of that model. Both steps involve complex subprocesses. For example, in inferring *H*'s model of *A*'s belief structure, *S* draws on all of the following:

(a) *S*'s knowledge of *H*'s interests
(b) General principles of common sense psychology
that *S* supposes that H believes
(c) Knowledge which *S* knows *H* to have about *A*

To illustrate, suppose *S* knows *H* to be interested in the behavior of *A* – for example, in whether *A*, while at a public function, will accuse Bernard J. Ortcutt of being a spy. Suppose further that *S* knows that *H* knows that *A* is unaware that Ortcutt is the man in the brown hat. Then by general principles of common sense psychology, which *S* supposes *H* to share, *S* may infer that *H* will deploy a fine-grained model of *A*'s psychology – one in which *A* has distinct representations for Ortcutt/the man in the brown hat.

[8] Most of this work assumes what philosopher's call a theory-theory of the mind. That is, it assumes that we attempt to construct theories of the mind of the agent that interests us. Recently this view has come under attack and it has been proposed that we do not construct theories of the mental states of other agents but rather that we attempt to simulate their mental states (see, for example, Davies and Stone (1995a, 1995b) for surveys of this literature). I'm not sure if the outcome of this debate affects the above proposal. Clearly, if the simulation theory is true, the speaker and hearer shall have to come to some sort of accord as to how best to simulate the mental state of the agent A. With this difference, reasoning should proceed as above.

In the second stage of selecting an ILF, S and H must agree on expressions used to speak of the components of H's model of A's belief structure. Expressions used in attitude ascriptions will be tacitly "negotiated" by participants in the discourse, following quite general principles holding of discourse of all kinds. The general process by which discourse participants negotiate a way to speak of objects (sometimes called "entrainment" by psychologists) is currently the subject of research in psycholinguistics (see Garrod and Anderson (1987), Clark (1992, Chapters 4 and 9), Brennan and Clark (1996) and Brennan (1996) for discussion). Applied to the current discussion, even if S and H are aware that Ortcutt is the man in the brown hat they will exercise care in deploying the expressions 'Ortcutt' and 'man in the brown hat' when describing A's belief state. Indeed they will no doubt employ these different expressions for speaking about A's distinct belief states. When no longer speaking of A's belief state S and H may return to using the expressions interchangeably.

As we will see in the next section, entrainment is a powerful tool for the ILF theorist, for it shows where one classical puzzle about belief ascription goes awry. First, however, we need to recap. It is not a compelling objection to the ILF theory that we use ILFs with English (or some other natural language) expressions to ascribe beliefs to Galileo, to babies, and to nonlinguistic animals. ILFs are not intended to describe objects in the agent's language of thought. Rather, ILFs are objects constructed for the benefit of the hearer to help inform the hearer about the agent's mental state. In a sense then, belief is only distantly a relation between an agent and an ILF – the relation is mediated by a great many considerations as the theory of belief ascription sketched above shows. Perhaps it is even a mistake to suppose that belief is relational. That would be consistent with the ILF theory. The key point is that you can believe an ILF with English expressions in it even if you have never had any contact with English, or even with a language that is formally similar to English.

3. Paderewski and the dynamic lexicon

Consider the case of Peter and Paderewski as discussed in Kripke (1979). Peter might come to believe that there are two Paderewskis – one a famous pianist, and the other his reclusive upstairs neighbor. Unknown to Peter, Paderewski the pianist just *is* his reclusive upstairs neighbor. Under such circumstances, is it not possible that we could report Peter's beliefs as (15) and (16)?

(15) Peter believes Paderewski is a pianist

(16) Peter believes Paderewski is not a pianist

And if that's the case, and if we can conjoin the that-clauses into a single belief, then we end up reporting that Peter inconsistently believes that Paderewski both is and is not a pianist. How is the ILF theory supposed to meet such a challenge, given that the only resources available for distinguishing beliefs are the objectual content (in this case Paderewski himself) and lexical items (like the name 'Paderewski')? Don't we need to introduce intensions or some additional modes of presentation in addition to the lexical items? According to Forbes (1996) such cases present "the hardest case" for theories, like the ILF theory, which are linguistically based. Contra Forbes, I think there is a natural solution to this puzzle. First, however, we need to look at a false start.

In (Larson and Ludlow, 1993) it was proposed that despite appearances Peter will in fact have two lexical items available, 'PaderewskiI' and 'PaderewskiII', and hence the form of the ILFs are different by virtue of this lexical difference. The idea was that in Peter's personal lexicon, at least, there are two distinct lexical entries for Paderewski, just as there are for the word 'bank'.

Others (e.g., Taylor, 1995; Forbes, 1996, fn. 12) have objected that this strategy is illicit since lexical items are supposed to be "common coin" items available to all. That is, the English lexicon is what it is, and while it may indeed contain two entries for 'bank', this information is widely shared. There is no such shared knowledge about there being multiple lexical entries for Paderewski, one to be used when speaking of him qua piano player and the other for speaking of him qua Peter's upstairs neighbor.

This objection rests upon a number of assumptions that I have rejected elsewhere (see Ludlow (1999), Chapter 1). In the first place, the common-coin argument rests upon what Chomsky (1986) calls an "E-language" perspective of the nature of language and hence of the lexicon. That is, it assumes that language is principally a social object established by convention by language users for purposes of communication. If we alternatively follow Chomsky and assume that linguistic forms and hence lexical entries are to be I-language representations (i.e. not external social objects, but rather represented in the mind/brain of the language user), then it is much more difficult to marshal arguments for the common-coin character of lexical items.[9] On the I-language perspective we each have our own lexicons, as it were, and we rely upon extensive (but not universal) overlap for communication to be possible.[10]

Alternatively, much of this discussion might be rendered otiose if we pursue certain other consequences of the ILF theory. One of the features of ILF construction noted above is that it involves the notion of "entrainment", whereby the uses of certain words are negotiated on the fly by discourse participants when ascribing attitudes. Studies on the nature of entrainment (e.g., by Garrod and Anderson

---

[9] The lexical theory drawn on in (Larson and Ludlow, 1993) is principally from (DiSciullo and Williams, 1987), but I now lean towards an approach that would incorporate the more dynamic view of the lexicon that one finds in the psycholinguistic research cited above.

[10] Importantly, on the I-language perspective it is not assumed that I-language is optimal for communication. It was not "built" for purposes of communication, but has merely been co-opted for that purpose.

(1987), Brennan (1996), and Brennan and Clark (1996)) are illuminating, for they show that words chosen as category labels are just fine-grained enough to reflect the relevant distinctions in a particular discourse.

To illustrate, experimental subjects might have the task of holding up certain pictures for their partner, who is to identify the picture (the correct way of identifying it is up to the experimental subjects). The labels chosen will depend upon the other pictures in the experiment. So, for example, in a trial where there is only one picture of a car, the label 'car' will suffice. In other trials, subjects will be more specific distinguishing 'Mercedes' from 'Porsche'. In the case of Peter, the prediction would be that a speaker S and hearer H would ordinarily employ distinct expressions for speaking of Peter's distinct belief states – at least if the two states are being discussed in a single conversation.

The critic of the ILF theory assumes that there are contexts in which it might be said both that "Peter believes Paderewski is a piano player" and "Peter does not believe that Paderewski is a piano player". But are there really such single contexts? We know there are contexts in which the former attribution might be made, and we know there are contexts in which the latter attribution might be made, but are there natural contexts in which both reports might be simultaneously made? Even if speaker and hearer are aware of the agent having multiple lexical entries for Paderewski, there is no way for the speaker to communicate separate beliefs in a single context without somehow signaling which entry is under discussion at the moment. The experimental evidence suggests that in such cases speakers will refine the expressions used, perhaps as 'Paderewski qua pianist' and 'Paderewski qua neighbor' or by some other mechanism (like explicitly pronouncing the numerical subscripts proposed by Larson and Ludlow).

Studies on entrainment also explode the myth of a common-coin lexicon by showing that even individuals who overhear or witness a conversation are in a much weaker position to understand what is being said than are the participants. Schober and Clark (1989), for example, show that addressees are much better than overhearers at understanding what is being said because addressees are involved in the tacit selection of the lexical items that will be employed in the evocation of certain concepts. The overhearer is not in a position to resolve unclarities in word choice and is not in a position to indicate when certain choices give rise to ambiguities for her. The point is that when there is danger of ambiguity, we become more precise in our choice of expression. Surely the same applies to belief attributions.

The point is that the lexicon is dynamic enough so that different word forms can be deployed in different contexts. These contexts may be as narrow as a single conversation. Obviously this bears some similarity to the theory articulated in (Davidson, 1986),[11] but it need not be taken as broadly or as destructively as

[11] Davidson basically argues that anytime two people meet and communicate another "language" is created on the fly. Taken to this extreme, it is a short step to rejecting the idea that there are such things as languages at all (in the traditional sense). And indeed, Davidson appears to take this last step.

Davidson does. Clearly there is a stable portion of our overlapping lexicons. The point here is that the lexicon is nonetheless dynamic, and that there is room for play when making fine distinctions in our belief attributions.

If this is right, then there is a kind of fallacy at work in Kripke's puzzle about belief. The fallacy involves the conjunction of two sentences (Fa and ~Fa) which, as it were, come from different languages. The fallacy, which in formal logic is obvious, is made here because we think of English as a kind of static external object that we are all speaking. In fact, if we are talking about I-language it isn't an external object that we learn to speak, and if I am right it isn't static at all - the lexicon can be bent to form slightly different "languages" in different contexts (and for different discourse participants in those contexts). Accordingly, conjunctions made across discourses need to be greeted with skepticism.

Summing up this section, we don't actually need to make the Larson and Ludlow move of introducing subscripts on lexical items like 'Paderewski', since in the practice of belief attribution this sort of bookkeeping will be done automatically. If multiple senses are under discussion, the discourse participants will either find a way to distinguish them verbally or communication will fail.

4. Conclusion

Once we see that attitude attribution is a very dynamic process extending also into the lexicon then a number of puzzles about belief dissolve. Belief reports do not describe objects that are in the agent's head, or even objects that the agent can be thought to be familiar with. Belief reports are constructed as a device for the speaker and hearer to get clear on the mental life of the agent, relative to the interests of the hearer. To this end, a number of resources are available to the speaker and hearer, including the coining of new lexical items for the purposes of a single conversation. The speaker and hearer are *not* limited to "common coin" lexical items. Indeed, it is their ability to creatively coin new lexical items on the fly which accounts for their ability to communicate successfully, even when they are discussing agents that are unaware that Hersperus is Phosphorus, Cicero is Tully, etc. Importantly, these abilities show how the practice of belief reporting has no need for intensional objects like senses and properties. All that is required are lexical items, and a dynamic theory of belief attribution.

References

Astington, J., Harris, P. and Olson, D. (eds) (1988), *Developing Theories of Mind*, Cambridge University Press, Cambridge.

Audi, R. (1973a), *The concept of wanting*, Philosophical Studies **24**, 1–21.

Audi, R. (1973b), *Intending*, Journal of Philosophy **70**, 387–403.

Brennan, S. (1996), *Lexical entrainment in spontaneous dialog*, Proceedings, 1996 International Symposium on Spoken Dialogue, ISSD-96, Philadelphia, PA, 41–44.
Brennan, S. and Clark, H. (1996), *Conceptual pacts and lexical choice in conversation*, Journal of Experimental Psychology: Learning, Memory and Cognition **22**, 1482–1493.
Cappelen, H. and LePore, E. (1997), *Varieties of quotation*, Mind, 429–450.
Chomsky, N. (1986), *Knowledge of Language*, Praeger, New York.
Clark, H. (1992), *Arenas of Language Use*, CSLI Publications and The University of Chicago Press, Chicago.
D'Andrade, R. (1987), *A folk model of the mind*, Cultural Models in Language and Thought, D. Holland and N. Quinn, eds, Cambridge University Press, Cambridge.
Davidson, D. (1986), *A nice derangement of epitaphs*, Truth and Interpretation: Perspectives on the Philosophy of Donald Davidson, E. LePore, ed., Blackwell, Oxford, 433–446.
Davies, M. and Stone, T. (eds) (1995a), *Folk Psychology: The Theory of Mind Debate*, Blackwell, Oxford.
Davies, M. and Stone, T. (eds) (1995b), *Mental Simulation: Evaluations and Applications*, Blackwell, Oxford.
den Dikken, M., Larson, R. and Ludlow, P. (1996), *Intensional 'transitive' verbs and concealed complement clauses*, Rivista di Linguistica **8**, 331–348.
DiSciullo, A. and Williams, E. (1987), *On the Definition of Word*, MIT Press, Cambridge.
Fiengo, R. and May, R. (1996), *Interpreted logical forms: a critique*, Rivista di Linguistica **8**, 349–374.
Forbes, G. (1996), *Substitutivity and the coherence of quantifying in*, Philosophical Review **105**, 337–372.
Frye, D. and Moore, C. (eds) (1991), *Children's Theories of Mind: Mental States and Social Understanding*, Lawrence Erlbaum Associates, Hillsdale, NJ.
Garrod, S. and Anderson, A. (1987), *Saying what your mean in dialogue: A study in conceptual and semantic co-ordination*, Cognition **27**, 181–218.
Harman, G. (1972), *Logical form*, Foundations of Language **9**, 38–65.
Higginbotham, J. (1986), *Linguistic theory and Davidson's program in semantics*, in E. LePore, *Truth and Interpretation: Perspectives on the Philosophy of Donald Davidson*, Basil Blackwell, Oxford.
Higginbotham, J. (1989), *Elucidations of meaning*, Linguistics and Philosophy **12**, 465–418.
Higginbotham, J. (1991), *Belief and logical form*, Mind and Language **6**, 344–369.
Kaplan, D. (1990), *Words*, Proceedings of the Aristotelian Society, Suppl. Vol. 64, 93–119.
Kripke, S. (1979), *A puzzle about belief*, Meaning and Use, A. Margalit, ed., D. Reidel, Dordrecht, 239–283.
Larson, R. and Ludlow, P. (1993), *Interpreted logical forms*, Synthese **95**, 305–355.
Larson, R. and Segal, G. (1995), *Knowledge of Meaning: Semantic Value and Logical Form*, Bradford Books/MIT Press, Cambridge, MA.
Ludlow, P. (1999), *Semantics, Tense, and Time*, MIT Press, Cambridge, MA.
Pietroski, P. (1993), *Possible worlds, syntax, and opacity*, Analysis **53**, 270–280.
Pietroski, P. (1994), *Similarity and innocent semantics*, McGill Papers in Cognitive Science, #294, McGill University.
Pietroski, P. (1996), *Fregean innocence*, Mind and Language **11**, 338–370.
Reiber, S. (1997), *A semiquotational solution to the substitution puzzles*, Philosophical Studies **86**, 267–301.
Richard, M. (1990), *Propositional Attitudes*, Cambridge University Press, Cambridge.
Schober, M. and Clark, H. (1989), *Understanding by addressees and overhearers*, Cognitive Psychology **21**, 211–232. Reprinted as Chapter 6 of Clark (1992).
Segal, G. (1989), *A preference for sense and reference*, Journal of Philosophy **86**, 73–89.
Segal, G. (1996), *Frege's puzzle as some problems in science*, Rivista di Linguistica **8**, 375–388.
Seymour, D. (1996), *Content and Quotation*, Rivista di Linguistica **8**, 309–330.
Taylor, K. (1995), *Meaning, reference, and cognitive significance*, Mind and Language **10**, 129–180.

Tedeschi, J., Lindskold, S. and Rosenfeld, P. (1985), *Introduction to Social Psychology*, West Publishing Co., St. Paul.

Wellman, H. (1990), *The Child's Theory of Mind*, MIT Press, Cambridge.

CHAPTER 4

Beyond Sense and Reference: An Alternative Response to the Problem of Opacity *

Lenny Clapp

Department of Philosophy, Illinois Wesleyan University, Bloomington, IL 61702-2900, USA

Contents

*I am grateful to Mark Richard, Sylvain Bromberger, Alex Byrne, Irena Heim, Cara Spencer, Michael Glansberg, Rob Streifer, Robert Stainton, Andrew Botterell, Jason Stanley, Jessica Wilson, Harry Deutsch, Mary Reed and the philosophy graduate students at MIT for helpful comments and criticisms.

PRAGMATICS OF PROPOSITIONAL ATTITUDE REPORTS
Current Research in the Semantics/Pragmatics Interface, Vol. 4
Edited by K.M. Jaszczolt

1. Introduction

Semantic theorists working within the traditions of Davidson and Montague have followed Frege (1893) in presupposing what I will call the principle of *sentential compositionality*: the truth conditions of an occurrence of a declarative sentence must be determined by (i) the syntactic structure of the sentence,[1] and (ii) the semantic values assigned to the words and other semantically relevant syntactic elements in the sentence. In this theoretical tradition the task of a semantic theory is to illustrate how the truth conditions of a sentence are a *function* of its syntactic structure and the semantic values it invokes. More precisely, each semantically relevant syntactic element of a sentence, including perhaps *phonetically unrealized* elements, is mapped, relative to a context of utterance, to a semantic value. The theory is directed by this mapping, and the syntactic structure of the sentence, to determine how all the semantic values invoked by the occurrence are combined to determine its truth conditions.[2] Though it is widely recognized that due to context sensitive expressions such as indexicals, demonstratives and tensed verbs, context plays a significant role in determining the truth conditions of an utterance, the role played by context has been limited to that of determining the semantic values of context sensitive expressions. Thus, though it is widely recognized that most if not all declarative sentences determine truth conditions only relative to a context, it is nonetheless presupposed that context is relevant *only* for determining what semantic values are invoked by an occurrence; *sentential compositionality* is preserved.

It is within the constraints imposed by sentential compositionality that *the problem of opacity* for propositional attitude ascriptions arises. Consider an all too familiar example:

(1) John believes that Twain wrote *Huckleberry Finn.*

(2) John believes that Clemens wrote *Huckleberry Finn.*

Sentences (1) and (2) seem to have the same syntactic structure. Moreover, since 'Twain' and 'Clemens' refer to the same man, it at least seems that (1) and (2) invoke the same semantic values in the same order. But if occurrences of (1) and (2) have the same syntactic structure, and invoke the same semantic values in the same order, then *sentential compositionality* dictates that they have the same truth conditions. This is problematic because competent speakers judge that some occurrences of (1) and (2) have distinct truth conditions.

---

[1] In contemporary syntactic theory the relevant level of syntactic representation is called "LF". There is not universal agreement, however, concerning precisely what information appears at LF. Such controversies are not directly relevant to my purposes here, and so I merely assume that those committed to sentential compositionality presuppose the existence of *some* syntactic structure that interacts with a semantic theory as described above.

[2] Commitment to, and motivation for, sentential compositionality is clear in recent textbooks on semantics. See Heim and Kratzer (1998), pp. 1–2, and Larson and Segal (1995), pp. 11–16.

If sentential compositionality is taken for granted, and it is assumed that (1) and (2) have the same syntactic structure, then there are only two plausible strategies for responding to this problem.[3] First, one can maintain that though (1) and (2) have the same syntactic structure, despite initial appearances they do not invoke the same semantic values. This is the strategy adopted by Frege. Frege claimed that expressions occurring with the complement clauses of attitude ascriptions do not have their ordinary referents as semantic values, but instead they shift semantic values so that they have extraordinary entities – senses – as their semantic values. So according to Frege embedded occurrences of 'Twain' and 'Clemens' refer to distinct senses. In this way Frege solves the problem of opacity, for on Frege's analysis occurrences of (1) and (2) invoke different semantic values, and thus it is not problematic that they have distinct truth conditions. I shall say that any proposed solution to the problem of opacity that follows Frege in claiming that, despite appearances, ascriptions such as (1) and (2) do not invoke the same semantic values utilizes *Frege's strategy*. The second strategy of response is to deny that the problem ever really arises. According to this strategy, ascription pairs such as (1) and (2) cannot differ in truth value, and our judgments to the contrary are due to a conflation of *semantic* factors which are limited to considerations of reference and truth value, and mere *pragmatic* factors such as the *appropriateness* of the utterance, and whether or not it is *misleading*. As this second strategy is developed in detail by Salmon (1986) I will call it *Salmon's strategy*.[4]

In my view neither of these strategies of response is adequate, and the only adequate response is to reject the general theoretical constraint that gives rise to the problem: sentential compositionality must be rejected. Salmon's strategy is inadequate not so much because it is implausible, but because it is incompatible with the central task of a semantic theory. The central task of a semantic theory is to explain and predict the judgments of competent speakers concerning the truth conditions of sentences. Denying the veracity of such judgments is not a viable option. Consequently I will here be concerned primarily to demonstrate that Frege's strategy cannot succeed. In what follows I first explain in general terms why *any* proposed solution to the problem of opacity that utilizes Frege's strategy will be inadequate. I then demonstrate in detail how this general problem arises for Richard's (1990)

[3] I will assume throughout this paper that at the relevant level of syntactic representation (1) and (2) have the same syntactic structure. This assumption is incompatible with the claim that the difference in truth conditions is a result of a *structural ambiguity*. If one grants that (1) and (2) have same syntactic structure, one cannot explain the difference between (1) and (2) as being some sort of *de re/de dicto* distinction resulting from differences in quantifier scope.

[4] It might be maintained that "paratactic" analyses, as developed for *oratio obliqua* by Davidson (1968) and extended to attitude ascriptions by LePore and Lowerer (1989), constitute a third plausible strategy. Though I will not consider such paratactic analyses here, they clearly fall within the bounds of Frege's strategy. This because the essential feature of paratactic analyses is their assignment of appropriate semantic values – *utterances* and/or mental event tokens – to the complementizers of complement clauses. Similar remarks apply to the "Interpreted Logical Form" analyses of attitude ascriptions proposed by Larson and Ludlow (1993), and others.

overt indexical analysis of attitude ascriptions. After thus completing my objection to Frege's strategy, I sketch a *discourse holistic* account of the truth conditions of attitude ascriptions that does not presuppose sentential compositionality.

2. The general difficulty with Frege's strategy

Though none of the more recently proposed solutions to the problem of opacity simply posits *senses* and claims that they are the semantic values of occurrences of embedded terms, many recently proposed solutions follow Frege in positing some sort of extraordinary entity to distinguish the truth conditions of ascriptions such as (1) and (2) in keeping with sentential compositionality. That is, though these proposals differ from Frege's in various ways, they all utilize Frege's strategy for solving the problem of opacity. I will briefly explicate two such proposals.

Mark Richard's (1990) "overt indexical" analysis invokes mental representations, expressions of mentalese, to play a role similar to the role played by Frege's senses. But Richard's ingenious analysis differs from Frege's in that Richard analyzes attitude verbs as indexicals; on Richard's analysis attitude verbs designate different relations in different contexts. This added overt indexical feature of Richard's analysis is designed to account for the context sensitivity of attitude ascriptions – it is designed to account for the fact that the same attitude ascription can have different truth conditions in different contexts of utterance. The details of Richard's analysis are somewhat complex, and I will present a more detailed explication of his analysis below, but the basic idea is this: An occurrence of (1) is true if and only if John holds the relation designated by this particular occurrence of 'believes' toward the sentence (type) 'Twain wrote Huck Finn' that occurs embedded in the complement clause. And John holds this particular relation toward 'Twain wrote Huck Finn' if and only if John has a sentence of mentalese Σ on his "belief blackboard" such that *in the context of utterance* 'Twain wrote Huck Finn' *appropriately translates* Σ. It is the semantic value of 'believes' in a context that determines what counts as *appropriate translation* in that context. Different occurrences of 'believes' determine more or less stringent *constraints* on what qualifies as an appropriate translation. If an occurrence of 'believes' determines very lax constraints, then it designates a more transparent *believes* relation, and if it determines very stringent constraints, then it designates a more opaque *believes* relation. So on Richard's analysis an attitude ascription uttered in a context *c* is true if and only if the sentence embedded in the complement clause *appropriately translates* in *c* a sentence of mentalese instantiated by the subject, and what qualifies as an *appropriate translation* in *c* is determined by what relation is designated by the attitude verb in *c*. How does Richard's analysis purport to solve the problem of opacity? Suppose that in a context *c* (1) is true, and (2) is false. Richard's analysis explains this possibility, in keeping with sentential compositionality, as follows: in *c* 'believes' designates a relation such that 'Twain wrote *Huck Finn*' appropriately translates some sentence of mentalese on John's belief blackboard, whereas 'Clemens wrote *Huck Finn*' does not appropriately translate some sentence of mentalese on John's belief blackboard. So John does hold the relation designated by 'believes' in c toward 'Twain wrote *Huck Finn*', though he does not hold this relation toward 'Clemens wrote *Huck Finn*'. So in c (1) is true and (2) is false.

Crimmins and Perry's (1989, 1992) "hidden indexical" analysis posits *cognitive particulars* to play a role very similar to the role played by Frege's senses. But Crimmins and Perry's analysis differs from Frege's and Richard's in that their analysis is *semantically innocent.* According to Frege's and Richard's analyses, terms embedded inside complement clauses of attitude ascriptions *shift* semantic values. On these analyses embedded terms do not have their ordinary referents as semantic values, but instead have senses, expressions of mentalese, or the very expressions themselves, as their semantic values. Crimmins and Perry's analysis, however, does not rely on embedded terms *shifting* semantic values in this way. Rather Crimmins and Perry reject "the doctrine of full articulation," which maintains that every semantic value invoked by an occurrence must be "the content of some [phonetically realized] expression in the sentence" (1992, p. 10). Rejection of full articulation allows Crimmins and Perry to maintain that, while embedded articulated terms retain their ordinary referents, *cognitive particulars* are referred to by a "hidden indexical" element of an ascription. As I will interpret Crimmins and Perry's analysis, it really does posit a "hidden indexical". That is, I will interpret their analysis as positing in the syntactic structure of attitude ascriptions (perhaps at the level of LF) *phonetically unrealized* indexical elements that have cognitive particulars (or properties thereof) as semantic values.[5] Occurrences of propositional attitude ascriptions are thus analyzed as asserting that a three-place relation obtains between an agent, a Russellian proposition, and a complex cognitive particular (or *kind* of cognitive particular), where the complex cognitive particular (or kind) is "tacitly referred to" by phonetically unrealized syntactic elements. And in this way Crimmins and Perry's analysis also purports to distinguish the truth conditions of occurrences of (1) and (2) in keeping with sentential compositionality: An occurrence of (1) is true if and only if the three-place *believes* relation is satisfied by $\langle \text{John}, P, \Sigma_1 \rangle$, where P is the Russellian proposition that Twain wrote *Huckleberry Finn*, and Σ_1 is a complex cognitive particular in John's

---

[5] Crimmins (1992) seems to allow, ironically enough, that there be no "hidden indexical" elements. That is, Crimmins seems to allow that an utterance of an attitude ascription might invoke cognitive particulars as semantic values, even though these cognitive particulars are not the semantic values of any phonetically realized *or even phonetically unrealized* syntactic elements. Thus Crimmins allows (something like) that an occurrence as a whole somehow "tacitly refers" to cognitive particulars. But this allowance is merely an unmotivated attempt to preserve the spirit of sentential compositionality, while avoiding the (implausible) commitment to phonetically unrealized syntactic elements that could have cognitive particulars as semantic values. There is no reason to think that what Crimmins calls "tacit reference" is a sort of *reference*. I therefore ignore Crimmins' allowance, and interpret the "hidden indexical" analysis as described above.

brain that includes one of John's Twain-ish cognitive particulars. An occurrence of (2), in contrast, is true if and only if the three-place *believes* relation is satisfied by ⟨John, P, Σ_2⟩, where Σ_2 is a complex cognitive particular in John's brain that includes one of John's Clemens-ish cognitive particulars.

Both of these analyses utilize Frege's strategy; i.e. they each attempt to distinguish the truth conditions of occurrences of (1) and (2) in keeping with sentential compositionality by positing an extraordinary sort of entity and appealing to such entities to distinguish the semantic values invoked by the occurrences. But because these analyses utilize Frege's strategy, they fall prey to the same general difficulty. The difficulty, in essence, is that any analysis that utilizes Frege's strategy will be pulled in two incompatible directions. The pull in one direction arises from the requirement that the posited extraordinary entities be individuated finely enough to solve all instances of the problem of opacity. The pull in this direction forces the posited entities to be identified with very finely individuated, esoteric, mental entities. The pull in the other direction arises from the requirement that an analysis of attitude ascriptions preserve the legitimacy of our ordinary attitude ascribing practices. Ordinary people who lack detailed knowledge, or even beliefs, concerning one another's mental states are able to utter true attitude ascriptions about each other, and thereby give true explanations of one another's behavior. But this ability of ordinary speakers requires that the posited extraordinary entities be more coarsely individuated and publicly accessible. As nothing could satisfy these competing requirements, nothing could play the role of the posited extraordinary entities. I will first explicate this general difficulty in terms of something like Frege's theory of sense and reference, though the difficulty clearly arises for any analysis of attitude ascriptions that utilizes Frege's strategy.

Frege claims that occurrences of ascriptions such as (1) and (2) differ in truth conditions because the embedded occurrences of 'Twain' and 'Clemens' refer to distinct senses. But, granting the existence of senses, if the embedded occurrences of 'Twain' and 'Clemens' refer to the *same* sense, then Frege's theory fails to solve the problem of opacity. That is, if the occurrences of (1) and (2) have *distinct* truth conditions, yet the embedded occurrences of 'Twain' and 'Clemens' refer to the *same* sense, then the truth conditions of the occurrences of (1) and (2) are *not* a function of (i) their syntactic structure and (ii) the invoked semantic values, and thus Frege's theory of sense and reference would fail to preserve sentential compositionality. So merely positing senses to serve as "secondary referents" is not in itself sufficient to solve the problem of opacity. In order to solve the problem of opacity the posited senses must be individuated finely enough so that for any possible pair of ascription occurrences such as (1) and (2) that differ in truth conditions, there are expressions in the complement clauses of these ascriptions that refer to distinct senses. Let us make this slightly more precise. Consider all actual and possible attitude ascription occurrences that are of the general form, $\ulcorner n V$s that $\Phi(\alpha)\urcorner$. A pair of such occurrences constitutes an *instance of opacity* if and only if

(i) the occurrences have the same syntactic structure;
(ii) the occurrences invoke the same *ordinary* semantic values, in the same order; and
(iii) the occurrences are judged by competent speakers to have distinct truth conditions.

In order for senses to be *appropriately individuated*, the following constraint must be satisfied:

> *The Individuation Constraint*: If two occurrences of attitude ascriptions O_1 and O_2 constitute an instance of opacity, then there must be some sense referred to by some expression in the complement clause of O_1 that is not referred to by any expression in the complement clause of O_2.[6]

If (something like) Frege's theory of sense and reference is to solve the problem of opacity, then it must individuate senses finely enough so that the individuation constraint is satisfied.

Satisfying the individuation constraint is hardly a trivial matter, and I am skeptical that an *independent* account of senses (sentences of mentalese, cognitive particulars, whatever) that satisfies this constraint can be formulated.[7] My central objection against theories that utilize Frege's strategy, however, does not presume that such a theory cannot provide an independent account of senses that satisfies this constraint. My central objection depends only upon the much weaker thesis, for which I argue below, that such a theory can satisfy the individuation constraint only if it identifies its posited entities, senses or whatever, with "ways of thinking," where these "ways of thinking" are individuated by appeal to particular details concerning the subject's mental life. If this is correct, then Frege's theory cannot maintain that 'Twain' has only one secondary referent; i.e. Frege's theory cannot maintain that all embedded occurrences of 'Twain' refer to the same *sense*, where a sense is something like a *linguistic meaning* known by all competent speakers. Rather it must allow distinct embedded occurrences of 'Twain' to refer to distinct "ways of thinking," where details concerning the subject's mental life determine which "way of thinking" ought to be referred to by a given ascription. But this result is incompatible with the pull in the other direction: ordinary speakers are

---

[6] This statement of the *individuation constraint* is not quite right, as occurrences of 'John believes that Twain likes Clemens' and 'John believes that Clemens likes Twain' constitute instances of opacity, yet there need not be a sense referred to by some expression in one complement clause that is not referred to by an expression in the other. It is relatively easy to amend the individuation constraint so that it accounts for such special instances of opacity, though for the sake of simplicity I will not do so.

[7] It would of course be trivial to provide a *dependent* account of senses that satisfies the individuation constraint, i.e. an account that individuates senses by appeal to opacity. For example, one could build into one's account of senses that if there is an instance of opacity involving occurrences of two embedded terms α and β, then these occurrences of α and β *must*, by *fiat*, express distinct senses. Such a *dependent* account would no doubt satisfy the individuation constraint, but it would also render the Fregean theorist's explanation of opacity circular, and therefore vacuous.

able to use and understand attitude ascriptions despite their ignorance of, and lack of intentions to refer to, such esoteric entities.

As examples such as Kripke's (1979) story involving Paderewski illustrate, there are *extreme* instances of opacity in which distinct occurrences of the same attitude ascription (type) have different truth conditions; i.e. there are many cases in which competent speakers would judge that one occurrence of an attitude ascription is true, while a different occurrence of the very same sentence, seemingly referring to the very same entities in the same order, is false. The phenomenon of extreme opacity does not require a setting as complex as Kripke's story involving Paderewski. Such cases are easy to construct using ascriptions containing indexicals and demonstratives. For example, competent speakers might judge one occurrence of 'John believes that *he* is an author' to be true, and another occurrence of this same sentences to be false, where the two occurrences of 'he' refer to the same person. Moreover, as is pointed out by Bach (1997, and this volume), "*any* 'that'-clause could be used, given the right circumstances, to describe something that someone believes and to describe something he disbelieves, and do so without imputing any incoherence to him" (1997, p. 233). So for example, even if John's mental state is held fixed, in the right circumstances one occurrence of 'John believes that Twain wrote *Huckleberry Finn*' can be true, and another occurrence of this very same ascription can be false, and yet no *irrationality* is thereby imputed to John. Consideration of the phenomenon of extreme opacity makes it clear that if (something like) Frege's theory is to satisfy the individuation constraint, it must individuate senses more finely than the *meanings* of expressions of natural language, and even more finely than such expressions themselves. So an advocate of Frege's analysis cannot maintain that senses are something like meanings or expressions of natural language. Rather he must identify the posited extraordinary entities with "ways of thinking" of some kind, and he must deny that every word (type) of natural language expresses only one such "way of thinking."[8]

But how are such "ways of thinking" to be individuated? At the heart of the problem of opacity lies the phenomenon of recognition failure. Where there is an instance of recognition failure, instances of opacity are not far to seek. The phenomenon of recognition failure occurs when a rational subject is twice cognizant of the same entity, and yet is not aware that both cognitions are *about* the same entity. For example, one might read about Chelsea Clinton in the newspaper, and then see her on Martha's Vineyard, and not be aware at the time of the seeing that the person one is seeing is the person one read about. At the core of Frege's strategy there lies this familiar model of recognition failure: If on a given occasion a subject fails to recognize an entity, then that subject must on that occasion instantiate

[8] Even Frege (1893) allowed names to express different senses for different people. Frege famously suggested that for some the sense of 'Aristotle' is given by the description 'the pupil of Plato and the teacher of Alexander the Great', while for others the sense is given by the description 'the teacher of Alexander the Great who was born in Stagira'. Frege also suggested that such variance in sense was a defect of natural language.

two "ways of thinking" (senses, modes of apprehension, whatever) of the entity, and fail to "connect" these "ways of thinking." The upshot is that "ways of thinking" must be individuated finely enough to account for every possible instance of recognition failure. For given any two cognitive acts in which a person thinks about the same entity, later circumstances *could* conspire to provide him with overwhelming, though misleading, evidence that during the two cognitive acts he was not thinking about the same entity. So given almost any two acts of cognizing in which a subject thinks about the same entity, the subject *might* not recognize the entity he thinks about in one act as the entity he thinks about in the other. But to allow for the this *possibility* of recognition failure, the advocate of Frege's strategy must posit two actual "ways of thinking" that the subject might fail to "connect" (or might later "disconnect").[9] But this entails that for almost every cognizant act in which a subject thinks about an entity there must correspond a unique "way of thinking." Consequently, if the individuation constraint is to be satisfied, "ways of thinking" must be individuated as finely as particular cognitive acts of thinking of entities. So, for example, John might have one (or several) "way of thinking" of Twain associated with his reading *Huckleberry Finn*, another with his reading *Tom Sawyer*, another with a certain visual experience of Twain, and yet another with a distinct visual experience of Twain, and so on.

If Frege's theory is to satisfy the individuation constraint, and thereby preserve sentential compositionality, it must identify the posited extraordinary referents with such finely individuated "ways of thinking." That is, it must analyze an occurrence of an ascription of the form $\ulcorner n\,V\text{s that } \Phi(\alpha)\urcorner$ as asserting that the subject referred to by n holds the attitude referred to by V toward a thought (sentence of mentalese, whatever) referred to by the embedded $\Phi(\alpha)$. The ascription is true if and only if this thought (sentence of mentalese, whatever) is composed of particular "ways" in which *the subject* thinks of the ordinary referents of the embedded terms.[10] (I ignore ascriptions in which one or more of the embedded terms lacks an ordinary referent.) Consequently the referents of an embedded occurrence will be *particular to the occurrence*. Different embedded occurrences of α will have to refer to different "ways of thinking," depending upon who the subject is, how they

[9] Richard (1990, p. 184), Crimmins (1992, p. 78), and even Salmon (1986, p. 107) note that their posited entities must be individuated finely enough to account for recognition failure.

[10] The amended version of Frege's analysis we have arrived at seems to be what is suggested in Fodor (1978). It is a version of what Richard (1990) and Forbes (1990) refer to as the "subject oriented" analysis of attitude ascriptions. On this analysis the sense referred to by a referring term appearing in the complement clause of a true ascription is a "way" in which the *subject* thinks of the referent of the term. (Problems of course arise for "empty" embedded terms, and for ascriptions that have more than one person as subject, but nevermind.) A potential alternative to the subject oriented analysis is the "speaker oriented" analysis, which maintains that embedded terms refer to a way in which the *speaker* thinks of the referent of the embedded term. I here consider only the subject oriented proposal, as the speaker oriented proposal clearly gets the truth conditions of attitude ascriptions wrong, and thus does not solve the problem of opacity.

think of the ordinary referent of α, and what the particular circumstances of the ascription are.

But now Frege's analysis has been pulled too far in one direction. If the posited extraordinary referents are identified with such finely individuated "ways of thinking," then the legitimacy of our ordinary attitude ascribing practices is undermined.[11] In uttering attitude ascriptions ordinary speakers are not referring to one another's finely individuated "ways of thinking." Given how little we know about the details of our own and each other's mental states, we *could not* be referring to such esoteric entities.[12] Indeed, the value of folk psychology lies in the fact that it produces relatively accurate predictions and explanations in the *absence* of such specialized knowledge.

Consider an occurrence of

(3) Dostoevsky believed that Shakespeare was a great author.[13]

Frege's analysis maintains that a speaker who utters (3) is attempting to use 'Shakespeare' as it appears in the complement clause to refer to a "way" in which the subject, Dostoevsky, thought of Shakespeare, and that an occurrence of (3) is true (or false) only if the speaker succeeds in so referring to a particular "way" in which Dostoevsky thought of Shakespeare. But ordinary speakers who are perfectly competent in uttering and interpreting (3) have little knowledge, or even belief, concerning the "ways" in which Dostoevsky thought of Shakespeare. Thus Frege's analysis requires too much for the truth of attitude ascriptions.

That Frege's analysis requires too much for the truth of attitude ascriptions is made evident when one considers the *felicity* conditions of attitude ascriptions. According to Frege's analysis, a speaker who utters (3) is, among other things, intending (perhaps "tacitly intending") to refer to a particular "way" in which Dostoevsky thought of Shakespeare, and thus a hearer knows the truth conditions of such an utterance only if she is able to identify which one of Dostoevsky's "ways of thinking of Shakespeare" is being referred to. These claims are extremely implausible, but let us grant them for the time being, so that we might consider what

[11] Frege himself was well aware of the problems that would arise if the sense expressed by a term was permitted to vary intersubjectively. In a letter to Jourdain Frege wrote,

> Now if the sense of a name was something subjective, then the sense of the [sentence] in which the name occurs, and hence the thought, would also be something subjective, and the thought that one man connects with this [sentence] would be different from the thought another man connects with it; a common store of thoughts, a common science would be impossible. It would be impossible for something one man said to contradict what another man said, because the two would not express the same thought at all, but each his own. (Frege, 1980.)

[12] Schiffer (1992) presents this problem as "the meaning intention problem".

[13] The objection presented briefly here is developed in more detail against Crimmins and Perry's (1989, 1992) "hidden indexical" analysis in Clapp (1995). Similar objections against Crimmins and Perry's "hidden indexical" analysis, and Richard's "overt indexical" analysis are presented in Saul (1997).

will happen when the speaker *fails* to refer to a relevant "way of thinking." So suppose that the utterer of (3) fails to refer to a "way" in which Dostoevsky thought of Shakespeare. This might occur for a number of reasons: perhaps Dostoevsky did not think about Shakespeare at all, and thus there is no relevant "way of thinking." Or perhaps, as seems likely given how little speakers know concerning one another's "ways of thinking," the speaker's intentions fail to determine a *unique* "way" in which Dostoevsky thought of Shakespeare. To clarify the case, let us assume that Dostoevsky did not think about Shakespeare at all. Under this assumption, our judgments dictate that an occurrence of (3) would be *false*; if Dostoevsky did not think of Shakespeare at all, then he certainly did not believe that Shakespeare was a great author. But Frege's analysis predicts that an occurrence of (3) would be *infelicitous*, as it would suffer from reference failure. (If one maintains, incorrectly in my view, that occurrences that suffer from reference failure are *false*, then our version of Frege's theory would incorrectly predict that an occurrence of the *negation* of (3) would be false.) The general problem is that our version of Frege's analysis requires too much for the truth of an occurrence of (3). If Dostoevsky believed that Shakespeare was a great author, if, say, he was disposed to declare sincerely that Shakespeare was a great author, and so on, then an occurrence of (3) is *true*. The speaker's (alleged) intentions to refer to this or that particular "way of thinking of Shakespeare" are *irrelevant* to the truth conditions of her utterance.[14]

An advocate of Frege's strategy might attempt to avoid the problem of requiring too much for the truth of ordinary attitude ascriptions by rejecting the idea that in making ordinary attitude ascriptions a speaker is intending to refer to a specific "way" in which the subject thinks of an entity. Instead it might be claimed that in making ordinary attitude ascriptions speakers are merely *describing* the subject's "ways of thinking."[15] For example, an occurrence of (3) might be analyzed as asserting something like this:

(3*) $\exists w(P(w)\ \&\ \text{Believes}\langle\text{Dostoevsky},\ w^\wedge S(\text{`was a great author'})\rangle)$.

Here 'w' ranges over "ways of thinking of Shakespeare," and '$S()$' designates a function from expression types to their senses – for convenience I assume that predicates are associated with only one "way of thinking." And '$^\wedge$' designates a concatenation device for "ways of thinking"; '$^\wedge$' designates a partial function from atomic "ways of thinking" to molecular "ways of thinking" (thoughts, sentences of mentalese, whatever). The predicate '$P()$' designates a property, or constraint, on "ways of thinking." For example '$P()$' might designate something like, "is a way

[14] Similar problems are raised by general ascriptions such as 'Nobody believes that Twain wrote' and 'Everybody believes that Twain wrote'. The problem posed by such sentences is that there is no particular subject whose "way of thinking of Twain" could serve as the extraordinary referent of 'Twain'.

[15] Crimmins and Perry (1989) utilize versions of the descriptive analysis. Crimmins (1992), however, eschews the descriptive analysis in favor of a referential analysis.

of thinking of Shakespeare as being an author." If '$P()$' is so interpreted, then (3*) is appropriately *false*, instead of infelicitous, in the situation where Dostoevsky has no thoughts about Shakespeare at all, since no "way of thinking" satisfying '$P()$' exists. Moreover, the above descriptive analysis does not require the speaker to have intentions sufficient for determining a unique "way" in which Dostoevsky thought of Shakespeare. The above analysis requires only that the speaker have intentions sufficient for determining a (potential) property of Dostoevsky's "ways of thinking of Shakespeare."

An advocate of Frege's strategy is pulled toward the above sketched *descriptive* analysis because of the problem of preserving the legitimacy of our ordinary attitude ascribing practices. The problem is that if "ways of thinking" are individuated as finely as they must be to satisfy the individuation constraint, then, because ordinary speakers lack detailed knowledge concerning one another's "ways of thinking," Frege's analysis will incorrectly predict that many true (or false) occurrences of attitude ascriptions suffer from reference failure. The descriptive analysis is invoked to make up for the fact that ordinary speakers lack the knowledge, beliefs, or even abilities, required for *referring* to one another's particular "ways of thinking." In effect, the descriptive analysis individuates the posited "ways of thinking" more coarsely in an attempt to preclude reference failure and/or to ensure that the subjects of attitude ascriptions will have a requisite "way of thinking." Understood in this way then it is not surprising that the problem of opacity re-emerges for the *descriptive* analysis. That is, if Frege's theory adopts the descriptive analysis, then it cannot solve all instances of the problem of opacity. Suppose that Dostoevsky in fact thought that Shakespeare was a lousy author. Suppose that he regularly asserted that Shakespeare was a lousy author, and so on. Under this assumption our semantic intuitions dictate that (3) is false. Further suppose, however, that Dostoevsky was once shown a picture of someone, and told that the person in the picture was a great author. Dostoevsky had no reason to doubt what he was told, and thus he came to believe that the author depicted, whoever it was, was a great author. Unknown to Dostoevsky the author depicted in the picture was, of course, Shakespeare. Thus there is some "way of thinking of Shakespeare" w that satisfies '$P()$'; i.e. Dostoevsky instantiates some "way of thinking of Shakespeare" w that is a "way of thinking of Shakespeare as being an author." Moreover, w is a constituent in a thought (sentence of mentalese, whatever) expressing that Shakespeare was a great author, and this thought is believed by Dostoevsky. So in this situation (3*) is true, though (3) is false. Hence (3*) is not an adequate analysis of (3). The *descriptive* analysis attempts to preclude the problem of reference failure and thereby takes steps toward preserving the legitimacy of our ordinary attitude ascribing practices, but in so doing it becomes susceptible to the problem of opacity.

The advocate of Frege's strategy might respond by pointing out that the above objection depends upon an unfortunate interpretation of '$P()$', and thus such problems can be avoided so long as '$P()$' is always appropriately interpreted to include certain "ways of thinking," yet exclude others. It is probably correct that if one *assumes* our semantic intuitions concerning an occurrence of an attitude ascription, one can, based upon these intuitions, construct an appropriate interpretation for '$P()$'. But if this is how the interpretation of '$P()$' is to be fixed, our version of Frege's theory fails to provide any sort of *explanation* of the phenomenon of opacity. The advocate of Frege's theory cannot explain and/or predict that occurrences of (1) and (2) have different truth conditions *because* they invoke different properties of "ways of thinking," and then justify the claim that they invoke these different properties by appealing to the fact that (1) and (2) have different truth conditions.[16] If the advocate of Frege's strategy is to justify his claim that in uttering attitude ascriptions ordinary speakers are somehow designating *just the right* properties of "ways of thinking," he must show that *something* about the communicative intentions of the speaker serves to determine *which* property of "ways of thinking" is designated. But the advocate of Frege's strategy cannot do this, for ordinary speakers simply lack the requisite intentions. It is no more plausible to suggest that in uttering attitude ascriptions ordinary speakers intend to designate specific properties of "ways of thinking" than it is to suggest they intend to refer to individual "ways of thinking." Saul puts the point exactly right: "The only plausible intention which could yield the right readings... would be an intention to get the truth conditions right. While this surely is an intention of any speaker who is concerned with truth conditions, allowing this intention to determine semantic content merely evades, rather than solves, the problem of propositional attitude semantics" (1997, p. 435).

A subject can think of an entity in myriad different "ways"; the more a subject knows, or believes, about an entity, the more "ways of thinking about the entity" he will employ. According to analyses that utilize Frege's strategy, if a speaker is to make a true attitude ascription concerning what a subject believes (etc.) about an entity, he must be able to either refer to an individual "way" in which the subject thinks of the entity, or to designate a specific property that is possessed by just the right individual "ways" in which the subject thinks of the entity. But given how little ordinary speakers know, or even believe, concerning one another's "ways of thinking" ordinary speakers will rarely if ever possess such ability.

3. The general difficulty and Richard's overt indexical analysis

The general difficulty described above will plague *any* analysis that utilizes Frege's strategy, but I cannot establish this by examining every analysis that utilizes Frege's strategy. So in this section I will provide evidence in support of this general claim by examining Richard's (1990) ingenious indexical analysis and illustrating

[16] This response on behalf of Frege's strategy in effect violates the *independence* condition on the posited extraordinary entities. See note 7 above.

how the general difficulty arises for it. I have chosen Richard's analysis because Richard is sensitive to the general difficulty with Frege's strategy. In fact, Richard (1990) argues that his overt indexical analysis is superior to Frege's analysis because it does not fall prey to these sorts of difficulties.[17] And in his more recent (1997) paper, Richard amends his earlier analysis in response to difficulties similar to those described above. Thus my purpose in this section is, first, to demonstrate that despite what is claimed for it Richard's (1990) analysis falls to the general difficulty with Frege's strategy, and second, to demonstrate that the amendments proposed in Richard (1997) fail solve the problem.

Let us consider Richard's (1990) proposal in terms of the following example, which I borrow from Richard (1997). Suppose that late at night you and Mary are observing a man whom you both know to be Ortcutt. Ortcutt is dressed in black, and he is sneaking around Ralph's house. Ralph, who is inside his house, looks out his window and seems to catch a fleeting glimpse of Ortcutt, who immediately ducks behind a bush. You then observe Ralph calling the CIA. Mary now utters

(4) Ralph believes that Ortcutt is a spy.

On Richard's overt indexical analysis Mary's utterance is true if and only if the complement clause of the utterance *appropriately translates* some sentence of mentalese on Ralph's "belief blackboard." And whether or not the complement clause does *appropriately translate* some such sentence of mentalese varies with context. According to Richard "context supplies some 'instructions for translation' to get from the mental idiom of [Ralph] to the spoken idiom of [Mary]" (1997, p. 106). So the context of Mary's assertion might determine that, for Ralph, 'Ortcutt' is to be used to translate or represent ω, where ω is a "way of thinking" of Ortcutt consisting of Ralph's recent fleeting glimpse of a man in his yard. Thus Mary's utterance of (4) in this context is true if and only if, roughly, Ralph has a sentence of mentalese on his belief blackboard that expresses the Russellian proposition that Ortcutt is a spy, and in that sentence of mentalese ω plays the role of 'Ortcutt'. (And a similar account applies to the other terms in the complement clause of (4).)

Let us be slightly more precise, so that it is apparent how Richard's (1990) account can preserve sentential compositionality. Richard maintains that 'believes' is an indexical – it designates different relations in different contexts. Glossing some irrelevant details, Richard can be interpreted as claiming that, relative to a context, 'believes' designates a relation between believers and ordered pairs of sentences and Russellian propositions, where for each such pair the first member – the sentence type – expresses (in the context) the second member – the Russellian proposition.[18] Let 'believes$_c$' stand for the particular relation designated

[17] See Richard (1990), Chapters 2 and 3.

[18] Richard actually states (1990, p. 142) that occurrences of 'believes', etc., designate relations between agents and RAMs (Russellian Annotated Matrices). RAMs are structures composed of pairs of

by 'believes' in a context c. According to Richard context c determines a set t of translation instructions for every relevant subject (believer) b. A set t of translation instructions for a believer b will specify which of b's "ways of thinking" are represented by various natural language expressions. For example, a set of translation instructions for John determined in a context c might specify that in c 'Twain' represents, or translates, w_1, w_2, and w_3, where w_1, w_2, and w_3 are expressions of mentalese referring to Twain, or "ways in which John thinks of Twain." Say that set of instructions t for a believer b *translates* b's mentalese sentence m just in case the instructions in t specify expressions of natural language that can be used in c to represent, or translate, m. Now we can state that a believer b stands in believes$_c$ to a sentence-proposition pair $\langle s, r \rangle$ if and only if there is some sentence of mentalese m on b's belief blackboard such that m expresses r and the instructions t for b translate m. So, in terms of our example, Mary's utterance of (4) is true just in case Ralph holds the particular believes relation designated in the context toward the Russellian proposition expressed by 'Ortcutt is a spy'. Suppose, as was assumed above, that the operant translation instructions for Ralph require, among other things, that 'Ortcutt' be used to translate w, where w is a "way of thinking" of Ortcutt consisting of Ralph's recent fleeting glimpse of a man in his yard. Under these assumptions, Mary's utterance of (4) is true if and only if, roughly, Ralph has a sentence of mentalese on his belief blackboard that expresses the Russellian proposition that Ortcutt is a spy, and w plays the role of 'Ortcutt' in this sentence of mentalese.

In Richard's analysis the relations designated by 'believes' ('doubts', etc.) vary across contexts because the operant sets of *translation instructions* are essential to the designated relations, and what translation instructions are operant varies from context to context. Consequently, in order for one to understand Mary's utterance of (4), one must know the semantic value of the relevant occurrence of 'believes'; i.e. one must know what relation is designated by this occurrence. But to know what relation is designated by this occurrence, one must know what translation instructions are operant in the context. And in order to know (perhaps tacitly) that a particular set of translation instructions are operant for a subject, one must know that the subject utilizes the "ways of thinking" that are specified in these instructions. For example, if one is to know that in a context c, for a believer b, 'Twain' translates any of w_1, w_2, or w_3, then one must know that w_1, w_2, and w_3 are "ways in which b thinks of Twain." But the claim that such knowledge is required for competently uttering and interpreting attitude ascriptions is extremely implausible, for competent speakers typically lack any sort of detailed knowledge (or belief) concerning one another's "ways of thinking." Moreover, it cannot be that such knowledge is required, for the truth conditions of attitude ascriptions simply do not depend upon such translation instructions.

---

term types and associated semantic values, and thus are more complex than the sentence-proposition pairs I use in explicating Richard's view. But the additional complexity is not relevant to my purposes here, so I ignore it for sake of simplicity.

Suppose that the impression you and Mary had of the situation involving Ralph and Ortcutt was somewhat mistaken. Perhaps Ralph did not catch a fleeting glimpse of Ortcutt; perhaps Ralph's wife, unseen by you and Mary, saw Ortcutt, and she subsequently alerted Ralph of the trespasser's presence. So no such visual "way of thinking" as w exists. Consequently either (i) Mary's utterance of (4) is predicted to be false, as Ralph does not have an appropriate sentence of mentalese on his belief blackboard, or, what I think is more plausible, (ii) Mary's utterance is infelicitous, as Mary's intentions fail to determine an appropriate set of translation instructions, and as a result the relevant occurrence of 'believes' fails to designate an appropriate relation. But both predictions are incorrect. If at the time of Mary's utterance Ralph is prone to utter sincerely things like 'That guy out there is a spy!' and so on, then Mary's utterance of (4) is true. Granted, Mary is slightly confused since she incorrectly thinks that Ralph caught a fleeting glimpse of Ortcutt when he actually did not. But in uttering (4) Mary is not asserting a belief to the effect that Ortcutt recently caught a glimpse of a man in his yard; in uttering (4) Mary is asserting her belief that Ralph believes Ortcutt to be a spy.

Or suppose Ralph actually caught several discontinuous glimpses of shadowy figures flitting about his yard, so unbeknownst to you and Mary, there is not a unique "visual way of thinking" of Ortcutt w instantiated by Ralph, but rather several such "visual ways of thinking." If this, very likely, circumstance obtains, then Mary's intentions again do not determine an appropriate translation manual for the context, as there is no *unique* visual "way of thinking" w. And consequently Mary again fails to designate an appropriate relation by her utterance of 'believes' in (4). So again Mary's utterance would be predicted to lack a truth value. The problem, which should by now be familiar, is that Richard's (1990) overt indexical proposal requires too much for the truth of attitude ascriptions. As a result it requires ordinary speakers to know far more about the details of one another's mental lives than they typically do know.[19]

If Richard is to avoid this sort of problem, he must somehow preclude such misconceived *translation instructions* from ever being determined by a context. That is, he must not require ordinary speakers to have such detailed knowledge of one another's individual "ways of thinking." One way to do this would be, again, to make the translation instructions *descriptive*; instead of specifying how individual "ways of thinking" can be represented, translation instructions might describe how

[19] Richard's (1990) proposal requires ordinary speakers to know what natural language expressions can be used to translate *representations*, where a *representation* is, roughly, a class of *unified* individual "ways of thinking." Two "ways of thinking" are *unified* for a subject just in case he "connects" them, i.e. just in case he takes them to be representations of the same entity. (See Richard, 1990, pp. 184–190.) Thus *representations* are even more esoteric than are "ways of thinking." If translation instructions tell a speaker/listener how such *representations* can be translated with natural language expressions, then knowing what relation is designated by an occurrence of 'believes' will require the speaker/listener to know about *all* of a subject's "ways of thinking," *and* to know which one's are *unified* with which other ones. Requiring this much knowledge is extremely implausible.

kinds or *types* of "ways of thinking" can be represented. For example, perhaps the operant translation instructions for Mary's utterance of (4) do not require that 'Ortcutt' be used to represent an individual "way of thinking" such as w, but instead require merely that 'Ortcutt' be used to represent, say, any one of Ralph's "ways of thinking" of Ortcutt that was somehow caused by a perception of Ortcutt. As our story goes, Ralph does utilize a "way of thinking" of Ortcutt of this kind: Ralph's wife did see Ortcutt in the yard, and this perception caused her to say something to Ralph, and this saying in turn caused Ralph to instantiate a particular "way of thinking" of Ortcutt. Hence, if at the time of Mary's utterance Ralph is prone to say things like, 'That guy out there is a spy!' and so on, then this revised account correctly predicts that Mary's utterance of (4) is true.

What the revised *descriptive* account essentially does, again, is to make the "ways of thinking" invoked by Richard's analysis more coarsely individuated, and therefore more accessible to ordinary speakers who have very limited knowledge of one another's mental states. But we know from the above discussion of Frege's analysis that by more coarsely individuating "ways of thinking," the proposed solution to the problem of opacity is undermined. The same point applies, *mutatis mutandis*, to the descriptive version of Richard's analysis. Suppose that the translation instructions determined by the context are descriptive, as suggested above: suppose the operant translation instruction require, among other things, that 'Ortcutt' be used to represent a "way of thinking" of Ortcutt that was somehow caused by a perception of Ortcutt. Then Mary's utterance of (4) is predicted to be true if and only if, roughly, there is a sentence of mentalese on Ralph's belief blackboard that expresses the Russellian proposition that Ortcutt is a spy and is such that a "way of thinking" of Ortcutt that was somehow caused by a perception of Ortcutt plays the role of 'Ortcutt' in this mentalese sentence. But now suppose that Mary's utterance is false; suppose that at the time of Mary's utterance Ralph is *not* prone to say things like, 'That guy out there is a spy!' and so on. Suppose he thinks the guy out there is an escaped criminal, and he calls the CIA because, in his anxious state, he confuses the CIA and FBI. Also suppose, however, that five years ago Ralph's friend Smiley who worked for MI5, pointed Ortcutt out to Ralph and said, 'that guy is the best spy we've got'. (Ortcutt was of course wearing a clever disguise at the time.) Ralph believed his friend Smiley, and thus there is (still) a sentence of mentalese on Ralph's belief blackboard that expresses the Russellian proposition that Ortcutt is a spy and is such that a "way of thinking" of Ortcutt that was somehow caused by a perception of Ortcutt plays the role of 'Ortcutt' in this mentalese sentence. Hence relative to this situation the proposed *descriptive* version of Richard's analysis incorrectly predicts that Mary's utterance of (4) is true. By making the translation instructions more general and therefore more accessible to ordinary speakers, Richard's solution to the problem of opacity is undermined.

One might respond on behalf of the descriptive version of Richard's (1990) analysis by pointing out that the above objection succeeds only because of an unfortunate choice of property, or "way of thinking" kind. If Mary's utterance is interpreted as adverting to a property of "ways of thinking" that is more discriminating than *being a way of thinking of Ortcutt somehow caused by a perception of him*, then Mary's utterance of (4) can be assigned appropriate truth conditions. But, again, if Richard's defender is to justify his claim that in uttering attitude ascriptions ordinary speakers are adverting to *just the right* properties of "ways of thinking," he must show that *something* about the communicative intentions of the speaker serves to determine which property of "ways of thinking" features in the operant translation instructions. But, again, ordinary speakers simply lack the requisite intentions for determining such a property. In uttering (4) Mary does not intend to advert to any particular property of Ralph's "ways of thinking" of Ortcutt, and thus she does not advert to any such "way of thinking."

In a recent paper Mark Richard presents and responds to an objection similar to the one presented above.[20] The objection Richard considers is this:

> (a) There is practically *no* use of an attitude ascription where it is determinate that a particular representation or property thereof is the intended object of reference (or adversion). (b) A meaningful expression cannot be mired in this sort of indeterminacy. In particular, if uses of a device generally fail to achieve determinate reference, then the device isn't referential. But (c) if contextualism and (a) are correct, then predicates such as 'believes that Ortcutt is a spy' are mired in such indeterminacy. So contextualism is wrong. (Richard, 1997, p. 105.)

(Richard's term 'contextualism' broadly refers to analyses of attitude ascriptions according to which different finely individuated "ways of thinking" or properties thereof are "adverted to" in different contexts. Hence our amended version of Frege's analysis, Crimmins and Perry's hidden indexical analysis, and Richard's overt indexical analysis are all *contextualist*.)

Richard presents a number of objections against this argument,[21] but I will focus on his rejection of (c). Richard rejects (c) on the grounds that even if something

[20] Richard's (1997) paper presents a number of criticisms of the broadly Fregean analysis of propositional attitudes proposed in Devitt (1996). Devitt responds to Richard's criticisms in Devitt (1997). This exchange between Richard and Devitt perfectly illustrates the general difficulty with Frege's strategy. Richard argues, quite correctly, that if the posited extraordinary entities are to do what they are posited to do, viz. solve the problem of opacity, they must be individuated very finely, more finely than Devitt's "*d*-senses." And Devitt argues, also quite correctly, that Richard's analysis, which posits very finely individuated extraordinary entities, is unable "to explain how hearers use linguistic conventions together with accessible context to understand ascriptions" (Devitt, 1996, p. 199; 1997, p. 124).

[21] Richard rejects (a) on the grounds that there are many occurrences of attitude ascriptions where "a particular property of [ways of thinking] is distinguished enough that it may... be identified as an object of reference" (p. 105). Richard does not, however, adequately support this claim. Richard states, "If I say 'After she heard the lecture on Cicero and read a poem signed 'Tully' she believed that Cicero orated, but not Tully,' it is clear to [what sort of "way of thinking"] I mean to advert..." (p. 105). But it is not clear. Even if we assume that Richard's utterance "adverts" to some sort of "way of thinking" of Cicero that she acquired during the lecture, it is not clear, for she no doubt acquired many sorts of "ways of thinking of Cicero" during the lecture. *Which* acquired during the lecture sort of "way of thinking"

like Crimmins and Perry's hidden indexical theory fails because ordinary speakers lack the knowledge and intentions required for referring to "ways of thinking," or properties thereof, still there will be ways of utilizing Frege's strategy that do not suffer from this problem. In what follows I briefly explicate Richard's more recent (1997) proposal, and demonstrate that it fares no better then his earlier (1990) proposal.

In his more recent (1997) paper Richard seems to concede that the above considered descriptive version of the overt indexical analysis would require the speaker, Mary, to have intentions she simply does not have. He suggests, quite rightly, that Mary "need not have a particular way of identifying Ralph's representations in mind; she means only to be relaying something about Ralph's attitudes..." (p. 106). In response to the problem posed by Mary's lack of the requisite intentions, Richard proposes what I will call the "unintended majority" version of his overt indexical analysis. Richard claims that despite Mary's lack of the requisite intentions, nonetheless "there can still be a collection *C* of 'best candidates' for the property of representations which, in Mary's context, one of Ralph's Ortcutt representations needs to have, in order to be acceptably translated using 'Ortcutt'. Roughly, *C* is the collection of properties expressed by what Mary would offer as ways to fill in the ellipsis in *This belief of Ralph's is one which involves a way of thinking of Ortcutt ...*" (p. 106). Richard goes on to suggest that *being a representation caused by perceiving him*, and *being a representation of Ortcutt involved in the belief that caused Ralph to call the police* are plausible candidates to be in *C*. On this latest proposal the translation instructions do not specify how *individual* "ways of thinking" are to be translated. Nor do they even specify how *kinds* of "ways of thinking" are to be translated. Richard concedes that such translation instructions could not be determined by the context, as Mary lacks the requisite knowledge and intentions. Rather the translation instructions appeal to sets of "best candidate" properties of "ways of thinking," where unmanifested dispositions of the speaker determine such sets of properties. Richard proposes the following translation instruction as an example:

> So far as Ralph is concerned, use 'Ortcutt' to translate a representation of Ortcutt that has most of the properties in *C* (p. 107).

Thus, under the unintended majority version of Richard's analysis, a context determines two things: First, it determines – via the speaker's unmanifested dispo-

---

is adverted to? Aurally acquired "ways of thinking" of Cicero she acquired during the lecture? Aurally or visually acquired "ways of thinking" of Cicero she acquired during the lecture? Suppose the lecturer uttered the name 'Tully', with an ancient Roman pronunciation, several times during the lecture. Are the "ways of thinking" she acquired as a result of such utterances to be included, or excluded from the type adverted to? If they are excluded, how are they excluded? It is not at all clear what sort of "way of thinking" Richard would be "adverting" to with his utterance of 'After she heard the lecture on Cicero and read a poem signed 'Tully' she believed that Cicero orated, but not Tully'. The truth conditions of such an utterance, however, would be relatively clear. And so much the worse for contextualism.

sitions – sets of best candidate properties of "ways of thinking." Second, it determines translation instructions that constrain how natural language expressions can be used to represent "ways of thinking" that have *most* of the properties in this set. On this proposal Mary's utterance is true if and only if, roughly, there is some sentence of mentalese on Ralph's belief blackboard that expresses the Russellian proposition that Ortcutt is a spy, where the individual "way of thinking" playing the role of 'Ortcutt' in this sentence of mentalese has *most* of the properties in the determined candidate set.

The unintended majority version of the overt indexical analysis is well motivated in that it attempts to avoid saddling ordinary speakers with intentions that they do not, and cannot, possess. It is unlikely, however, that ordinary speakers will *always* have the sorts of dispositions that Richard supposes would determine the sets of best candidate properties. If Mary is a typical speaker, she may not be disposed to fill in the relevant ellipsis in any way at all. Moreover, it is even more unlikely that ordinary speakers, or *hearers* for that matter, have *knowledge* (even tacit knowledge) of these dispositions that would enable them to determine the relevant set of best candidate properties. And since such knowledge would be required for determining the truth conditions of occurrences of attitude ascriptions, Richard's unintended majority proposal is incompatible with the fact that ordinary language users typically *do* know the truth conditions of attitude ascriptions. But beyond these problems, or rather *because* of these problems, Richard's unintended majority proposal simply fails to make correct predictions concerning the truth conditions of attitude ascriptions.

First, let us suppose, as seems likely, that the number of best candidate properties in C is relatively large, say around fifty or one hundred. The larger the number of properties in C, the more likely it is that *none* of the subject's relevant "ways of thinking" will have *most* of the properties in C. In terms of Mary utterance of (4), suppose that the context determines a set C that contains exactly one hundred properties. But suppose that none of the individual "ways of thinking" of Ortcutt utilized by Ralph has more than fifty of these properties. In this case the unintended majority version of Richard's analysis predicts that Mary's utterance is false; Ralph does not hold the attitude designated by Mary's utterance of 'believes' toward the pair $\langle$'Ortcutt is a spy', $p\rangle$, where p is the Russellian proposition that Ortcutt is a spy. But Mary's utterance could well be true; if at the time of Mary's utterance Ralph is prone to say things such as 'That guy out there is a spy!' and so on, then Mary's utterance is true, regardless of how many properties in C are possessed by Ralph's "ways of thinking" of Ortcutt. Putting many properties in C is in effect to individuate "ways of thinking" very finely, and, as we have seen, when this is done the legitimacy of our ordinary attitude ascribing practices is undermined.

If, on the other hand, it is claimed that C contains relatively few best candidate properties, then the proposal will be unable to account for all instances of the problem of opacity. To make C contain fewer properties is in effect to individuate "ways of thinking" more coarsely. And, as we have seen, when an analysis utilizing

Frege's strategy coarsely individuates the posited "ways of thinking," the ability of the analysis to solve the problem of opacity is undermined. Suppose that John does not know that Twain is Clemens. He thinks, as he would put it, that both men were authors, but he thinks that Twain wrote *Huckleberry Finn*, while Clemens wrote *Tom Sawyer*. Moreover, John believes that Clemens smoked, but that Twain did *not* smoke; he is prone to utter sincerely things such as 'Clemens smoked', and 'Twain did not smoke', and so on. And further suppose that Ralph and Mary know that John does not believe that Twain and Clemens are the same person, but, as is typical, they do not know, nor even believe, much more than that; they assume that John believes that Twain was a famous author, but they really have no idea what John thinks of Clemens. Now, for whatever reason, Mary utters

(5) John believes that Twain smoked.

Assuming the above description of John's mental states, Mary's utterance of (5) is false. Given Mary's limited knowledge and assumptions concerning John's mental states, it is as plausible as any other proposal that *C* contains the following best candidate properties of John's "ways of thinking" of Twain:

C:
(a) Being a "way of thinking" of Twain involved in a belief toward the Russellian proposition that Twain was an author.
(b) Being a "way of thinking" of Twain involved in a belief toward the Russellian proposition that Twain wrote *Huckleberry Finn*.
(c) Being a "way of thinking" of Twain involved in a belief toward the Russellian proposition that Twain wrote *Tom Sawyer*.

According to the unintended majority version of Richard's analysis, Mary's utterance of (5) is true if and only if, roughly, there is a sentence of mentalese on John's belief blackboard that expresses the Russellian proposition that Twain smoked, where the individual "way of thinking" that plays the role of 'Twain' in this sentence of mentalese has *most* of the properties in *C*. So in this situation the unintended majority proposal makes the wrong prediction concerning Mary's utterance of (5): because John believes that Clemens smoked, and that Clemens was an author who wrote *Tom Sawyer*, there is a sentence of mentalese on John's belief blackboard that expresses the Russellian proposition that Twain smoked where the individual "way of thinking" that plays the role of 'Twain' in this sentence of mentalese has *most* of the properties in *C*. More specifically, because John believes that Clemens smokes and that Clemens was an author who wrote *Tom Sawyer*, John utilizes a relevant "way of thinking" of Twain that has properties (a) and (c) in *C*, and thus he does utilize a relevant "way of thinking" of Twain that has *most* of the properties in *C*. And thus the unintended majority proposal incorrectly predicts that Mary's utterance of (5) is true.

Richard might respond to these last two objections against his unintended majority proposal by noting that they presuppose an unfortunate set C of best candidate properties, and thus such problems could be avoided so long as appropriate sets C of best candidate properties are always somehow determined by the context. But, again, this response is not really to the point. It is probably correct that if one assumes our semantic intuitions concerning an occurrence of an attitude ascription, one can, based upon these intuitions, construct an appropriate set C of best candidate properties. But, again, if this is how an appropriate set C of best candidate properties is to be determined, Richard's analysis fails to provide any sort of *explanation* of the phenomenon of opacity. Richard cannot explain and/or predict that occurrences of (1) and (2) have different truth conditions *because* the contexts of the occurrences determine different appropriate sets C of best candidate properties of "ways of thinking", and then justify the claim that they invoke these appropriate sets by appealing to the fact that (1) and (2) have different truth conditions. Moreover, while it is probably true that an appropriate set C *can always be constructed*, there is no reason to believe that an appropriate set C *will always be determined*. That is, there is no reason to believe that the set C of best candidate properties actually determined in a context, together with the detailed facts concerning the subject's mental state, will *always* yield appropriate truth conditions. Given how little ordinary speakers know about the details of one another's mental lives, it seems likely that *often* their dispositions would determine *in*appropriate sets of best candidate properties.

I have not established that every analysis that utilizes Frege's strategy will fall to the general difficulty presented above. But the above discussion provides very strong evidence in support of this conclusion. The general difficulty with Frege's strategy is that the identity conditions for the posited extraordinary entities are pulled in incompatible directions. In order to account for all instances of the problem of opacity, the posited entities must be identified with very finely individuated "ways of thinking". But if this is done, then the legitimacy of our ordinary attitude ascribing practices is undermined. Even if it is granted that such "ways of thinking" exist, ordinary language users simply do not have the knowledge required for identifying, describing, or referring to such entities. But, conversely, if the posited entities are more coarsely individuated, then an analysis that utilizes Frege's strategy cannot account for all instances of opacity. This general difficulty cannot be avoided by identifying "ways of thinking" with different sorts of entities. Nor can it be avoided by positing another new semantic mechanism – in addition to "reference shifting", "hidden indexicals", or analyzing attitude verbs as overt indexicals – to account for how such "ways of thinking" (or properties thereof) are invoked by attitude ascriptions. This strongly suggests that Frege's strategy is inadequate, and an alternative strategy for responding to the problem of opacity ought to be formulated.

4. An alternative strategy for responding to the problem of opacity

The proper response to the problem of opacity is not to posit extraordinary entities and special referential mechanisms to somehow achieve the result that occurrences of (1) and (2) invoke different semantic values. Rather the proper response is to deny that the truth conditions of occurrences of ascriptions such as (1) and (2) are a function of only (i) their syntactic structures, and (ii) the semantic values they invoke. If sentential compositionality is rejected, then it is not *especially* problematic that occurrences of (1) and (2) have the same syntactic structure and invoke the same semantic values in the same order, yet have distinct truth conditions.

Two kinds of evidence are needed to support this response to the problem of opacity. First, it ought to be demonstrated that semantic phenomena independent of attitude ascriptions are incompatible with sentential compositionality. For if this cannot be demonstrated, the rejection of sentential compositionality can be legitimately objected to on the grounds that it is *ad hoc*. Second, and more importantly, an alternative analysis of attitude ascriptions that does not presuppose sentential compositionality must be formulated and shown to be superior to its rivals. I will not here attempt to provide evidence of the first kind.[22] I will, however, take some preliminary steps toward providing evidence of the second kind by sketching an analysis of attitude ascriptions that does not presuppose sentential compositionality.

Attitude ascriptions are very context sensitive. Even if the facts concerning a subject's mental states are held fixed, there are some contexts of utterance in which an attitude ascription concerning the subject would be true, and other contexts in which an occurrence of the same ascription, referring to the same subject, would be false. Creating these *extreme* instances of opacity, however, requires a significant amount of what Devitt (1997) calls "stage setting". In order for us to assign distinct truth conditions to different occurrences of the same ascription, the occurrences must be embedded within carefully constructed discourses of the sort that philosophers excel at constructing. Moreover, creating even a *standard* instance of the phenomenon of opacity requires a bit of clever story telling. Even getting firm judgments that occurrences of sentence pairs such as (1) and (2) have distinct truth conditions requires a significant amount of "stage setting". I propose that the stage setting essential to the context sensitivity of attitude ascriptions be taken much more seriously. I propose that the preceding discourse environment of an occurrence of an attitude ascription (and other sorts of sentences as well) is an essential semantic feature of the occurrence: The occurrence cannot be given an adequate semantic analysis independently of this previous discourse environment, *even after all the semantic values invoked by the occurrence are determined.* On this proposal the previous discourse environment does not merely serve to facilitate

[22] Such evidence against sentential compositionality can be found in Travis (1985), Carston (1988), Recanati (1989), Sperber and Wilson (1986), Bach (1994), Stainton (1994), Culicover and Jackendoff (1995), and Saul (1993).

assignment of semantic values to the relevant syntactic elements; rather the previous discourse environment itself is essential to determining the truth conditions of a sentence occurring later in a discourse. Thus this proposal is incompatible with sentential compositionality: the truth conditions of an occurrence need *not* be a function of (i) the syntactic structure of the sentence, and (ii) the semantic values assigned to the semantically relevant syntactic elements in the sentence. Rather on this proposal, which I will call *discourse holism*, the truth conditions of an occurrence need only be a function (i) the syntactic structure of the occurrence, (ii) the semantic values assigned to the words and other semantically relevant syntactic elements in the sentence, and (iii) relevant features of the discourse environment.

The fundamental idea of *discourse holism* has been developed in some detail by theorists working within *Discourse Representation Theory* (DRT) and associated programs in *dynamic semantics*.[23] In what follows I will introduce and use, albeit in a simplistic and informal way, the machinery of DRT to illustrate how a discourse holistic approach can distinguish the truth conditions of occurrences of sentences very similar to (1) and (2).[24]

The underlying idea of DRT is this: In the process of natural language discourse competent speakers construct a *context*, where a context is a set of beliefs that are mutually shared by the discourse participants. A context is a mutually constructed cognitive model of reality. The semantic effect of an utterance within a discourse is to amend the context being constructed, but exactly how an utterance affects the context relative to which it occurs is partly a function of what is already in the context at the time of utterance. The machinery of DRT is a means of representing formally, with "Discourse Representation Structures" (DRSs), how this recursive process of context construction occurs. At the heart of DRT is the "discourse construction algorithm" which constitutes a function from previous DRSs and current utterances to subsequent DRSs. This process is described by Kamp and Ryle as follows:

---

[23] The general idea of discourse holism was, I believe, first proposed by Stalnaker (1978). The formal machinery of "Discourse Representation Theory" is introduced in Kamp (1984), and developed in some detail in Kamp and Reyle (1993). A somewhat similar approach is developed in Fauconnier (1994). The DRT analysis of attitude ascriptions I sketch below owes much to Kamp (1990) and Asher (1986), though it also differs in a number of important respects. In particular, in the analysis sketched here DRSs represent (partial) mutually believed contexts, whereas Kamp and Asher take DRSs to represent (partial) cognitive states of individual discourse participants.

[24] The discourse holistic proposal has some affinity with the "descriptivist" account proposed by Bach (1997 and this volume). Bach claims that attitude ascriptions such as (1) and (2) "though semantically equivalent, are also *semantically incomplete*. That is, they do not express complete propositions, and to that extent they are like such sentences as ['Fred is ready']" (1997, p. 228). Yet Bach, unlike Crimmins and Perry, denies that the requisite completion involves reference to anything like "ways of thinking." According to Bach, the complement clause of a belief report does not *specify* the content believed, but merely *describes*, or *characterizes*, one of the subject's beliefs, where precisely how a given complement clause characterizes a belief varies from context to context.

> ... when the algorithm is applied to a sequence of sentences $S_1, \ldots, S_n$ it deals with sentences in order of appearance. It first incorporates S_1 into starting DRS K_0, then it incorporates S_2 into DRS K_1 resulting from the first incorporation, etc. The first step of the process by which S_i gets incorporated into K_{i-1} consists in adding the syntactic analysis $\lceil S_i \rceil$ of S_i to the set of conditions of K_{i-1} : ... K_{i-1} acts as a context of interpretation for S_i. (Kamp and Reyle, 1993, p. 85.)

Thus according to DRT semantic competence is knowledge of how to construct contexts in the process of natural language discourse. Or in Kamp and Reyle's terminology, what competent speakers know is how to construct DRSs from utterances of sentences and previous DRSs via the discourse construction algorithm.

In DRT truth conditions are directly assigned to DRSs, and thereby indirectly assigned to the utterances from which the DRSs resulted. Thus, since DRS K_{n+1} of a discourse is a function of the utterance of a sentence S_{n+1} together with the previous DRS K_n, the truth conditions of the utterance of S_{n+1} are *not* a function of only (i) the syntactic structure of S_{n+1} and (ii) the semantic values of the words and relevant syntactic features of S_{n+1}. Rather it is more accurate to say that in DRT the truth conditions of S_{n+1} are determined by the discourse construction algorithm as a function of (i) the syntactic structure of S_{n+1} and (ii) the semantic values of the words and relevant syntactic features of S_{n+1}, and (iii) the location of S_{n+1} in a discourse, or more specifically, the relations that obtain between S_{n+1} and the previous sentences in the discourse of which S_{n+1} is a part. According to DRT a discourse creates "a semantic 'web' that cannot in general be equated with a simple conjunction of propositions expressed by the individual sentences" (Kamp, 1990, p. 34).

I cannot here develop the proposal in detail, but discussion of a simple case will suffice to demonstrate that discourse holism constitutes a plausible alternative to Frege's strategy. Suppose that Ralph and Mary are engaged in a discourse which concerns their friend John and his confusion concerning the identity of Twain and Clemens. The following much simplified DRS (see DRS 1) represents the original context of the discourse. It represents some of the relevant mutual beliefs of Ralph and Mary.

DRS 1

$u\ v\ w$
(c1) is named 'John' (u) (c2) is named 'Twain' (v) (c3) is named 'Clemens' (w) (c4) is a great author (v) (c5) wrote *Huck Finn* (v) (c6) (v) is the same person as (w)

The letters 'u', and 'v' and 'w' at the top of DRS 1 are *reference markers*, and the set $\{u, u, v\}$ is the "universe" of DRS 1. A DRS can be thought of as a sort of cognitive model, and reference markers are the things in the model. Thus reference markers are not referents, rather they are representations that may or may not correspond to actual referents. The reference markers also function in the process of DRS construction as "pegs" on which the discourse participants can "hang" property ascriptions. These property ascriptions are represented by the *conditions* (c1)–(c6). The conditions represent some of the things that the discourse participants believe about the entities that, at least allegedly, correspond to the discourse referents. If the mutual beliefs represented by the DRS are accurate, the reference markers in the universe of the DRS will correspond with actual individuals who have the properties represented by the conditions. Thus DRS 1 represents the mutual beliefs of Ralph and Mary that somebody named 'John' exists, that somebody named 'Twain' exists, that somebody named 'Clemens' exists, and the person named 'Twain' was a great author, and the person named 'Twain' wrote *Huck Finn*. Condition (c6) represents that Ralph and Mary mutual belief that Twain *is* Clemens, or more precisely, that the person named 'Clemens' is the person named 'Twain'.[25]

Now suppose that relative to the initial context represented by DRS 1, Ralph utters the following:

> John thinks that Twain and Clemens are different people. He believes that Twain was a great author, but he thinks that Clemens was just an eccentric who never wrote anything.

Ralph's utterances change the context of the discourse between Ralph and Mary. The new context which is brought about by Ralph's utterance, as directed by the discourse construction algorithm, is represented by the following DRS (see DRS 2), which contains all the information contained in DRS 1 plus the information added by Ralph's utterances.

The discourse construction algorithm constructs DRS 2 from DRS 1 together with Ralph's utterances roughly as follows. From the first sentence Ralph utters the algorithm introduces the new reference marker p into the universe of the DRS, and creates (c7) and (a preliminary version of) (c8). Reference marker p represents an (alleged) attitudinal state, or at least a component of a subject's attitudinal state. Condition (c7) in effect states that the (alleged) attitudinal state represented by 'p' is a belief state of John's. Condition (c7), which introduces a *subDRS*, states a condition on this attitudinal state; it states the "content" of John's attitudinal state. A subDRS is required in (c7) because Ralph's first utterance is an attitude

[25] There are some complicated issues raised here, as believing that somebody named 'Twain' exists is not the same thing as believing that Twain exists. One might say that the former is *de dicto*, while the latter is *de re*. These difficulties can be resolved in the framework of DRT (see Kamp, 1990), but they are not relevant to the fundamental point I am making here. So for the sake of simplicity I ignore them.

DRS 2

	$u\ v\ w\ p$
(c1) is named 'John' (u)	
(c2) is named 'Twain' (v)	
(c3) is named 'Clemens' (w)	
(c4) is a great author (v)	
(c5) wrote *Huck Finn* (v)	
(c6) (v) is the same person as (w)	
(c7) believes $\langle u, p\rangle$	
(c8) p:	$x\ y$ (c1') x is *not* the same person as y (c2') was a great author (x) (c3') was just an eccentric who never wrote anything (y)
(c9) $v \Leftrightarrow x$	
(c10) $w \Leftrightarrow v$	

ascription, and hence what it expresses is Ralph's beliefs about John's beliefs, and thus what is results is a subDRS – a cognitive model of a cognitive model.

Ralph's second utterance further develops the subDRS in (c7). That the occurrences of the pronoun 'he' in Ralph's second utterance is interpreted as coreferring with 'John', and not 'Twain' or 'Clemens', is implicitly represented in DRS 2 by the conditions (c1′)–(c3′) being introduced into the subDRS describing u's (i.e. John's) attitudinal state. In DRT every occurrence of a definite noun must be associated with a reference marker already present in the previous DRS, otherwise the utterance containing the definite noun is infelicitous. This is known as *the familiarity constraint*. The conditions (c1′)–(c3′) represent that Ralph and Mary mutually believe that John believes that there are two people, one of whom wrote *Huck Finn*, the other of whom was just an eccentric who never wrote anything. Note that the subDRS does *not* represent that John is familiar with the names 'Twain' and 'Clemens'. This is as it should be: Ralph's utterances could be true, for example, even if John has never heard the names 'Twain' and 'Clemens', and is familiar only with the first names 'Mark' and 'Samuel'.

The embedded occurrences of 'Twain' and 'Clemens' in Ralph's utterances introduce *new* reference markers x and y into the subDRS of (c8′). Sentences containing *unembedded* occurrences of 'Twain' and 'Clemens' would have merely introduced new conditions on v and w. But because the occurrences of 'Twain' and 'Clemens' in Ralph's utterances are embedded in attitudinal complement clauses, they cannot merely be associated with already present reference markers u and v. For this would represent that John shares Ralph and Mary's mutual beliefs concerning Twain; but Ralph's utterances *contrast* John's beliefs about Twain with those of himself and Mary. Ralph's utterances, however, are nonetheless about John's beliefs concerning *Twain*, the guy believed by Ralph and Mary to be the same person as Clemens. Moreover, the familiarity constraint requires that the embedded occurrences of the definite nouns 'Twain' and 'Clemens' in Ralph's utterances be associated with reference markers already present in DRS 1. For these reasons the reference markers x and y of the subDRS are *linked* via (c9) and (c10) to reference markers v and w of the main DRS, which are in turn associated with the names 'Twain' and 'Clemens'. That x and y are *linked* to v and w represents that the embedded occurrences of the names 'Twain' and 'Clemens' in Ralph's ascriptions refer to *Twain*, and because reference markers x and y are linked to already present reference markers u and v, Ralph's utterances satisfy the *familiarity constraint*.[26]

Ralph's utterances are true just in case the DRS constructed by his utterances accurately models reality, i.e. just in case *there are* real individuals a, b, c and attitudinal state d, where a plays the role of reference marker u, b plays the role of reference marker v, c plays the role of reference marker w, and d plays the role of reference marker p.[27]

Slightly more precisely, Ralph's utterances are true if and only if

> $\exists a \exists b \exists c \exists d$ [is named 'John'(a) & is named 'Twain'(b) & is named 'Clemens'(c) & was a great author(b) & wrote *Huck Finn*(b) & b is the same person as c & believes$\langle a, d\rangle$ & (d is true iff $\exists e \exists f$ [e is not the same person as f & was a great author(e) & was just an eccentric who never wrote anything(f)])]

Now let us consider what happens to the context when, in response to Ralph's utterances, Mary utters sentences relevantly similar to ascriptions (1) and (2). Let us first suppose that, in response to Ralph's utterances, Mary utters an ascription relevantly similar to (2):

> He believes that Clemens wrote *Huck Finn*.

Mary's utterance of this sentence evaluated relative to DRS 2 brings about DRS 3a. Mary's utterance amends the subDRS that represents Ralph and Mary's mutual beliefs concerning John's belief state. Thus the subDRS, which is a condition on p, is amended to incorporate the information expressed by Mary's

---

[26] Clearly much more needs to be said concerning linking conditions. In Fauconnier (1994) the idea is developed in much more detail, though in Fauconnier linking is accomplished via "connectors" that map between "triggers" and "targets." The same sorts of issues that arise in attempting to state what exactly it is for reference markers to be linked arise in possible world semantics under the rubric of "transworld identity conditions for objects."

[27] Kamp and Asher define truth for DRSs relative to models in terms of assignment functions, where an assignment function is a (perhaps partial) function from the discourse referents in a DRS to individuals in the universe U of the model. Thus, roughly, a DRS K is true in a model $\langle U, I\rangle$ iff there is some assignment function f such that f is a *proper embedding* for K in $\langle U, I\rangle$. And f is a proper embedding for K in $\langle U, I\rangle$ iff, for every condition in K of the form $C(x)$, where $C()$ is a unary condition and x is a reference marker, $f(x) \in I(C)$. (A recursive clause is required for the case in which C itself is a DRS.)

DRS 3a

$u\ v\ w\ p$	
(c1) is named 'John' (u)	
(c2) is named 'Twain' (v)	
(c3) is named 'Clemens' (w)	
(c4) is a great author (v)	
(c5) wrote *Huck Finn* (v)	
(c6) (v) is the same person as (w)	
(c7) believes $\langle u, p\rangle$	
(c8) p:	$x\ y$ (c1′) (x) is *not* the same person as (y) (c2′) was a great author (x) (c3′) was just an eccentric who never wrote anything (y) (c4′) wrote *Huck Finn* (y)
(c9) $v \Leftrightarrow x$	
(c10) $w \Leftrightarrow y$	

utterance. More specifically, condition (c4′) is added to the subDRS. Reference marker y, rather than x, is associated with Mary's embedded utterance of 'Clemens' because 'Clemens' is familiar to the discourse, and is associated with reference marker w, which is internally linked via (c10) to reference marker y. That Mary's utterance is so linked is required by the familiarity constraint. Mary's utterance of 'He believes that Clemens wrote *Huck Finn*', relative to DRS 2, is thus true if and only if

> $\exists a \exists b \exists c \exists d$ [is named 'John'(a) & is named 'Twain'(b) & is named 'Clemens'(c) & was a great author(b) & wrote *Huck Finn*(b) & b is the same person as c & believes$\langle a, d\rangle$ & (d is true iff $\exists e \exists f$ [e is not the same person as f & was a great author(e) & was just an eccentric who never wrote anything(f) & wrote *Huck Finn*(f)])][28]

The central point here is that relative to the context created by Ralph's previous utterances, Mary's utterance is true only if John is in a belief state that accurately represents the world only if somebody who never wrote anything wrote *Huck Finn*. Thus, unless John is seriously confused, Mary's utterance of 'He believes that Clemens wrote *Huck Finn*' in the above discourse is false.

Now let us suppose that instead of uttering 'He believes that Clemens wrote *Huck Finn*', in response to Ralph's utterances, Mary were to utter an ascription that is relevantly similar to (1):

> He believes that Twain wrote *Huck Finn*.

[28] For the sake of simplicity I ignore the contribution that (c9) and (c10) make to the truth conditions of Mary's utterance. These conditions require, roughly, that the possible persons that could make John's belief state true be *counterparts* to the actual individual Twain.

When an utterance of this sentence is evaluated relative to DRS 2 a significantly different DRS results (see DRS 3b).

DRS 3b

$u\ v\ w\ p$
(c1) is named 'John' (u) (c2) is named 'Twain' (v) (c3) is named 'Clemens' (w) (c4) is a great author (v) (c5) wrote *Huck Finn* (v) (c6) (v) is the same person as (w) (c7) believes $\langle u, p\rangle$
(c8) p: [$x\ y$ (c1′) (x) is *not* the same person as (y) (c2′) was a great author (x) (c3′) was just an eccentric who never wrote anything (y) (c4*) wrote *Huck Finn* (x)]
(c9) $v \Leftrightarrow x$ (c10) $w \Leftrightarrow y$

Again, Mary's utterance amends the subDRS that represents Ralph and Mary's mutual belief concerning John's belief state. More specifically, condition (c4*) is added to the subDRS. This time reference marker x, rather than y, is associated with Mary's utterance of 'Twain' because, again, 'Twain' is familiar to the discourse, and is associated with reference marker v, which is in turn linked via (c9) to reference marker x. That Mary's utterance of 'Twain' be so linked is, again, required by the familiarity constraint. Mary's utterance of 'He believes that Twain wrote *Huck Finn*' relative to DRS 2, is thus true if and only if

> $\exists a \exists b \exists c \exists d$ [is named 'John'(a) & is named 'Twain'(b) & is named 'Clemens'(c) & was a great author(b) & wrote *Huck Finn*(b) & b is the same person as c & believes$\langle a, d\rangle$ & (d is true iff $\exists e \exists f$ [e is not the same person as f & was a great author(e) & was just an eccentric who never wrote anything(f) & wrote *Huck Finn*(e)])]

Thus in this simplistic DRT analysis 'He believes that Clemens wrote *Huck Finn*' uttered in response to Ralph's utterances does not have the same truth conditions as does an utterance of 'He believes that Twain wrote *Huck Finn*'. In particular, such an occurrence of 'He believes that Clemens wrote *Huck Finn*' is true only if John is in a belief state that accurately represents the world only if somebody who never wrote anything wrote *Huck Finn*, while the truth of such an utterance of 'He believes that Twain wrote *Huck Finn*' does not require that John have such an absurd belief.

The above sketched DRT analysis is inadequate because it is incomplete. It merely assumes the results of the discourse construction algorithm, and it provides only a rough picture of how the truth conditions of DRSs are determined. An adequate DRT analysis of attitude ascriptions would have to overcome these deficiencies. But despite its incompleteness the above sketched DRT analysis suffices to illustrate an important advantage that a discourse holistic analysis has, or would have, over analyses that utilize Frege's strategy: A discourse holistic analysis will not face the general difficulty with Frege's strategy. Because a discourse holistic analysis rejects sentential compositionality, it has no need to posit finely individuated extraordinary entities – "ways of thinking" of whatever sort – to account for the truth conditions of attitude ascriptions. The discourse holist, because he rejects sentential compositionality, need not claim that occurrences of (1) and (2) that have distinct truth conditions somehow invoke distinct extraordinary entities. Rather he can maintain that the difference in truth conditions is due to *overt* differences in the discourse environments of the occurrences. In particular, as is illustrated by the DRT analysis sketched above, the discourse holist can appeal to anaphora-like intersentential connections between occurrences of proper names to explain why the truth conditions of ascriptions such as (1) and (2) differ. Thus, as is proper, a discourse holistic analysis of ordinary attitude ascriptions need not presuppose the existence of any sort of "ways of thinking", whose existence may or may not be supported by future empirical evidence. Moreover, a discourse holistic analysis need not suppose that in using attitude ascriptions ordinary speakers are referring to, or otherwise "adverting to", such esoteric entities, and therefore it need not suppose that ordinary speakers have intentions they do not, and cannot, have.

One might object that the proposal of discourse holism confuses *semantic* and *pragmatic* considerations. It might be objected that any effect that the surrounding discourse environment has on what is communicated by an occurrence of an attitude ascription can be only a *pragmatic*, and not a *semantic*, matter. According to this objection the domain of semantics is limited to properties and factors *internal* to a sentence occurrence that are relevant to determining *what is said*.[29] And thus if there is information communicated by an occurrence that is communicated only because of features of the discourse environment *external* to the sentence, then this information is not within the domain of semantics, but is instead "merely pragmatic." Therefore, if our judgment that occurrences of (1) and (2) can differ in truth value is due in part to features of the discourse environment and is not determined by only (i) the syntactic structure of the occurrences, and (ii) the semantic values of the words and other semantically relevant syntactic elements in the occur-

[29] Some, such as Bach (1987), define semantics so that "the semantics of an expression give the information that a competent speaker can glean from it independently of any context of utterance" (p. 5). On this construal, reference and truth are not within the domain of semantics. Another common usage, probably stemming from Grice (1975), includes within semantics everything relevant to determining *what is said* by an occurrence, as opposed to what is (merely) *implicated* by the occurrence. This latter usage would include reference and truth in the domain of semantics. The imagined objector uses 'semantics' in this latter, Grice inspired, way.

rences, then occurrences of (1) and (2) cannot literally *say* different things – they cannot have distinct truth conditions. And judgments to the contrary are based on a confusion of *semantic* and merely *pragmatic* matters. And so, the objection concludes, the discourse holistic proposal simply leads us back to *Salmon's strategy*, briefly mentioned at the outset.

It should now be clear what is wrong with this sort of objection. The objection not only commits us to an analysis of attitude ascriptions that disregards our semantic judgments and is thus incompatible with the central task of a semantic theory, but it *presupposes* sentential compositionality and thereby begs the question against discourse holism. On the discourse holistic proposal sketched above *what is said* by an occurrence – its truth conditions – need *not* be determined by (i) its syntactic structure, and (ii) the semantic values assigned to its semantically relevant syntactic elements. There can be no significant objection to reserving the term 'semantic' for properties determined by such *intrinsic* features of an occurrence. But if that is how the term is to be used, then all the *semantic* properties of an occurrence need not determine *what it says* – need not determine the truth conditions of the occurrence. To merely assert otherwise is to beg the question against the discourse holistic proposal.

References

Asher, N. (1986), *Belief in discourse representation theory*, Journal of Philosophical Logic **15**, 137–189.

Bach, K. (1987), *Thought and Reference*, Oxford University Press, Oxford.

Bach, K. (1994), *Conversational impliciture*, Mind and Language **9** (2).

Bach, K. (1997), *Do belief reports report beliefs?*, The Philosophical Quarterly **78**, 215–241.

Carston, R. (1988), *Implicature, explicature, and truth-theoretic semantics*, Mental Representations: The Interface Between Language and Reality, R. Kempson, ed., Cambridge University Press, Cambridge.

Clapp, L. (1995), *How to be direct and innocent: A criticism of crimmins and perry's theory of attitude ascriptions*, Linguistics and Philosophy.

Crimmins, M. (1992), *Talk About Beliefs*, MIT Press, Cambridge.

Crimmins, M. and Perry, J. (1989), *The Prince and the Phone Booth*, Journal of Philosophy.

Culicover, P. and Jackendoff, R. (1995), *'Something else' for the binding theory*, Linguistic Inquiry **26** (2), 249–275.

Davidson, D. (1968), *On saying that*, Synthese **19**, 130–136.

Devitt, M. (1996), *Coming to Our Senses: A Naturalistic Program of Semantic Localism*, Cambridge University Press, Cambridge.

Devitt, M. (1997), *Meanings and psychology: A response to Mark Richard*, Nous **31** (1), 115–131.

Fauconnier, G. (1994), *Mental Spaces: Aspects of Meaning Construction in Natural Language*, Cambridge University Press, Cambridge.

Fodor, J. (1978), *Propositional attitudes*, The Monist **61** (4). Also in J. Fodor (1981), Representations: Philosophical Essays on the Foundations of Cognitive Science, MIT Press, Cambridge.

Forbes, G. (1990), *The indispensability of Sinn*, Philosophical Review **99**, 535–564.

Frege, G. (1893), *Über Sinn und Bedeutung*, Zeitschrift für Philosophie und Philosophische Kritik **100**, 25–50.

Frege, G. (1980), *Philosophical and Mathematical Correspondence* (Gabriel, Hermes, Kambartel, Theil and Veraart, eds, McGuinness, abr., and Kaal, tr.), University of Chicago Press, Chicago.

Grice, P. (1975), *Logic and conversation*, Speech Acts, Syntax and Semantics **3**, P. Cole and J. Morgan, eds, Academic Press, New York.

Heim, I. and Kratzer, A. (1998), *Semantics in Generative Grammar*, Blackwell Publishers, Oxford.

Kamp, H. (1984), *A theory of truth and semantic representation*. Truth, Representation and Information, J. Groendijk, T. Janssen and M. Stokhof, eds, Foris, Dordrecht.

Kamp, H. (1988), *Comments on Stalnaker*, Contents of Thought, Grimm and Merrill, eds, University of Arizona Press, Tucson, 156–181.

Kamp, H. (1990), *Prolegomena to a structural theory of belief and other attitudes*, Propositional Attitudes, A. Anderson and J. Owens, eds, CSLI Lecture Notes 20, pp. 27–90.

Kamp, H. and Reyle, U. (1993), *From Discourse to Logic: Introduction to Model Theoretic Semantics of Natural Language, Formal Logic and Discourse Representation Theory*, Kluwer, Dordrecht.

Kripke, S. (1979), *A puzzle about belief*, Meaning and Use, A. Margalit, ed., Reidel, Dordrecht.

Larson, R. and Ludlow, P. (1993), *Interpreted logical forms*, Synthese **95**, 305–355.

Larson, R. and Segal, G. (1995), *Knowledge of Meaning: An Introduction to Semantic Theory*, MIT Press, Cambridge.

LePore, E. and Loewer, B. (1989), *You can say* that *again*, Contemporary Perspectives in the Philosophy of Language II, P. French, T. Uehling and H. Wettstein, eds, Midwest Studies in Philosophy **14**, University of Notre Dame Press, Notre Dame, 338–356.

Recanati, F. (1989), *The pragmatics of what is said*, Mind and Language **4**.

Richard, M. (1990), *Propositional Attitudes: An Essay on Thoughts and How We Ascribe Them*, Cambridge University Press, Cambridge.

Richard, M. (1997), *What does commonsense psychology tell us about meaning?*, Nous **31** (1), 87–114.

Salmon, N. (1986), *Frege's Puzzle*, MIT Press, Cambridge.

Saul, J. (1993), *Still an attitude problem*, Linguistics and Philosophy **16**, 423–435.

Saul, J. (1997), *Substitution and simple sentences*, Analysis **57** (2), 102–108.

Schiffer, S. (1992), *Belief ascription*, Journal of Philosophy **89**, 499–521.

Sperber, D. and Wilson, D. (1986), *Relevance: Communication and Cognition*, Blackwell, Cambridge.

Stainton, R. (1994), *Using non-sentences: An application of relevance theory*, Pragmatics and Cognition **22**, 269–284.

Stalnaker, R. (1978), *Assertion*, Syntax and Semantics, Vol. 9: Pragmatics, Cole, ed., Academic Press, New York.

Travis, C. (1985), *On what is strictly speaking true*, Canadian Journal of Philosophy **15**, 187–229.

CHAPTER 5

How Do We Know What Galileo Said?

M.J. Cresswell

PRAGMATICS OF PROPOSITIONAL ATTITUDE REPORTS
Current Research in the Semantics/Pragmatics Interface, Vol. 4
Edited by K.M. Jaszczolt

It is now thirty years since the appearance of Donald Davidson's paper 'On saying that' (Davidson, 1969). Perhaps all that needs to be said has been said – yet even if so, Davidson's paratactic account of *that* clauses still exerts a very strong pull on semantic theorists, and for that reason alone another paper might not be completely otiose.

When I first read Davidson's paper I was struck, as many others must have been, by the dependence of his analysis on a notion of 'samesaying'. Davidson's analysis, recall, of

(1) Galileo said that the earth moves

is that an utterance of (1) consists of an utterance of two sentences

(2) The earth moves

and

(3) Galileo said that

where in (3) *that* is a demonstrative referring to (2), and that (3) is to be analysed as (*op. cit.*, p. 169)

(4) $\exists x$(Galileo's utterance x and my last utterance make us samesayers).

The relation of samesaying is introduced on p. 168. Davidson admits that samesaying involves 'a judgement of synonyms, but not as the foundation of a theory of language, merely as an unanalysed part of the content of the familiar idiom of indirect discourse'.

I want to focus on the claim that samesaying is 'unanalysed'. We are told little more about what precisely Davidson means, but what I shall do is present a question for Davidson's account. The question is this. Does a semantic theory along Davidsonian lines entail that samesaying is determined by the semantics of the languages involved – in (1) Italian and English – or does it not? Put in another way my question could be understood as the question of whether samesaying is a semantic phenomenon – a consequence of your semantic theory – or a pragmatic phenomenon independent of that theory. This question has been touched on in one way or another in a number of discussions of Davidson's account, e.g., in (Bigelow, 1980; Boër, 1990) and on pp. 135–137 of (Schiffer, 1987). My aim is to pose it in as precise a form as I am able.

Davidson's account of saying that is often seen as in competition with an *intensional* account, by which I shall mean an account which considers the job of semantics to be the assignment of such non-linguistic intensional entities as propositions to be the *meanings* of linguistic expressions. In an intensional semantics (2) would have a meaning assigned to it, as would the words ***Galileo*** and ***says***; and (1) would be true iff the meaning of ***Galileo*** (presumably Galileo) stands in the relation which is the meaning of ***says*** to the meaning of (2). According to such an account the meaning of (1) is determined *semantically* from the meanings of all the words in it. If Davidson's theory is to be judged against such an account it has to be construed as providing an alternative explanation – one not involving 'meanings' – of how someone can understand (1) simply by understanding English.

If samesaying is not determined by a semantic theory (and this seems perhaps the most plausible way of taking Davidson's remarks) then I will argue that, whatever task a Davidsonian semantics may be accomplishing, it is not the same task as is being attempted by semantical theories which postulate intensional entities to be the meanings of sentences, and therefore cannot be seen to be in competition with such theories. I shall then go on to look at what the effect would be of the requirement that a semantical theory *should* determine the samesaying relation, and I will argue that to achieve this a Tarski-style truth theory, of the kind Davidson favours (see Davidson, 1967) would need to involve reference to entities of the kind that Davidson's analysis of saying that is intended to avoid, if it is to give an adequate account of the semantics of *that*-clauses.

In this paper I shall concern myself with one question only – the question of whether samesaying is a semantic or a pragmatic notion. Davidson's account of saying that has been discussed from a number of other points of view, and I will at this point mention three of them, if only to make clear their independence of my own question. The first is the question of the syntactic plausibility of Davidson's 'paratactic' account. Two recent syntactic criticisms appear in (Segal and Speas, 1986) and (Hand, 1991). There is also a discussion in (Higginbotham, 1986) and (Segal, 1988). It certainly seems clear that Davidson is wrong at the level of surface syntax, and perhaps also at the level of logical form, though that may be more controversial. The second problem for the paratactic account is the problem of quantifying in. Hand (1991, p. 361) discusses

(5) Each boy said that he wants a baseball glove for Christmas.

I have no wish to defend a paratactic account of (5), but if I had to I would incline to the view that it involves a *de re* sense of ***says*** which relates each boy to an object (in (5) himself) and the utterance of a predicate (in (5) the predicate 'wants a baseball glove for Christmas'). That one can use an utterance to display a predicate may make Davidson's account more abstract than his defenders would be happy with, but could prove a possible move.

The more serious philosophical criticisms of Davidson have usually been that it is not at all clear how to generalize his account to other propositional attitudes. A response to such criticisms occurs in (LePore and Loewer, 1989), but I shall not attempt to evaluate either the criticisms or the replies. What underlies these criticisms may be the thought that the important semantic issues concern respects in which other attitudes are *different* from indirect discourse. Some may even want to claim that saying that is not even a propositional attitude at all. While it may be true that important questions in the philosophy of mind concern differences between indirect discourse and, say, belief and desire, yet one of the themes of

(Cresswell, 1985) (especially Chapters 12 and 13) is that indirect discourse is semantically every bit as difficult as any other attitude. For the semantic problem is the problem of how to account for the *content* of an attitude, whether this content is said, hinted, believed, feared, wanted, or is the object of any other attitude.

It is important to see that Davidson's approach is not a quotational approach. Davidson correctly points out that analysing indirect discourse in terms of a relation between a person and a sentence presupposes reference to a 'language' (by which he has to mean an interpreted language) and 'languages are at least as badly individuated as propositions' (p. 164). I certainly have no quarrel with this, and have argued against quotational approaches, for much the same reasons, in Chapters 6 and 7 of (Cresswell, 1988). But Davidson also rejects an intensional account, for reasons which he claims are 'essentially Quine's' – that there is too much indeterminacy in language to enable us to attribute to a sentence anything which could count as its meaning. It is not clear to me that Davidson's own proposal avoids the problem of indeterminacy, but I shall not take up that issue in this paper. On the contrary I shall begin by setting out a version of an intensional semantics. The kind of language that I shall discuss is a modification of the kind of language $\mathcal{L}$ presented in more detail in Chapters 1 and 2 of (Cresswell, 1994).

(6) $\mathcal{L}$ contains a category of *names*. Let these include ***Galileo*** and ***Terra***.

(7) $\mathcal{L}$ contains a category of *predicates*. Let these include ***moves***, ***supports*** and ***says***.

(8) $\mathcal{L}$ contains a *name-forming operator* **that**.

Category (7) may be further subdivided. ***moves*** is a *one-place* predicate, while ***supports*** and ***says*** are two-place predicates. The grammatically well-formed sentences of $\mathcal{L}$ are those and only those finite sequences of the symbols in (6)–(8) which satisfy the following formation rules:

FR1 If N is a name and F is a one-place predicate then NF is a sentence.

FR2 If N and M are names, not necessarily distinct, and F is a two-place predicate, then NFM is a sentence.

FR3 If α is a sentence then ***that*** α is a name.

To represent a natural language $\mathcal{L}$ would obviously need to be augmented by symbols to represent other names and predicates, as well as sentential operators, quantifiers, adverbs, prepositions and the like. But $\mathcal{L}$, as defined here, contains enough symbols for present purposes.

In (Cresswell, 1978) I claimed that to know what a sentence means is to know the difference between a world in which the sentence is true and one in which it is false. So we begin with a set W of world-time pairs. But $\mathcal{L}$ doesn't only talk about world-time pairs, it also talks about things. Assume that D is the domain or universe of things. Symbols of $\mathcal{L}$ have semantic values. Further, a crucial feature of language is its *conventionality*. What this means is that the semantic value of a symbol – its meaning if you like – is not part of the intrinsic nature of the symbol. So an *interpretation* for $\mathcal{L}$ will include a specification V of the semantic value of each symbol and will consist of a triple $\langle W, D, V \rangle$. The meanings of names are, as far as $\mathcal{L}$ goes, just members of D. Suppose that Galileo and the earth are in D, and suppose that the meaning of ***Galileo*** is Galileo, and that the meaning of ***Terra*** is the earth. That is, $V(\textit{\textbf{Galileo}}) =$ Galileo, and $V(\textit{\textbf{Terra}}) =$ the earth.

Meanings of whole sentences of $\mathcal{L}$ are sets of world-time pairs. But whole sentences are complex expressions, and their meanings depend on the meanings of the symbols in them, together with the rules for combining those meanings together. It is true that the individual words of our language have the meaning that they do by convention, but it is part of that very same convention to determine the meanings of the complex items, in particular the meanings of sentences and of names formed using ***that***. By FR1 a one-place predicate turns a name into a sentence. Among the set of all world-time pairs there will be those at which the earth is moving. Call this set p. There will also be the set of world-time pairs at which Galileo is moving. Call this set q. It will be a constraint on the V which models English that

(9) $V(\textit{\textbf{Terra moves}}) = p$

and

(10) $V(\textit{\textbf{Galileo moves}}) = q$.

What would the meaning of ***moves*** be? Let me first mention an enterprise that I am not engaging in. There is a view of semantics according to which I ought now to say something about what moving is. Perhaps I should decompose it into a number of 'semantic primitives', or perhaps I should locate it in a map of 'features'. I shall do nothing like this. When I spoke just now of the sets p and q I was relying on the fact that there is a set of worlds in which the earth is moving. The earth moves in all the worlds in p and not in the ones out of p. And there is a set of worlds in which Galileo is moving. The commitment of this kind of semantics to such things as possible worlds is admittedly controversial; indeed it was precisely to avoid such a commitment that Davidson developed the theory I am discussing in this paper. But if you grant that there are ways the world might have been but isn't, and if you grant that knowing the meaning of a sentence involves having the ability to distinguish among these, then there will be such sets as p and q, and further we know what they are. For that is simply to admit that we have the ability to know what it is for the earth to be moving, and what it is for Galileo to be moving. It is not the task of semantics, as I understand it, to say what it is for something to move. Things do move, and we can know what it is they do when they move. Notice too that the ability to know what moving is is not a linguistic ability. The linguistic ability is the additional ability to connect moving with a particular word or phrase.

English speakers connect moving with the word ***moves***, while speakers of other languages connect it with quite different words. But speakers of all languages in which there is a word for moving have to know what moving is.

How than can knowledge of p and q take us to a knowledge of the meaning of ***moves***? If you think about it you will see that part at least of what the meaning of ***moves*** does is get you from the earth to p, and from Galileo to q. So the meaning of a one-place predicate is a function whose domain is taken from D and whose values are all subsets of W. Suppose ω is such a function. This means that

(11) $\omega(\text{the earth}) = p$

and

(12) $\omega(\text{Galileo}) = q$.

It should be obvious how to deal with the sentence

(13) ***Terra moves***.

The rule is quite simple:

(14) $V(\textbf{\textit{Terra moves}}) = V(\textbf{\textit{moves}})(\text{V}(\textbf{\textit{Terra}}))$.

$V(\textbf{\textit{moves}})$ we suppose is ω and $V(\textbf{\textit{Terra}})$ is the earth. So $V(\textbf{\textit{moves}})(V(\textbf{\textit{Terra}}))$ is simply

(15) $\omega(\text{the earth})$

and this we recall is p, the set of world-time pairs at which the earth moves. The principle used for (13) applies to all sentences made up in accordance with FR1.

(16) $V(NF) = V(F)(V(N))$.

That is, the value of NF according to V will be the result of taking the function which is the value of F, and this we know is a function from D to subsets of W, and applying that function to the member of D which is the value according to V of the name N. The meaning rule for FR2 is the obvious extension of that for FR1.

(17) $V(NFM) = V(F)(V(N), V(M))$.

Thus

(18) $V(\textbf{\textit{Terra supports Galileo}})$

will be

(19) $V(\textbf{\textit{supports}})(V(\textbf{\textit{Terra}}). V(\textbf{\textit{Galileo}}))$.

V(***supports***) will be a two-place function which takes a and b to the set of world-time pairs at which a supports b, and so $V((19))$ will be the set of world-time pairs at which the earth supports Galileo.

To complete the description of $\mathcal{L}$ I shall consider the name-forming operator ***that*** and the two-place predicate ***says***. The purpose of ***that*** is principally syntactic. Its semantics is very simple. For $p \subseteq W$,

(20) $V(\textbf{\textit{that}})(p) = p.$

For this to work we need to require that D contain all sets of world-time pairs. This is in effect a decision to regard propositions (sets of world-time pairs) as 'things'.

We are finally in a position to provide a sentence in $\mathcal{L}$ to represent (1). It is

(21) ***Galileo says that Terra moves***.

If we were to take seriously the past tense of (1) we would need to introduce a one-place sentential tense operator ***past*** with the semantics:

(22) Where α is any wff of $\mathcal{L}$, and w is a world-time pair having the form $\langle w^*, t\rangle$ in which w^* is a possible world and t a time (interval) then $w \in V(\textbf{\textit{past}}\ \alpha)$ iff for some t' earlier than t, $\langle w^*, t'\rangle \in V(\alpha)$.

Clearly if we have an adequate semantics for (21) then we can deal with its past tense version in terms of (22). In accordance with (20) we have that V(***that Terra moves***) is the set of world-time pairs at which the earth moves. To give a semantics for ***says*** we shall, in the interests of simplicity, invoke an (inessential) idealisation. We are treating a proposition simply as a set of world-time pairs. It is notorious that in this sense of proposition all logically equivalent propositions are identical, and so (21) would have Galileo asserting all propositions logically equivalent to V(***Terra moves***). This problem has been addressed in intensional semantics by myself and others (e.g., Lewis, 1972; Cresswell, 1985; Richard, 1990) and any of those solutions could be invoked, if required, here. However, for the purposes of this paper the idealisation is not relevant, and we may assume an idealised set of language users who are not only completely rational, but also logically omniscient.

The semantics of ***says*** will need to refer to what a speaker means, and this causes the following difficulty. If an interpretation for a language is no more than a pairing of expressions with their meanings then the fact that certain expressions are paired with certain meanings will be a *mathematical* (or logical) fact. But it is obvious that someone who knows no English is not suffering a deficiency of mathematical knowledge. The empirical fact is that a certain formal structure correctly models the behaviour of a linguistic population in ways in which alternative structures do not. Thus an interpretation in which the word ***moves*** refers to moving is correct in a sense in which an interpretation in which ***moves*** refers to resting is wrong. The conclusion of (Cresswell, 1994) was that, even if we are unable to say what it is about linguistic behaviour which gives the words that we use the meanings they have, yet there is a fact of the matter, and the assumption behind the intensional approach to semantics is that these facts are semantic facts. In the case of $\mathcal{L}$, if we assume that W and D are a constant feature of the universe we may refer to an interpretation simply as V, since this will be the only component of $\langle W, D, V\rangle$ which will vary from language to language. So, for any person a and world-time pair w we shall assume that there is a V which best models the language spoken by a at w. We shall often refer to this as V^a. To 'say' a proposition, on the present account, is to express it in an interpreted language – i.e. in a language $\mathcal{L}$ together with an interpretation V. Given this, the meaning of ***says*** may be represented as follows, where a and $b \in D$, and $w \in W$:

(23) $w \in V(\boldsymbol{says})(a, b)$ iff a (assertively) produces an utterance u of a sentence α of $\mathcal{L}^a$ such that, where V^a models the language $\mathcal{L}^a$ that a is speaking at w in producing u, $V^a(\alpha) = b$.

I have put 'assertively' in parentheses so as not to have to take sides on whether ***says*** involves asserting. b will be a set of world-time pairs, but we have put all such sets into D. Given (23), (21) will be true at w iff at w Galileo (assertively) produces an utterance of a sentence α of $\mathcal{L}^{\text{Galileo}}$ such that $V^{\text{Galileo}}(\alpha) = V($***that Terra moves***$)$. And this, as we have seen, is the set of world-time pairs at which the earth moves. So (21) is true iff Galileo produces an utterance of a sentence which means, in his language, that the earth moves. A word may be in order here about the reference to V^a in (23), since this might suggest that $V($***says***$)$ involves a relativity to another language beside V. The reason it does not is that V^a is in fact a bound variable. An analogy is with ***supports***. If I ask whether a supports b I am asking whether a relation holds between two things. If I ask whether a supports *something* I am asking whether a certain one-place property, the property of supporting something, belongs to a. Even though I may be asked to understand what supporting something is in terms of the (two-place) relation of supporting, the property I arrive at is not relative to anything but a. (23) says that a 'says' b iff there is some language that a is speaking and a sentence in it means that b – and since no reference is made to any particular language $V($***says***$)$ is simply a two-place relation between a and b. $V($***says***$)$ may seem circular in its reference to an interpretation for a whole language (including ***says***) but there is no ontological circularity, since $V($***says***$)$ is, ontologically, simply a function from an individual and a set of worlds to a set of worlds. (But see Chapter 12 of (Cresswell, 1985), especially pp. 108–110.) It is convenient to define a function f from an utterance and a world to a set of worlds.

(24) Let $f(u, w) = p$ iff, where V^a is the language used by the utterer a of u in w, and α is the sentence of which u is an utterance, then $V^a(\alpha) = p$.

At least this is so provided a cannot be simultaneously producing, by one and the same utterance, a sentence α in two different (interpreted) languages. We may read $f(w, u) = p$ by saying that u *expresses* in w the proposition p. (Although f is defined in terms of world-time pairs, it is only the world component of the pair which is relevant – assuming that in any world an utterance can occur at only one time.) In this way the world-utterance pairs may be used to encode propositions. It might be worth repeating that the nature of p does not matter. I have chosen it to be a set of world-time pairs, but if a finer notion of proposition is required then that may be used as the value of $f(w, u)$. Notice that although f is defined in terms of the semantics of the language used by the utterer of u in w, it is a function whose two arguments are just w and u, and is not a language-relative function – for the same reasons as $V($**says**$)$ according to (23) is not language-relative. In the perceptive criticism of Davidson in (Arnaud, 1976), Arnaud points out on p. 294 that what an utterer says in an utterance depends on the language being used. This is certainly correct, but does not prevent us from speaking of the semantic properties of an utterance without providing an extra argument place for a language.

So suppose that I know all of the following:

(25) I know which V^{Galileo} models the language $\mathcal{L}^{\text{Galileo}}$ that Galileo was speaking.

(26) I know which sentence of $\mathcal{L}^{\text{Galileo}}$ Galileo uttered when producing an utterance u.

(27) I know which V models the language $\mathcal{L}$ that I am speaking.

(28) I know which sentence of $\mathcal{L}$ I uttered when producing an utterance u'.

On the intensional picture, if I know (25)–(28) then I know whether, in producing u and u' respectively, Galileo and I are samesayers. This is because, on the intensional picture, samesaying is a derivative notion, defined by reference to V in such a way that u and u' make their utterers samesayers in w iff

(29) where α is the sentence of $\mathcal{L}$ uttered in u in w, and β the sentence of $\mathcal{L}^*$ uttered in u' in w and V models the language spoken in u in w, and V^* models the language spoken in u' in w then $V(\alpha) = V^*(\beta)$.

(29) does raise a question about the nature of utterances. Consider an utterance u. In an intensional framework u will take place in a possible world w. The question is whether the very same utterance u can express different propositions in different worlds. I shall not take sides on this question, though I am inclined to think that an utterance might not have meant what it does in fact mean. If this possibility is rejected then f as defined in (24) will depend only on u and not also on w.

In place of an intensional theory of meaning for a language Davidson uses a Tarski-style truth theory. Such a theory cannot accommodate the word ***that*** as used in (20), and I shall later look at how Davidson proposes to treat it. In Davidson's terms, corresponding to (25)–(28) we would have the following:

(30) I know the truth theory of Italian.

(31) I know the truth theory of English.

(32) I know that Galileo uttered 'Eppur si muove'; (utterance u.)

(33) I know that Galileo was speaking Italian in uttering u.

(34) I know that I uttered 'The earth moves'; (utterance u'.)

(35) I know that I am speaking English in uttering u'.

My question for Davidson is simply this. Does the truth (30)–(35) entitle me to conclude that

(36) Galileo's utterance of u, and my utterance of u' make us samesayers?

The first response is to take Davidson's claim about the unanalysability of same-saying as answering no to this question. (36) may well be *true*, and may well be known to be true, but, according to this response, its truth is not something which follows merely from (30)–(35). Additional information is needed to conclude that (36) is true. Now the intensional theories described above assume that if we have semantic knowledge of two languages – as represented in (25)–(28) then we *do* have the knowledge which will enable us to answer yes to (36). This means that these theories give an account of more linguistic knowledge than a Davidsonian theory does, assuming a 'no' answer to the question I posed. It is not my purpose to take any sides on what kind of knowledge a semantic theory *ought* to explain, and it may indeed be theoretically important that there is a level of linguistic knowledge which does not entail an affirmative answer to (36). But just as the fact that a Davidsonian semantics is intended to explain less of our linguistic knowledge than an intensional semantics does cannot be used as an argument against Davidsonian semantics, so the fact that an intensional semantics is intended to explain more of our linguistic knowledge than a Davidsonian semantics does cannot be used as an argument against an intensional semantics. Since the theories are addressing different questions, a comparison between them cannot be used in deciding whether intensional entities are needed in semantics.

But suppose that a Davidsonian theory is supposed to answer 'yes' to (36). What I shall try to do in the next part of the paper is to consider whether it can succeed. In order to do this I will amend the kind of languages introduced above so that they incorporate a Davidson-style solution to the problem of the semantics of *that*-clauses. The principal amendment to the syntax of $\mathcal{L}$ to accommodate Davidson's account of saying that is to incorporate its paratactic nature, as indicated in (2) and (3). Let $\mathcal{L}^\dagger$ be a language which has FR1 and FR2 but lacks FR3. In its place the word ***that*** is added to the class of names. In place of (21) we then have the pair of sentences

(37) ***Terra moves***

and

(38) ***Galileo says that***.

Although in $\mathcal{L}^\dagger$ ***that*** functions syntactically as a name its semantics makes it more like a free individual variable in a first-order language. To be precise its meaning is supplied by context. This requires a slightly different model theory – one which is closer to those provided for first-order logic in the style of Tarski (1936). A model will now consist of a triple $\langle U, D, E\rangle$, where U is simply the set of times, and does not include reference to worlds. On p. 319f of (Davidson, 1967), Davidson appears happy with this kind of relativity to times and refers to it in note 24 of (Davidson, 1969). He treats indexical relativity as equivalent to taking a semantic theory to apply to utterances rather than to sentences. Curiously Montague regarded an utterance as a pair consisting of a sentence and a context. In (Montague, 1974, p. 230), Montague says 'The useful idea of construing a token as a pair consisting of a type and a point of reference originates with Bar-Hillel'. Taylor (1977), working in the Davidsonian tradition, treats tensed sentences as open sentences with free temporal variables. Such a treatment is semantically equivalent to the indexical account assumed here.

I have used E in place of V since, in an extensional language, the value of a predicate is simply an extension – the set of things which satisfy the predicate. In $\mathcal{L}^\dagger$ this is not quite accurate, since the use of temporal indices makes E behave just like V except in using indices from U instead of from W. Nevertheless, in comparing $\mathcal{L}$ with $\mathcal{L}^\dagger$ it will be vital not to confuse the different kinds of semantic value, and the use of a different letter to denote the meaning assignment will hopefully enable the different kinds of value to be kept separate. If N is a name (except for ***that***) then, just as with V, $E(N) \in D$. If F is a one-place predicate then $E(F)$ is a function from D to subsets of U. In the case of ***moves***, for $u \in D$ and $t \in U$, $t \in E(\textbf{\textit{moves}})(u)$ iff u moves at t. If F is a two-place predicate $E(F)$ is a function from pairs from D to subsets of U. In the case of ***supports*** if a and b are in D and $t \in U$, $t \in E(\textbf{\textit{supports}})(a, b)$ iff a supports b at t, and so on. The other principal difference between a semantics for $\mathcal{L}$ and for $\mathcal{L}^\dagger$ is that a meaning assignment for $\mathcal{L}^\dagger$ is relative to a context. In evaluating wff of first-order logic a context would be a sequence of individuals representing the values of all the free variables of the wff. In $\mathcal{L}^\dagger$ there is only one such symbol, and so a context can consist of a single individual, considered as the utterance of the sentence in that context. So in place of $V(\alpha)$ we shall now write $E_u(\alpha)$. Where α is a sentence of $\mathcal{L}^\dagger$, $E_u(\alpha)$ will be a subset of U, which means that it is simply a set of times. For any symbol α except ***that***, $E_u(\alpha) = E(\alpha)$.

(39) E_u $(\textbf{\textit{that}}) = u$.

The rules for evaluating sentences in $\mathcal{L}^\dagger$ are the obvious generalizations of the rules for $\mathcal{L}$:

(40) $E_u(NF) = E_u(F)(E_u(N))$.

(41) $E_u(NFM) = E_u(F)(E_u(N), E_u(M))$.

One important symbol which has a value in $\mathcal{L}^\dagger$ which is not merely an extensionalized version of its value in $\mathcal{L}$ is ***says***. To avoid confusion with (23) I will refer to the meaning of ***says*** in $\mathcal{L}^\dagger$ as $E^\dagger$(***says***). In order to state $E^\dagger$(***says***) I shall introduce the notation $\approx_s$.

(42) $u \approx_s u'$ iff u and u' make their utterers samesayers.

We can then give a meaning for ***says*** in $\mathcal{L}^\dagger$. For any $t \in U$,

(43) $t \in E^\dagger$(***says***)(a, u) iff a produces (assertively) at t an utterance u' such that $u \approx_s u'$.

(1) is then analysed as (38) in a context u in which u is an utterance of (37).

We can now address the question of whether the truth theory of $\mathcal{L}^\dagger$ determines samesaying. In one sense it might seem that it clearly does. On the intensional account, to know the meaning of the words spoken in a given context is to know which of the infinitely many possible V's is the one which best models the linguistic behaviour of a population. If this criterion is used for $\mathcal{L}^\dagger$ then, on the assumption that the E which models the language in which (37) and (38) are uttered satisfies (43), knowing the meaning of ***says*** in a context u will be knowing which set of pairs $\langle a, u' \rangle$, is such that a produces (assertively) at t an utterance u' such that $u \approx_s u'$. So knowing $E^\dagger$(***says***) will indeed entail knowing whether the samesaying relation holds between utterances. Of course, as Schiffer (1987) points out, merely knowing the nature of u may not enable us to know what has been said. On p. 134 Schiffer offers the following little dialogue:

(44) *Pierre:* La neige est blanche.
Donald: Tarski said that.

In this case a monolingual English hearer can conclude that Tarski and Pierre are samesayers without knowing what Tarski said. This does seem to be a serious problem for Davidson, but suppose that we have somehow ensured that (37) and (38) are by a single utterer and that the utterer of (37) and (38) knows what u means. This certainly provides enough knowledge. The problem is that it provides too much. For it entails that I know whether Galileo and I are samesayers on the basis of knowing what ***says*** means in *my* language. Look again at (25)–(28). If we leave off (25) then it should be clear that merely knowing (26)–(28) will not suffice for knowing whether Galileo and I are samesayers. To know *that* I have to know in addition what his utterance meant in *his* language, and knowledge of my language won't provide that.

In fact there is a problem in general about a Tarski-style semantics – what is it to know a particular truth theory? Take ***moves***. One can know the meaning of ***moves*** without knowing which things move. So knowing the meaning of ***moves*** cannot be knowing which E models the language spoken. Presumably what one knows is that, in the language spoken by a linguistic population P,

(45) ***moves*** is true of a at t iff a moves at t.

I shall first take seriously that (45) is something that we *know* when we know a language, and that a semantic theory will involve an account of what it is to know something. Further, I shall assume an intensional account of knowing. Davidson presumably would not accept an intensional analysis of knowing, but such analyses are possible, and, even those who would not accept the entities such accounts use have to admit that they get the truth conditions right under the idealised notion of proposition that is used in (23). Since our aim is to compare Davidsonian and intensional semantic theories, it will be instructive to see how such an analysis fares, in our attempt to see whether knowing the truth theory for a language enables one to know what samesaying is. On the intensional account of knowing, a person a knows that p in a world w iff p is true in every world w' not ruled out by what a knows in w. This is codified by a relation R of *epistemic accessibility* which goes back at least to Hintikka (1962). wRw' iff, for all that a knows in w, the world could be w'. On the intensional interpretation of (45) the right hand side gives no problems. It is the set of worlds in which u moves at t, and does not involve reference to linguistic facts. But the left hand side does involve reference to linguistic facts, since whether or not ***moves*** is true of any particular thing depends on what (interpreted) language the relevant P are speaking. How then should we give an intensional analysis of the knowledge of a Tarski-style truth theory for P's language? A first suggestion is that to know (in w) that (45) is true of the language spoken by P would be:

(46) In every w' such that wRw' the E that gets closest to the language of population P in w is such that $t \in E(\textbf{\textit{moves}})(u)$ iff u moves at t in w'.

The problem with (46) is that in a Tarski-style semantics $E(\textbf{\textit{moves}})$ is simply a function from things to times – in fact the things which move at t in w – and there is no reason to suppose that the same things move in w and w'. One might try to get closer to an acceptable analysis of (45) by supposing that E can vary from world to world. So that (46) would read

(47) In every w' such that wRw' the E that gets closest to the language of population P in w' is such that $t \in E(\textbf{\textit{moves}})(u)$ iff u moves at t in w'.

This will certainly allow different things to move in w and w', but if E represents the meaning of ***moves*** according to the language P use in w' (47) will not allow different things to move in any w' in which P speak the same language as they speak in w. To rectify this problem one would need to take it that P's language in w is to be represented, not by a single extensional E, but by a family V of different

E's, one for each w' such that wRw'. If we write $V_{w'}$ for the E which constitutes the w' version of the language P speak in w then (47) becomes

(48) In every w' such that wRw', $t \in V_{w'}(\textbf{\textit{moves}})(u)$ iff u moves at t in w'.

But (48) then emerges as little more than a notational variant of the intensional semantics itself, with $V_w(\alpha)$ in place of $V(\alpha, w)$. For that reason I shall proceed to consider what a Davidsonian analysis of saying that would look like in an explicitly intensional framework.

We must adapt slightly the intensional semantics presented above since it was for $\mathcal{L}$ rather than $\mathcal{L}^\dagger$, and did not incorporate a mechanism for treating ***that*** as a demonstrative. So our next task will be to provide an intensional semantics for $\mathcal{L}^\dagger$ in order to see what kind of an answer to (36) it would give. No doubt Davidsonians would not be sympathetic toward such an enterprise, but there are after all two quite separate questions. One is whether possible worlds or other intensional entities should be used at all in semantic theories; and the other is whether a samesaying relation between utterances is the correct way to account for the meaning of ***says***. It is the latter question I shall address right now. I shall return to the former question later in the paper. An intensional semantics for $\mathcal{L}^\dagger$ is provided by an interpretation $\langle W, D, V\rangle$ in which W is the set of all world-time pairs, and truth is relative both to a world-time pair w, and also to a context u. The meanings of names (except ***that***) are still members of D, and the meanings of predicates (except ***says***) are as in (12) and (11). The rules for determining the values of sentences are as in (40) and (41), but involving W and V rather than U and E. For any symbol α except ***that***, $V_u(\alpha) = V(\alpha)$. V_u (***that***) $= u$. As a first attempt at an intensional semantics for ***says*** in $\mathcal{L}^\dagger$ we might try, where w is a world-time pair, and a and u are in D,

(49) $w \in V^\dagger(\textbf{\textit{says}})(a, u)$ iff a produces (assertively) at w an utterance u' such that $u \approx_s u'$.

In (49) $\approx_s$ is as defined in (42), and is treated as not world-dependent. This precludes the possibility that $u \approx_s u'$ at w but not at w'. I shall later look at what happens if $u \approx_s u'$ is allowed to hold at some worlds but not others.

In comparing an intensional semantics for $\mathcal{L}^\dagger$ with that originally presented for $\mathcal{L}$ I shall assume the correctness of (23) in the following sense – that saying relates a person and a set of world-time pairs, and holds when a person utters a sentence which, in their language, has that set of world-time pairs as its semantic value. The assumption of correctness is not question-begging, since the motivation for a Davidsonian account is not that (23) is *incorrect* – indeed it is surely obvious that, if samesaying is a semantic rather than a pragmatic relation, then *something* like (23) must be right – but rather that the effect of (23) can be obtained without appeal to such things as meanings or propositions. The aim of this part of the paper is to consider whether a Davidsonian semantics can achieve the same results as an intensional semantics in which $V(\textbf{\textit{says}})$ works according to (23). Consider a representation of (1). First assume that it is just (38). Let V^* be just like V except that $V^*(\textbf{\textit{Terra}})$ = the sun. (38) does not contain the word ***Terra***, and so $V_u((38)) = V_u^*((38))$. But this is wrong, since Gallileo said that the earth moves, not that the sun moves. The problem of course is that in analysing (38) in V_u we are assuming that u is an utterance of (37) in a language in which ***Terra*** means the earth, while in analysing it in V^* we are assuming that u is in a language in which ***Terra*** means the sun. What has gone wrong is that in a report of what Galileo said we have to choose the right context in terms of the previous utterance. One might wish to say that this alone makes the analysis of indirect discourse in $\mathcal{L}^\dagger$ a pragmatic matter. It is certainly pragmatic in Richard Montague's sense (see Montague, 1974, Chapters 3 and 4) whereby any indexical relativity is pragmatic. Montague attributes this view to (Bar-Hillel, 1954), but it is at least arguable that some indexicality should be regarded as semantic, as for instance 'I' in an utterance of an English sentence refers to the utterer of that sentence.

Presumably one should say that the representation of (1) should be a pair of sentences, in fact (37) and (38). The truth conditions of (1) will be those of (38) in a context u which consists of an utterance of (37). But that is not sufficient, since u will not be an acceptable context for the truth of (37) at w unless the utterer of u at w is speaking in accordance with V, rather than with V^*. Suppose that,

$$V_u(\textbf{\textit{Terra moves}}) = p$$

and

$$V_u^*(\textbf{\textit{Terra moves}}) = q.$$

(Since ***Terra moves*** does not contain ***that*** its value is not sensitive to u.) The result we require is that $V_u((38))$ is the set of world-time pairs at which Galileo utters a sentence which in his language means that p. Now $w \in V_u((38))$ iff

(50) $w \in V^\dagger(\textbf{\textit{says}})(\text{Galileo}, u)$

and, if we use (49) for ***says***, (50) will hold iff Galileo (assertively) produces at w an utterance u' such that $u \approx_s u'$.

We can now consider whether (38), in the appropriate context, has the same meaning as (21), where an appropriate context is a u which expresses p, i.e. using the function f introduced in (24), a u such that $f(w, u) = p$. (Recall that we are at present assuming that f is not world-dependent, and so the choice of w makes no difference.) First note that (23) can be stated as

(51) $w \in V(\textbf{\textit{says}})(a, b)$ iff a (assertively) produces at w an utterance u such that $f(w, u) = b$.

Using (49) we have that $w \in V_u((37))$ iff at w Galileo (assertively) produces an utterance u' such that $u \approx_s u'$. If an utterance u is essentially tied to the expression of a single proposition – a possibility mentioned in the discussion of (29) above –

then we will be able to choose a u such that $f(w, u) = p$ for any w. But to get a result which captures (21) we must require that where u expresses p then so must u'. This means that we need the principle

(52) If $u \approx_s u'$ then $f(w, u) = f(w, u')$.

How can (52) be achieved? If we define $\approx_s$ in some such way as in (29) then all we have produced is a roundabout method of getting the same result that (23) gets directly, and it is not clear in that case what advantages this indirect method has over the direct method used in (23) itself. Still, it is a way of interpreting Davidson which makes his theory compatible with an intensional account of saying that; and indeed, in reading the defence of Davidson in (LePore and Loewer, 1989) I am very tempted to take their stress on *knowledge* of a truth theory as advocating a view whose precise articulation could well be in the form of an intensional semantics which respects (52). If (52) is not a consequence of some such definition as (29) then $\approx_s$ must be explicitly required to satisfy (52) – but in that case it is unclear *why* this should be stipulated, since there does not seem to be any way in which (52) falls out of an unanalysed notion of samesaying. If Davidson's claim that samesaying is an unanlysed relation, not part of the theory of meaning for a given language, is a denial of (52) then we cannot guarantee that an intensionalized Davidsonian semantics in which the meaning of ***says*** is as in (49) will be equivalent to an intensional semantics in which the meaning of ***says*** is as in (23).

There are perhaps other ways of looking at the constraint expressed by (52). One would be that, instead of regarding (52) as a constraint on $\approx_s$ in terms of a function f induced by an initially provided V, why not say that the direction of fit is the other way round? Why not assume it as a given that certain utterances make their utterers samesayers with the utterers of certain other utterances, and then require that an interpretation V be so defined as to respect this? What this would entail would be that V(***Terra***) and V(***moves***) would have to be some kind of entities which would ensure that $V((37))$ would determine the class of utterances whose utterers would all be samesayers with someone who says that the earth moves. While such a semantics might be possible I doubt whether it is anything like what Davidson had in mind, and I know of no attempt to provide one. (Though see my comments on (Boër, 1990) in (Cresswell, 1985, p. 161).)

A more radical response to (52) would be to deny the assumption of the correctness of (23), on the ground that there is no such function as f, because of the indeterminacy of language. In that case (52) could not even be *stated*. I mentioned at the beginning of the paper that Davidson does indeed appear to favour the Quinean position on indeterminacy, and perhaps this would be his reply to (52). In making this response Davidson would be asking us to accept that, although there is no fact of the matter about what the sentences of a language mean which is sufficiently precise to determine whether Galileo's Italian sentence means the same as any English sentence, and no possibility of giving any recursive specification of this meaning in terms of the meanings of the words in Galileo's language and the structure of Galileo's sentence, yet there *is* a fact of the matter about whether Galileo's utterance means the same as the utterance of a certain English sentence. As I said earlier, it is not my intention to take up the question of indeterminacy, though, as I also said, Davidson's own proposal seems to me to be a victim of that same indeterminacy. But in any case this radical response to (52) seems to me a version of the response that samesaying is a pragmatic and not a semantic matter.

This discussion has assumed that an utterance cannot express different propositions in different worlds, and that $\approx_s$ is not world relative. But suppose we allow the possibility expressed in the discussion of (29) above that an utterance can change its meaning from world to world, and suppose we amend (49) to read.

(53) $w \in V^{\dagger}(\textit{\textbf{says}})(a, u)$ iff a produces (assertively) at w an utterance u' such that $u \approx_s u'$ at w.

Then $w \in V_u((38))$ iff

(54) Galileo produces (assertively) at w an utterance u' such that $u \approx_s u'$ at w.

The problem with (54) is that to get the right result we must choose a u which expresses p in every w, since otherwise the fact that $u \approx_s u'$ at w will not guarantee that u' counts as a saying that p. This means that we must require that $f(w, u) = p$ for every w. And this in turn entails that the meaning of (1) cannot be identified with $V_u((37))$ for any single u unless that u expresses p in every world. Since we are now assuming that an utterance *can* express different propositions in different worlds (53) will require amending.

What is going on here is that we begin with an utterance u, which in this world w expresses the proposition p, and then we proceed to consider the truth value of (38) in another world w' in which Galileo produces an utterance which in his language in w' means what (37) means in our language in w, viz. p. There is in fact a well-studied body of literature (see Cresswell, 1990) which investigates sentences like

(55) It might have been that everyone actually rich was poor

which depend for their evaluation on a pair of worlds. In the present case we need to refine $\approx_s$ in the following way on the assumption that what an utterance means can vary from world to world. Where w and w' are possible worlds (not world-time pairs) $\langle u, w\rangle \approx_s \langle u', w'\rangle$, will mean that the utterance of u in w and the utterance of u' in w' make their utterers samesayers.

In stating the semantics of a multiply-indexed language it would be best to be explicit and refer to the semantical indices as triples $\langle t, w_1, w_2\rangle$, at which t is a time interval and w_1 and w_2 are possible worlds. w_1 is known as the *evaluation world* – the world at which the wff is held to be true or false; and w_2 is known as the *reference world* – the world from whose perspective we are making the evaluation. In the present case, to evaluate (38) at $\langle t, w_1, w_2 \rangle$ would be to consider Galileo's utterance in w_1 as meaning the same as (37) means in w_2. Our present simplified language will not contain any ***actually*** operators, and for every symbol except ***says*** the reference world w_2 will simply be carried along as a parameter. The multiply-indexed semantics for ***says*** is an adaptation of (49):

(56) $\langle t, w_1, w_2 \rangle \in V^{\dagger}(\textit{\textbf{says}})(a, u)$ iff a produces (assertively) at t in w_1 an utterance u' such that $\langle u, w_2 \rangle \approx_s \langle u', w_1 \rangle$.

We can now consider whether (38), in the appropriate context, has the same meaning as (21), where an appropriate context in w_2 is a u which in w_2 expresses p, i.e. a u such that $f(w_2, u) = p$. Using (56) we have that $\langle t, w_1, w_2 \rangle \in V_u((37))$ iff in w_1 Galileo (assertively) produces an utterance u' such that $\langle u, w_2 \rangle \approx_s \langle u', w_1 \rangle$. To get a result which captures (21) we must require that, where u expresses p in w_2, then u' must express p in w_1. This means that we need the principle

(57) If $\langle u, w \rangle \approx_s \langle u', w' \rangle$ then $f(w, u) = f(w', u')$.

And exactly the same comments can be made about (57) as were made above about (52).

Perhaps analysing (45) intensionally in terms of what we know is a mistake. After all, one of the attractions of a Tarski-style truth theory is that it makes no reference to any intensional notions of the kind used in giving an account of what it is to know such things as (45) – though see Field (1972). I have treated (45) as something which may be true or false in a given world, and whose right hand side does not involve language at all. But of course (45) is stated in English, and one can regard that sentence itself as part of a semantic theory. Such a sentence is called a *T-sentence*, and a Tarski-style truth theory is frequently presented as an axiomatic theory from which may be derived as theorems sentences like (45). In the case of (45) itself, since it states a condition for one of the simple symbols of $\mathcal{L}^{\dagger}$, the predicate ***moves***, (45) might be one of the axioms of the truth theory for $\mathcal{L}^{\dagger}$. The axiom for ***says*** would be simply

(58) ***says*** is true of $\langle a, u \rangle$, at t iff a produces at t, an utterance u' such that $u \approx_s u'$.

In (58) there is no reference to worlds and $\approx_s$ is the purely extensional samesaying relation originally used in (14) for $\mathcal{L}^{\dagger}$.

In such a way of looking at the truth theory nothing is said about what it is to *know* (45) or (58), or about what it would be for (45) or (58) to be true in this or that possible world. All that we require is that the theory be *materially adequate*, i.e. that we have an object language $\mathcal{L}^{\dagger}$, and an interpreted metalanguage $M(\mathcal{L}^{\dagger})$ in which occur a finite (or at least effectively specifiable) set of axioms, from which may be derived all instances of the following schema, for any sentence α of $\mathcal{L}^{\dagger}$:

(59) α is true of u at t iff ... of u at t

where ... states in $M(\mathcal{L}^{\dagger})$ something which has the same truth value as α.

In order to discuss T-sentences I shall assume that a language $\mathcal{L}^{\dagger}$ is augmented by a one-place sentential operator ***not***. Call such a language $\mathcal{L}^{\boldsymbol{not}}$. The semantics of ***not*** in an intensional interpretation $\langle W, D, V\rangle$, is:

(60) $w \in V(\boldsymbol{not}\ \alpha)$ iff $w \notin V(\alpha)$.

Using (60) then

(61) ***not Terra moves***

is true in a world w iff the earth does not move in w. In an extensional semantics, where no reference to worlds is made, the meaning of ***not*** is given by its standard truth table:

α	***not*** α
True	False
False	True

On the basis of this table the axiom for ***not*** in a Tarski-style truth theory for $\mathcal{L}^{\boldsymbol{not}}$ would be:

(62) ***not*** α is true of u at t iff α is not true of u at t

In a semantical theory in the Tarski style, I take it to be important that truth and falsity have to mean actual real-world truth and falsity. Otherwise it cannot claim to avoid intensionality. I shall use the following fact: In 1996 there was a general election in New Zealand, which was not won by the Labour Party. Consider the operator

(63) Labour won in 1996 iff ...

Represent this operator by ***not****, and let $\mathcal{L}^{\boldsymbol{not}^*}$ be $\mathcal{L}^{\dagger}$ augmented with ***not****. Consider the sentence

(64) ***not* Terra moves***

In order to evaluate (64) in an extensional semantics we need a truth table for ***not****. Labour didn't win, so the table for ***not**** is

α	***not**** α
True	False
False	True

This is because, since Labour didn't in fact win, the truth value of ***not**** α will be the opposite of the truth value of α. And this will be so *for every sentence* α whatsoever; and therefore, in $\mathcal{L}^{\boldsymbol{not}^*}$ (62) can be replaced by

(65) ***not***** α is true of u at t iff α is not true of u at t

Thus the (extensional) truth theory for $\mathcal{L}^{not}$ will give exactly the same results as the (materially adequate) truth theory for $\mathcal{L}^{not^*}$ which uses (65); and so (61) and (64) are treated exactly alike. Yet (61) and (64) clearly have different meanings, and someone who utters one and someone who utters the other will not be samesayers. For take a world in which Labour *did* win. (There clearly are such worlds. Indeed in September 1996 we didn't then know whether they would or not.) In a world in which Labour won ***not***** has the table

α	***not***** α
True	True
False	False

Thus, (64) is true in a world w iff in w Labour won in 1996 and the earth moves or Labour did not win and the earth does not move, while (61) is true in a world w iff the earth does not move in w. And so utterers of (61) and (64) would not be samesayers.

The difference between the truth tables for ***not*** and for ***not***** is that although they coincide in the actual world, they differ in worlds in which Labour won. Unlike the tables for ***not***** the table for ***not*** reverses the truth value in *every* world. It might be tempting to respond that while ***not*** is a logical constant ***not***** is not. But from an extensional point of view they differ only orthographically, and it can hardly be the shape of its sign which makes something a logical constant. I believe that what happens is that although the official account of truth tables is purely extensional in only mentioning actual truth values, in reading the tables one tacitly assumes that they don't depend on what the actual world is like. But that reading is only legitimate if one is interpreting the tables intensionally, as holding in all worlds. (If I have understood Etchemendy (1990) correctly the intensional interpretation of the truth tables is part of what he calls the *representational* way of understanding validity in logic. Etchemendy makes his point in the context of Tarski's (1936) semantics for first-order logic, but if it is the same point as mine, it can be made even for propositional logic.) So a truth theory for $\mathcal{L}^{\dagger}$, interpreted as an axiomatic theory for generating materially adequate T-sentences, will not determine samesaying.

The situation would of course be different if (1) were treated syntactically as (21), as it is in $\mathcal{L}$, since the relevant T-sentence would be

(66) ***Galileo says that not***** ***the earth moves*** is true iff Galileo says that the earth does not move

and would not be true. Nor would

(67) ***Galileo says that not the earth moves*** is true iff Galileo says that the earth does not move

be true of a language in which ***not*** means what ***not****** means. But the paratactic account is designed precisely to rule out such sentences as (21) as the objects of a semantical theory, and succeeds only because it does so. And indeed there is one clear sense in which Davidson's enterprise does succeed. For, on the paratactic account, the language for which the truth theory is to be provided can be regarded as a version of the language of first-order logic, and it is standard that the semantics of first-order logic can be provided by a Tarski-style truth theory. The price is to regard an explanation of samesaying as a pragmatic rather than a semantic matter – or at least a matter not explained by the truth theory of the language in question.

As I have said, it is no part of my aim to dispute the viability of a project such as Davidson's. My point has been rather to investigate the extent to which his account might be intended to be doing the same job as the intensional account – but doing it better because it does not use intensional entities. If Davidson's task is a different one – as I have argued that it would have to be if it is to succeed – then it is not in competition with intensional semantics, and its success or failure in its own terms, has no implications either way for the success or failure of intensional semantics. In particular it does not shew that a *semantic* account of indirect discourse can get by without using intensional entities.

References

Arnaud, R.B. (1976), *Sentence, utterance, and samesayer*, Noûs **10**, 283–304.

Bar-Hillel, Y. (1954), *Indexical expressions*, Mind **63**, 359–379.

Bigelow, J.C. (1980), *Believing in sentences*, Australasian Journal of Philosophy **58**, 11–18.

Boër, S.E. (1990), *Names and attitudes*, Essays in Honor of Arthur Burks, M. Salmon, ed., Kluwer, Dordrecht.

Cresswell, M.J. (1978), *Semantic competence*, Meaning and Translation, F. Guenthner and M. Guenthner-Reutter, eds, Duckworth, London, 9–43. (Reprinted in (Cresswell, 1988, pp. 12–33).)

Cresswell, M.J. (1985), *Structured Meanings*, MIT Press, Bradford Books, Cambridge, MA.

Cresswell, M.J. (1988), *Semantical Essays*, Kluwer, Dordrecht.

Cresswell, M.J. (1990), *Entities and Indices*, Kluwer, Dordrecht.

Cresswell, M.J. (1994), *Language in the World*, Cambridge University Press, Cambridge.

Davidson, D. (1967), *Truth and meaning*, Synthese **17**, 304–323.

Davidson, D. (1969), *On saying that*, Words and Objections: Essays on the Work of W.V. Quine, D. Davidson and K.J.J. Hintikka, eds, Reidel, Dordrecht, 158–174.

Etchemendy, J. (1990), *The Concept of Logical Consequence*, Harvard University Press, Cambridge, MA.

Field, H. (1972), *Tarski's theory of truth*, Journal of Philosophy **69**, 347–375.

Hand, M. (1991), *On saying that again*, Linguistics and Philosophy **14**, 349–365.

Higginbotham, J. (1986), *Linguistic theory and Davidson's program in semantics*, Truth and Interpretation, E. LePore, ed., Basil Blackwell, New York.

Hintikka, K.J.J. (1962), *Knowledge and Belief*, Cornell University Press, Ithaca.

LePore, E. and Loewer, B. (1989), *You can say that again*, Midwest Studies in Philosophy, Vol. 14, University of Notre Dame Press, Notre Dame.

Lewis, D.K. (1972), *General semantics*, Semantics of Natural Language, D. Davidson and G. Harman, eds, Reidel, Dordrecht, 169–218.

Montague, R.M. (1974), *Formal Philosophy*, Yale University Press, New Haven.
Richard, M. (1990), *Propositional Attitudes: An Essay on Thoughts and How We Ascribe Them*, Cambridge University Press, Cambridge.
Schiffer, S. (1987), *Remnants of Meaning*, MIT Press, Cambridge, MA.
Segal, G. (1988), *A preference for sense and reference*, Journal of Philosophy **89**, 73–89.
Segal, G. and Speas, M. (1986), *On saying* ðət, Mind and Language **1**, 124–132.
Tarski, A. (1936), *The concept of truth in formalized languages*, Logic, Semantics and Metamathematics, Clarendon Press, Oxford, 1956, 152–278.
Taylor, B. (1977), *Tense and continuity*, Linguistics and Philosophy **1**, 199–220.

CHAPTER 6

A Puzzle about Belief Reports

Kent Bach

Contents

PRAGMATICS OF PROPOSITIONAL ATTITUDE REPORTS
Current Research in the Semantics/Pragmatics Interface, Vol. 4
Edited by K.M. Jaszczolt

I'd like to present a puzzle about belief reports that's been nagging at me for several years. I've subjected many friends and audiences to various abortive attempts at solving it. Now it's time to get it off my chest and let others try their hand at it.[1]

My puzzle is not to be confused with either Frege's or Kripke's. Frege's (1892) puzzle about attitude reports, which derived from his more famous puzzle about the informativeness of identity statements, concerns the effect of substitution of co-referring terms. Kripke's puzzle (1979) goes deeper than that, showing that there is a similar problem about belief reports even without substitution. In my view, their puzzles arise only on a certain seemingly innocuous assumption, that 'that'-clauses specify belief contents. More precisely, this 'Specification Assumption' says that for a belief report of the form '*A* believes that *p*' to be true, the proposition that *p* must be among the things that *A* believes. Frege and Kripke, despite their radically different views on the semantics of 'that'-clauses in belief reports, share this popular assumption. My puzzle arises once it is rejected.

First I will use Kripke's Paderewski case, along with a simple linguistic observation, to call the Specification Assumption into question. Next I will briefly sketch the main options available, given the Specification Assumption, for solving Frege's substitution puzzle, and suggest that these options present an unpalatable dilemma. And then I will explain how giving up that assumption offers prospects for an intuitively more plausible approach to the semantics of belief reports (and attributions of other propositional attitudes). However, this approach must confront a puzzle of its own. For it turns out that every case is a Paderewski case, at least potentially.

1. The specification assumption and Kripke's puzzle

What could be more plausible than the supposition that a belief report of the form, '*A* believes that *p*', is true only if the proposition that *p* is among the things that *A* believes? Belief reports of this form certainly appear to relate believers to things believed. Indeed, it is sometimes suggested that the clause 'that *p*' is a kind of singular term, whose reference is the proposition that *p* (the idea is that 'that' is a term-forming operator on sentences). Then we have a straightforward explanation of the apparent validity of such inferences as the following:

I1.	Jerry believes everything Hilary says.	$(x)(Shx \rightarrow Bjx)$
	Hilary says that water is wet.	Shp
	So, Jerry believes that water is wet.[2]	Bjp

[1] To make my puzzle clear, in giving the necessary but, I hope, familiar background I will often either omit details or relegate them to the footnotes and give references.

[2] Contrary to philosophical legend, water is not wet – it only makes things wet.

If the clause 'that water is wet' is a term, then I1 has the form indicated on the right, in which case it is not only valid but formally valid. The analogous point seems to apply to the following inference:

I2. Art believes that Paderewski had musical talent. Bap
Bart believes that Paderewski had musical talent. Bbp
So, there is something both Art and Bart believe. $(Ex)(Bax\&Bbx)$

But is it so clear that the 'that'-clause of a true belief report specifies something the believer believes? Consider Kripke's Paderewski case. On account of what Peter believes regarding a certain pianist, an utterance of (1) is true.

(1) Peter believes that Paderewski had musical talent.

Even so, an utterance of (2)

(2) Peter disbelieves that Paderewski had musical talent.

could be true too, because of what Peter believes regarding a certain statesman. It happens that these are the same man, Paderewski, but Peter does not realize this.[3] Kripke's puzzle is to explain how (1) and (2) can both be true (not that both would be uttered in the same context without qualification). They seem to have Peter believing and disbelieving the same thing. That's what they must do if the following inference is formally valid, with the form indicated:

I3. Peter believes that Paderewski had musical talent. Bap
Peter disbelieves that Paderewski had musical talent. Dap
So, there is something Peter believes and disbelieves. $(Ex)(Bax\&Dax)$

Kripke's puzzle arises from the fact that Peter's problem is ignorance, not bad logic. But that can't be right if (1) and (2) really do have him believing and disbelieving the same thing, or, equivalently, believing contradictory things. How could he believe contradictory propositions (simultaneously and consciously) without being illogical?

Kripke is so pessimistic about finding a satisfactory way to say what Peter believes that he is led to lament, 'When we enter into [this] area, we enter into an area where our normal practices of interpretation and attribution of belief are subjected to the greatest possible strain, perhaps to the point of breakdown' (1979, pp. 268–269). I say there's no such strain, once we see through the illusion that (1) and (2) have Peter believing and disbelieving the same thing.

The alternative is to reject the Specification Assumption and say that (1) and (2) are true but not because Peter believes and disbelieves the same thing. This

[3] As Kripke describes the situation, Peter uses the name 'Paderewski' for what he takes to be two different individuals, but it is inessential to the problem that Peter even be familiar with the name. Uses of (1) and (2) could be prompted by Peter's reaction to two different photographs, for example. Frege's substitution puzzle is also not essentially about names the believer uses.

is possible because the ‘that’-clause they contain does not specify anything he believes or anything he disbelieves – it merely characterizes something he believes and characterizes something he disbelieves, and these needn’t be the same thing. Compare the following sentences:

Peter likes a certain pianist.
Peter dislikes a certain pianist.

There is no implication here that Peter likes and dislikes the same pianist. Somewhat similarly, I suggest, (1) and (2) do not jointly imply that Peter believes and disbelieves the same thing. One and the same ‘that’-clause, even though it expresses but one proposition, can characterize (as opposed to specify) two distinct belief contents. This entails that a belief report can be true even if the believer does not believe the specific proposition expressed by the ‘that’-clause. With (1), for example, Peter must believe something such that Paderewski had musical talent, but he need not believe *that* proposition.

You might think that believing that p just *is* believing the proposition that p. After all, (2) seems equivalent to (2p),

(2p) Peter disbelieves the proposition that Paderewski had musical talent.

But the following are anything but equivalent:

(2′) Peter suspects/fears/realizes that Paderewski had musical talent.

(2p′) Peter suspects/fears/realizes the proposition that Paderewski had musical talent.

The oddity of (2p′) should make one wonder whether ‘that’-clauses in attitude contexts really do refer to propositions.

On the alternative ‘descriptivist’ view, ‘that’-clauses in belief reports do not specify but merely characterize things believed. If this view is correct, inference I3 above does not have the indicated form and is not formally valid. But in that case inferences I1 and I2 do not have the forms indicated for them and are not formally valid either. That they are is an illusion due to the Specification Assumption. Once we abandon that assumption, we can see that even though their respective ‘that’-clauses express the same proposition, (1) and (2) can both be true without Peter believing and disbelieving the same thing.

2. The specification assumption and Frege’s substitution puzzle

The pernicious effect of the Specification Assumption is evident if we consider the main options it allows for solving Frege’s substitution puzzle. As we will see, it forces a dilemma on us: we must choose between a solution that requires terms mysteriously to acquire special semantic roles in belief contexts and one which implausibly rejects the intuitive explanation of why the puzzle arises in the first place.

Ordinarily, replacing one term with another, co-referring term does not and cannot affect truth value. For example, if 'Superman can fly' is true, then so is 'Clark Kent can fly'. But in belief contexts, substitution seems to affect truth value. Even though Clark Kent is Superman, substituting 'Clark Kent' for 'Superman' in (3)

(3) Lois has always believed that Superman can fly.

seems to turn a truth into a falsehood:

(4) Lois has always believed that Clark Kent can fly.

The puzzle is to explain why substitution can fail in belief (and other attitude) contexts. How can being embedded matter? Whatever the answer, it should reckon with the apparent fact that (3) and (4) have Lois believing two different things, that Superman can fly and that Clark Kent can fly. Because she can believe one without believing the other, the truth values of (3) and (4) can differ accordingly. The problem is how to explain all this, or else explain it away.[4]

It is natural to suppose that the 'that'-clause in a belief report specifies something the believer believes and that substitution can affect what is specified. The two traditional views suppose this.

Fregean: This view denies that terms occurring in embedded clauses have their 'customary' references. It claims that they refer instead to their (customary) senses (their 'indirect' references). The embedded sentence refers to the 'thought' (or 'Fregean proposition') that the person is being said to believe. Unembedded, the sentence would express the thought but not refer to it.[5]

Metalinguistic: Like the Fregean view, this view denies that terms occurring in embedded sentences have their customary references. It claims instead that such terms refer to themselves, or, alternatively, to their translations in the believer's language (or perhaps to their translations in his mental language). On such a

[4] One thing to keep in mind is this. If you utter 'Superman can fly', you thereby say, and express the belief, that Superman can fly. However, you are not saying that you are saying this or that you believe this. If you uttered 'Clark Kent can fly' instead, your utterance would have the same propositional content but you would not be expressing the same belief. But you are not talking about the belief – you are talking about Clark Kent (or Superman). Ordinary statements express beliefs but, unlike belief reports, are not about beliefs.

[5] Frege held that the referent of an unembedded sentence is a truth value (the True or the False), but one could hold, more plausibly, that it is a proposition, of the sort composed of the referents of the constituents of the sentence, and still be something of a Fregean. To be sure, this would be not a 'Fregean' but a 'Russellian proposition'. Even so, as a Fregean one could still hold that the sentence 'expresses' a Fregean proposition, or what Frege himself called a 'thought'.

quotationalist or sententialist view, belief reports relate believers not to propositions but to sentences (or mental representations).[6]

Notice that both the Fregean and the metalinguistic views in effect reject the original terms of the substitution puzzle. They deny that substituting 'Clark Kent' for 'Superman' in a belief context really *is* a case of substituting one co-referring term for another – in such contexts the names do not have their usual references. This is the price these views are willing to pay in order to explain the effect of substitution (e.g., that the difference between (3) and (4) concerns what they have Lois believing). Unfortunately, these views do not give an independently motivated account of how and why such reference shifts should occur. One symptom of trouble is that in a sentence like (5),

(5) Lois believes that Clark Kent can't fly, but he can.

the pronoun 'he' refers to Clark Kent even though it is anaphoric on the embedded name, 'Clark Kent', which is supposed not to refer to Clark Kent in this context. This difficulty may be superficial, but it illustrates why positing a reference shift just doesn't ring true.

The contemporary approach is to avoid reference shifts and maintain that constituents of an embedded sentence have their usual references. But then, since 'Superman' and 'Clark Kent' have the same reference, it seems that the difference between (3) and (4) must consist in something other than what they have Lois believing. Indeed, the two main current views on the subject say precisely this. They both distinguish the 'how' from the 'what' of belief and claim that (3) and (4) differ not in what they have Lois believing but in how they have her believing it.[7] They both hold that an embedded sentence refers to a Russellian proposition, whose constituents are objects and properties (or relations).[8] Since the 'that'-clauses of (3) and (4) refer to the same proposition, the singular proposition that Superman/Clark Kent can fly, (3) and (4) as a whole have Lois believing the same thing.[9] Even so, utterances of (3) and (4) can differ in how they have her believing it. Speakers,

[6] A more extreme version of the metalinguistic view denies that constituents of embedded sentences refer at all and that belief reports relate believers to anything at all. I will ignore this view in what follows. Obviously such a view is not committed to the Specification Assumption. The most glaring difficulty with such a view is that it has to treat each belief-predicate (of the form 'believes that *S*') as semantically primitive.

[7] Both theories, though anything but Fregean – they claim that 'that'-clauses refer to Russellian propositions, not Fregean ones – still exploit Frege's notion of 'mode of presentation.' They distinguish individuals from ways of thinking of them, and (Russellian) propositions from ways of taking them. Ways of taking Russellian propositions (modes of presentation of them) are essentially Fregean propositions, or thoughts.

[8] In the case of (3) and (4), this is a 'singular' proposition, so-called because its subject constituent is an individual (or sequence of individuals). The simplest form of such a proposition may be represented as a sequence of the form: $\langle a, F \rangle$.

[9] This assumes that proper names such as 'Clark Kent' and 'Superman' are devices of direct reference, even as they occur in belief contexts. You might turn the point around and argue that the two 'that'-

by how they word the 'that'-clause in a belief report, convey information about ways of thinking of things and ways of taking propositions, but this information is not part of the semantic content of the 'that'-clause. In particular, using 'Clark Kent' rather than 'Superman' conveys different information about how Lois thinks of the individual both names name, so that using a 'that'-clause containing one name rather than the other conveys different information about how she takes the proposition that he can fly. The two views in question differ in how they regard the semantic status of such information.

Neo-Russellian: On this view, such information is merely 'pragmatically imparted', as Salmon (1986) puts it (he proposes an ingenious explanation of how this information is readily confused with semantic content). This view rejects the anti-substitution intuition, at least as far as the semantic contents of belief reports are concerned. (4) does follow from (3): to believe that Clark Kent can fly *is* to believe that Superman can fly, at least under some way of taking that proposition.

Hidden-indexical: Alternatively, information about ways of taking propositions, even though it is conveyed only tacitly, *is* part of the semantic contents of belief reports. [10] Claiming this requires denying that (3) and (4) have the logical form they appear to have: 'believe' (or any verb of propositional attitude) expresses not a dyadic but a triadic relation, involving not only persons and propositions but also ways of taking propositions, to which utterances of belief sentences make tacit reference. Then (3) is true relative to one implicitly referred to way of taking the singular proposition that Superman/Clark Kent can fly, and (4) is false relative to another.[11]

Both views are counterintuitive. The neo-Russellian view implausibly rejects the anti-substitution intuition that gives rise to Frege's puzzle in the first place. This intuition is so strong that, as Mark Richard suggests, it would take 'bribery, threats, hypnosis, or the like ... to get most people' to think that (3) and (4) have Lois

---

clauses refer to different propositions, hence that names are not devices of direct reference, at least in belief contexts. Rejecting the Specification Assumption, as we will do later, makes this issue moot. The alternative is to deny, e.g., that (3) is true because Lois believes the singular proposition its 'that'-clause expresses. One could deny this on grounds first given by Schiffer (1977), namely that singular propositions cannot comprise complete contents of beliefs.

[10] This proposal was first advanced by Schiffer (1977) and has since been developed in detail by Crimmins (1992). It claims, in effect, that belief sentences fail to express complete propositions independently of context, that they are semantically incomplete (for discussion of this notion, see Bach (1994)). Significantly different versions have been proposed by Forbes (1990) and by Richard (1990).

[11] (4) could be true relative to the way of taking that proposition relative to which (3) is true. However, because 'Clark Kent' is being used rather than 'Superman', a typical utterance of (4) would refer to a different way of taking that proposition, and relative to that way of taking it (4) is false.

believing the same thing (1990, p. 125).[12] The hidden-indexical theory purports to respect the anti-substitution intuition, but in fact it claims, contrary to a key element of that intuition, that (3) and (4) do have Lois believing the same thing – they differ only in how they have her taking that proposition. Moreover, it provides no linguistic explanation of where the extra argument place comes from.[13]

If the four views considered (and their variants) exhaust the options available on the Specification Assumption, then collectively they pose a dilemma with respect to the anti-substitution intuition. The first two, in an effort to explain why (3) and (4) have Lois believing two different things, both posit theoretically unmotivated reference shifts. The last two avoid reference shifts but deny the basis of the intuition, namely that (3) and (4) have Lois believing two different things. Escaping this dilemma requires explaining, without positing reference shifts, how (3) can be true because of one thing Lois believes and how (4), if it were true, would be true because of something else she believes.[14]

---

[12] Only the neo-Russellian view regards the inference from (3) to (4) as formally valid, having the following form:

$$Bl\langle s, F\rangle \quad k = s \quad \text{So, } Bl\langle k, F\rangle$$

The trouble is, taking I4 to have this form is tantamount to rejecting the anti-substitution intuition.

[13] This is one of several objections brought by Schiffer (1992) against the hidden-indexical theory. He calls this the 'logical form' problem. There is a related grammatical form problem: the hidden-indexical theory seems to violate the principle of Compositionality, which says, roughly, that the meaning of a sentence is determined by its syntactic structure and the meanings of its constituents. There is no evident syntactic basis for the alleged device (the "hidden" indexical) of tacit reference. The hidden-indexical theory at least respects the principle of Semantic Innocence, which says that embedding expressions in particular constructions, such as 'that'-clauses in belief reports, does not change their meaning or reference. These principles and how they tie in to Frege's puzzle are discussed in (Crimmins, 1992, Chapter 1). The Fregean and the metalinguistic views, with their claim of a reference shift, violate Semantic Innocence. Crimmins also explains the relevance of the principle of Direct Reference, which denies that determinants of reference, as opposed to the referents themselves, enter into semantic contents). Notice that Semantic Innocence is logically independent of Direct Reference, although proponents of the former generally endorse the latter.

[14] How do the four types of theory sketched above fare with the Paderewski case, which does not involve substitution? Here, it seems, the referentially shifty approaches have a real problem, inasmuch as (1) and (2) contain identical 'that'-clauses. The Fregean and metalinguistic views would like to claim that Peter is being said to believe one thing and to disbelieve something else. Its strategy in the substitution case was to claim that substitution (e.g., of 'Clark Kent' for 'Superman') changes the reference in a belief context. But the same move is not available in the Paderewski case, where there is no substitution. There is no linguistic difference between the 'that'-clauses of (1) and (2), nothing to capture the difference between what Peter is being said to believe and what he is being said to disbelieve. The neo-Russellian and the hidden-indexical theories claim that (1) and (2) have Peter believing and disbelieving the same proposition, but under two different ways of taking it. The trouble with this claim, quite simply, is that (1) and (2) *seem* to have Peter believing one thing and disbelieving something else. The puzzle with Peter seems to be what he believes, not how he believes it. The challenge in solving that puzzle is to reckon with the fact that there is no difference between the 'that'-clauses of (1) and (2), nothing to mark the difference between what Peter believes and what he disbelieves.

To appreciate how this can be, compare Lois's situation with that of Perry White, Clark Kent's editor at the Daily Planet. For him, believing that Clark Kent can fly amounts to the same thing as believing that Superman can fly. This is so because he was party to Superman's Clark Kent ploy in the first place. Perry has always believed that Superman can fly and also that Clark Kent can fly, but that is in virtue of only one belief of his. No wonder Perry believes that only one individual can fly. Things would be different with Lois even if she came to believe that Clark Kent can fly. Suppose she saw Clark, attired in a grey suit, suddenly soar into the air but she was still so smitten with Superman that she did not make the obvious inference. We would describe her as now believing that Clark Kent can fly, but the belief that makes this so would be distinct from her longstanding belief that Superman can fly. Together they lead her to believe that two individuals can fly. Unlike her, Perry believes that only one individual can fly.

3. Giving up the specification assumption: A new puzzle

Why does it take bribery, threats or hypnosis to get most people to think that (3) and (4) say the same thing? The reason is very simple. (3) and (4) have Lois believing two different things. It's not that she believes the same thing in two different ways – she believes two different things. An analogous point explains what's puzzling about the Paderewski case. The puzzle here concerns what Peter believes, not how he believes it. (1) is true because Peter believes one thing, and (2) is true because he disbelieves something else. So, we might ask, how can this be, if the same 'that'-clause occurs in both? That is my puzzle.

The solution begins with the rejection of the Specification Assumption. Once we realize that the 'that'-clauses in (1) and (2) do not specify anything Peter believes and disbelieves, we can see that (1) and (2) do not express relational propositions, of the form 'Bap' and 'Dap' respectively. 'Believes' and 'disbelieves' express dyadic relations all right, and Peter is one of the terms of that relation, but there is no reference to, or specification of, the other term of that relation. For the only thing that could be the other term is the proposition that Paderewski had musical talent, but that is not what Peter believes or disbelieves. What he believes is something that requires the truth of that proposition, but that proposition is not what he believes. Similarly, what he disbelieves is something that requires the truth of that proposition (he believes something that requires the falsity of that proposition). But neither what he believes nor what he disbelieves is specified by the 'that'-clause in (1) and (2). The puzzle, then, is to explain what makes (1) and (2) true anyway.

A solution must answer three questions:

Q1: What is the relation between the proposition expressed by the 'that'-clause in a true belief report and the belief(s) that it characterizes?

Q2: How can propositionally equivalent 'that'-clauses characterize different beliefs?

Q3: How can they characterize different beliefs in one context (as with Lois) and the same beliefs in another context (as with Perry)?

It is important to realize that my puzzle about belief reports is not limited to isolated cases like Paderewski. It is epidemic – every case is a Paderewski case, at least potentially. Kripke thinks that the puzzle cases are special cases (he is reluctant to draw conclusions from them because 'hard cases make bad law'), but there is nothing special about 'that Paderewski had musical talent' – it is a perfectly ordinary 'that'-clause. Similar puzzles arise with belief reports whose 'that'-clauses express general propositions rather than singular ones. For *any* 'that'-clause 'that *S*', there could be circumstances in which someone believes that *S* and disbelieves that *S* without being illogical. For it need not specify anything that he both believes and disbelieves.

It might seem that the problem here is merely one of insufficient detail. Make the 'that'-clause more specific in one way and you can say what Peter believes; make it more specific in another way and you can say what he disbelieves. Yes, we could embellish (3) and say that Peter believes that Paderewski the pianist had musical talent and embellish (4) and say that he disbelieves that Paderewski the statesman had musical talent, but ultimately this strategem does not work. Suppose that Peter hears two recordings, a beautiful performance of Rachmaninov and a horrible jazz improvisation, both by Paderewski. Then it wouldn't do any good to say that Peter believes that Paderewski the pianist had musical talent, because we could just as well have said that he disbelieves that Paderewski the pianist had musical talent. We could say that Peter believes that Paderewski the classical pianist had musical talent but that he disbelieves that Paderewski the jazz pianist had musical talent. But this ploy won't ultimately work either. Suppose Peter hears a recording of an atrocious performance of Mozart (by Paderewski) after the gorgeous performance of Rachmaninov. We could say that Peter disbelieves that Paderewski the classical pianist had musical talent, but this would not distinguish what he disbelieves from what he believes. We would need to say that Peter disbelieves that Paderewski the classical pianist playing Mozart had musical talent, and that Peter believes that Paderewski the classical pianist playing Rachmaninov had musical talent.... When it comes to saying what someone believes, we can always say more but, it seems, we can never say enough.

This deepens my puzzle about belief reports. Not only do 'that'-clauses merely characterize belief contents, they seem inherently incapable of fully specifying the contents of beliefs. Any belief report is potentially a Paderewski case. What, then, are belief contents, such that their contents can't be specified fully by 'that'-clauses, and how *can* belief contents be specified fully? Now that's a puzzle.

Acknowledgments

Thanks to David Sosa for his very helpful suggestions.

References

Bach, K. (1994), *Conversational impliciture*, Mind & Language **9**, 124–162.
Crimmins, M. (1992), *Talk about Beliefs*, MIT Press, Cambridge, MA.
Forbes, G. (1990), *The indispensability of Sinn*, Philosophical Review **99**, 535–563.
Frege, G. (1892), *On sense and reference*, Translations of the Philosophical Writings of Gottlob Frege, P. Geach and M. Black, eds, Blackwell, Oxford.
Kripke, S. (1979), *A puzzle about belief*, Meaning and Use, A. Margalit, ed., Reidel, Dordrecht.
Richard, M. (1990), *Propositional Attitudes: An Essay on Thoughts and How We Ascribe Them*, Cambridge University Press, Cambridge.
Salmon, N. (1986), *Frege's Puzzle*, MIT Press, Cambridge, MA.
Schiffer, S. (1977), *Naming and knowing*, Midwest Studies in Philosophy **2**, 28–41.
Schiffer, S. (1992), *Belief ascription*, Journal of Philosophy **89**, 490–521.

CHAPTER 7

Do Belief Reports Report Beliefs?

Kent Bach

Contents

PRAGMATICS OF PROPOSITIONAL ATTITUDE REPORTS
Current Research in the Semantics/Pragmatics Interface, Vol. 4
Edited by K.M. Jaszczolt

Short version

My thesis is very simple: belief reports do not report beliefs. But that needlessly sounds paradoxical. What I mean is that a belief report does not do quite what it appears to do, namely, say what someone believes. That is, it does not specify what the person believes but merely describes it. (1), for example, though true,

(1) The Joker thinks that Bruce Wayne is a wimp.

does not specify something the Joker thinks. For if it did do that, then (2) would be true too,

(2) The Joker thinks that Batman is a wimp.

since the proposition that Batman is a wimp is the same (singular) proposition as the proposition that Bruce Wayne is a wimp. But (2) is false – the Joker does *not* think that Batman is a wimp. QED: Belief reports do not specify beliefs but merely describe them.

Long version

The problem of belief reports (and other attitude attributions) has puzzled philosophers of language for over a century. There are basically two kinds of puzzle cases: those with and those without substitution. Substitution cases, of the Hesperus/Phosphorus, Cicero/Tully, Leningrad/St. Petersburg, and Superman/Clark Kent variety, are illustrated by (1) and (2).

(1) The Joker thinks that Bruce Wayne is a wimp. *[true]*

(2) The Joker thinks that Batman is a wimp. *[false]*

In these cases replacing a term with another, coreferring term changes the belief report's content, turning a true belief report into a false one. The problem is how to explain this.

Why does this need to be explained? Because given certain plausible, widely held principles – Semantic Innocence, Semantic Compositionality, and Direct Reference – which we will assume for the sake of discussion, it seems impossible that (2) could be false while (1) is true. It seems that substituting the name 'Batman' for 'Bruce Wayne' could never affect the truth value of sentences in which they occur (if used, not mentioned). If, for example, Batman is not a wimp, then Bruce Wayne is not a wimp (he might act like one but that's irrelevant). But if the Joker thinks that Bruce Wayne is a wimp, as (1) says, then how can (2) not be true too? How could it be false that he thinks that Batman is a wimp? Given our principles, and given that Bruce Wayne is Batman, (2) seems to have the Joker believing the same thing as (1) does, in which case (2) should be true too. Yet the substitution here does affect truth value – belief contexts are opaque. So how is this opacity possible?

Assumed Principles

1. *Direct Reference*: Singular terms contribute their referents to propositions expressed by sentences in which they occur.
2. *Semantic Innocence*: Embedding a term in a 'that'-clause does not change its semantic value.
3. *Semantic Compositionality*: The semantic value of a semantically composite expression is a function of its structure and the semantic values of its constituents.

1. Four familiar approaches

The effect of substitution cannot be explained by citing the believer's relation to the particular terms that occur in the two belief sentences. The difference between (1) and (2), for example, need not have anything to do with the Joker's relation to the names 'Bruce Wayne' and 'Batman', for they can differ in import even if the Joker has no familiarity with these (or any) names for the individual in question. The difference between what (1) and what (2) report might correspond, for example, to the difference between a tuxedo and a batsuit.

There have been four main ways in which philosophers have tried to explain (or in one case explain away) the opacity of belief reports. These correspond to four different theories of belief reports: the Fregean, the quotationalist-sententialist, the hidden-indexical, and the neo-Russellian theories. As we will see, none of them solves the problem of opacity. They do not keep opacity from leading to paradox (clash of irresistible intuitions with immovable principles). Three of the four give up at least one principle, and the fourth tries to explain away the anti-substitution intuition.

Fregean. According to Frege (1892), (2) can differ from (1) in truth value because embedding affects reference – an embedded term refers not to its "customary" reference but to its "customary" sense, which in this context is its "indirect" reference. Frege would have claimed that 'Batman' in (2) does not have the same semantic value as 'Bruce Wayne' in (1), and that would explain how (2) could be false even though (1) is true. His ingenious idea complies with Compositionality but only at the expense of violating Innocence (it also conflicts with Direct Reference). One cost of this violation is illustrated by (1+),

(1+) The Joker thinks that Bruce Wayne is a wimp, but he is not.

where the pronoun 'he', which is anaphoric on the name 'Bruce Wayne', is being used, and used literally, to refer to Bruce Wayne. Frege's theory predicts that it refers to the sense of the name 'Bruce Wayne', not to Bruce Wayne himself. This difficulty may not be insuperable, but it illustrates why denying semantic innocence just doesn't ring true.

Quotationalist-sententialist. Popular several decades ago, mostly among those of positivist bent, the metalinguistic or quotationalist-sententialist view also violates Innocence, for it claims that a 'that'-clause refers to a sentence. On the simplest version of this view, an embedded sentence refers to itself. On more lavish versions, an embedded sentence refers to a sentence in the believer's language, perhaps in his mental language. The quotationalist-sententialist view respects Compositionality – it holds that the constituents of a 'that'-clause also refer to linguistic items – but, as with Frege's view, its denial that they refer to their ordinary referents is a naked violation of Innocence.

Historically, the quotationalist-sententialist view seems to have been motivated by an aversion to propositions. It seems to me, though, that philosophy of language should not let metaphysical considerations so easily trump semantic ones, if only because a language might have bad metaphysics built into it. One might have scruples about the objective character of moral or aesthetic values, for example, but this should not lead one to suppose that adjectives like 'good' or 'beautiful' are to be treated differently, from a semantic point of view, from 'round' or 'reptilian'. Also, the quotationalist-sententialist view has the same sort of problem with (1+) that Frege's view has. The pronoun 'he' in (1+), which is anaphoric on 'Bruce Wayne', is not used to refer to the name 'Bruce Wayne' or to any other name of Bruce Wayne. It is being used to refer to Bruce Wayne himself. This fact becomes something of a mystery on the quotationalist-sententialist view.

Hidden-indexical. Introduced by Schiffer (1977), revived by Crimmins and Perry (1989), and developed by Crimmins (1992), the hidden-indexical theory respects Innocence by holding that an embedded sentence refers to the same proposition that it expresses unembedded. According to this theory, what explains how (1) and (2) can differ in truth value (and content) is not what they say explicitly, about *what* the Joker believes, but what they say implicitly, about *how* he believes it. (1) and (2) have him believing the same proposition but not taking it in the same way, and their different truth values (and contents) are relative to these different, implicitly referred to, ways of taking that proposition. The beliefs that (1) and (2) impute to the Joker differ not in their content, the singular proposition that Bruce Wayne/Batman is a wimp, but in the way in which he is being said to be taking that proposition.

Unfortunately, it seems that for the hidden-indexical theory to preserve Innocence it must give up Compositionality. It may assert that a certain way of taking the proposition expressed by the 'that'-clause is an "unarticulated constituent" of the proposition expressed by the entire belief report, but there is no syntactic basis for this contention. A sentence of the form '*S* believes that *a* is *F*' contains no empty category (in the linguist's sense) for this alleged unarticulated constituent. So it is gratuitous from a linguistic point of view to suppose that such a belief sentence expresses a proposition containing an unarticulated constituent for a way of taking the proposition expressed by its 'that'-clause. Crimmins claims that there are counterexamples to what he calls the "Principle of Full Articulation" (1992, pp. 15–21). Sentences like 'Fred is ready' and 'Jerry has finished', for example, are each missing an argument. But it doesn't follow that they express propositions with unarticulated constituents – they might not express propositions at all. Crimmins implicitly assumes that if a sentence is used to convey a proposition, it must have a proposition as its semantic value. He does not consider the possibility that such sentences are semantically incomplete and simply fail to express complete propositions (for discussion of this idea see Bach (1994)).

Violating Compositionality is not the only trouble with the hidden-indexical theory. As Schiffer (1992) has argued (see also Bach (1993)), its claim that belief reporters make reference to ways of taking propositions is not plausible psychologically. But the fundamental problem, also raised by Schiffer, is that the hidden-indexical theory implausibly treats 'believes' (and other verbs of propositional attitude) as expressing a triadic relation rather than the dyadic relation which, from a linguistic point of view, it appears to express.

This last problem is avoided by a variant of the hidden-indexical theory that was suggested originally by Schiffer (1977) and has since been developed by Recanati (1993, Chapter 18). This version treats the belief relation as the dyadic relation it appears to be, by claiming that 'that'-clauses are contextually sensitive. In particular, instead of claiming that a belief report with a 'that'-clause of the form 'a is F' refers explicitly to a singular proposition, $\langle a, F\rangle$, and tacitly to a way of taking that proposition, $\langle m_a, m_F\rangle$, it claims that the 'that'-clause itself refers to a "quasi-singular", mode-of-presentation-containing proposition of the form, $\langle\langle m_a, a\rangle, \langle m_F, F\rangle\rangle$. This notational variant of the hidden-indexical theory might be called the "overt-indexical" theory, since the 'that'-clause itself is claimed to be the vehicle of reference to modes of presentation. In this way the overt-indexical theory preserves Compositionality but, unfortunately, only at the expense of Innocence – it claims that embedded sentences undergo a shift in reference (in the case of a singular sentence of the form 'a is F', referring to a quasi-singular rather to a singular proposition).

Neo-Russellian. This view (Salmon 1986, 1989; Soames 1987, 1988) aims to respect Innocence (as well as Direct Reference) without violating Compositionality. The neo-Russellian theory agrees with the hidden-indexical theory that the 'that'-clause in a singular belief report refers to the singular proposition that the agent is being said to believe. It agrees further that to believe a proposition is to believe it under some mode of presentation – one must take the proposition in some way or other. But the neo-Russellian theory denies that ways of taking propositions enter into the semantic contents of belief reports. For, as noted above, nothing in ordinary belief sentences encodes information about ways of taking propositions (or modes of presentation of their constituents).

To avoid giving up any of our three principles, neo-Russellians bite the bullet and reject the anti-substitution intuition – they deny that (2) can be false while (1) is true. Instead, they claim that (2) must be true if (1) is, but that ordinarily we wouldn't assert (2). That is, if the Joker thinks that Bruce Wayne is a wimp, he thinks that Batman is a wimp, regardless of what we – or he – would say. What we say is sensitive to a pragmatic "requirement that the reporter be maximally faithful to the words of the agent unless there is reason to deviate" (Soames, 1988, p. 123). Relying on their pragmatic strategy, neo-Russellians contend that the common intuition stems from a confusion between what a sentence like (2) says and what uttering it conveys, namely that the believer accepts the sentence embedded in the 'that'-clause or otherwise takes the proposition expressed by that sentence in a way that is pragmatically associated with that sentence. In the box below, where all four views are schematized, the representation of the neo-Russellian view has modes of presentation in brackets, indicating that they are not part of the semantic content of the belief sentence.

Four Theories of Belief Reports

	form of described belief (that a is F)
1. Fregean	$\langle m_a, m_F \rangle$
2. quotationalist/sententialist	$\langle `a', `F' \rangle$
3. hidden-indexical	$\langle a, F \rangle, \langle m_a, m_F \rangle$
4. neo-Russellian	$\langle a, F \rangle, [\langle m_a, m_F \rangle]$

One counterintuitive consequence of their pragmatic strategy is that neo-Russellians must deny that negative reports like (2–) are literally true.

(2–) The Joker does not think that Batman is a wimp.

They would claim that there *is* a way of taking the proposition that Batman is a wimp, the one pragmatically conveyed by an utterance of (1), whereby the Joker *does* think that Batman is a wimp. Similarly, to vary the verb, they would say that if (1d) is true,

(1d) The Joker doubts that Bruce Wayne is a threat.

then so is

(2d) The Joker doubts that Batman is a threat.

and that if (1f) is true,

(1f) The Joker fears that Bruce Wayne is Batman.

then so is

(2f) The Joker fears that Batman is Batman.

In every case, neo-Russellians will explain away any anti-substitution intuition, no matter how strong, by distinguishing the proposition referred to by the 'that'-clause from the way of taking it which, in Salmon's phrase, is merely "pragmatically imparted".

The neo-Russellian approach has met with considerable skepticism. Mark Richard suggests that it would take "bribery, threats, hypnosis, or the like ... to get most people" to regard pairs of sentences like (1) and (2) as the same in content (1990, p. 125). Substitution in attitude contexts seems to be able to turn a truth into a falsehood, especially with verbs like 'doubt' or 'fear', as above, or with 'forget', 'know', 'notice', 'suspect', or 'realize'. So, for example, it seems just plain false that the Joker, even though he realizes that Bruce Wayne is rich, realizes that Batman is rich. He might suspect that Batman is on to him without suspecting that Bruce Wayne is. So the effect of substitution does not seem to be merely pragmatic, at least not in the way suggested by the neo-Russellian theory.

2. Rejecting the specification assumption

Both the hidden-indexical and the neo-Russellian theories exploit the distinction between the "what" and the "how" of belief, between propositions and ways of taking them. In so doing, they assume that the 'that'-clause in a belief report specifies the thing that the believer must believe if the belief report is to be true. Indeed, this assumption about the role of 'that'-clauses in belief reports is shared by all four theories considered above, despite their differences. I call this the Specification Assumption. In my view, it is the real trouble with all four theories. Its pernicious effect is evident from the dilemma that is presented by the theoretical choices considered so far: we must choose between a solution which assigns special, ad hoc semantic roles to terms in belief contexts and one which implausibly rejects the intuitive explanation of why the puzzle arises in the first place.

The Specification Assumption is an essential ingredient of what generically may be called the relational analysis of belief reports. This must be distinguished from the relational analysis of *belief*, which says that belief (and other propositional attitudes) is a relation to a proposition (opinions differ, of course, on the nature of propositions). The relational analysis of belief *reports* (RABR), which is shared by three of the above four views, the quotationalist-sententialist view excepted, says that a belief report (or attribution of any other propositional attitude) has just the logical form it appears to have: it expresses a relation between a person and a proposition, its 'that'-clause refers to a proposition, and this 'that'-clause specifies something that the person is being said to believe. On this analysis, a belief report of the form '*A* believes that *S*' (we are not talking about ones with nominal complements, like 'Art believes Goldbach's Conjecture') cannot be true unless the proposition that *S* is among the things that *A* believes (on the quotationalist-sententialist view this is a sentence rather than a proposition).

The Relational Analysis of Belief Reports

1. *Relationalism*: Belief reports express relations between persons and propositions.
2. *Propositionalism*: The semantic value of a 'that'-clause is a proposition.
3. *Specification Assumption*: Belief reports specify belief contents, i.e. to be true a belief report must specify a proposition the person believes.

The RABR is not generally argued for but it is widely held, as indicated by the following representative quotations; see the table below.

The Relational Analysis of Belief Reports: Apt Quotes

Tyler Burge: Sentences about propositional attitudes ... have the logical form of a relation ... between a person ... and something indicated by the nominal expression following the propositional attitude verb. (1980, p. 55)

Jerry Fodor: Propositional attitudes should be analyzed as relations. In particular, the verb in a sentence like 'John believes it's raining' expresses a relation between John and something else, and a token of that sentence is true if John stands in the belief-relation to that thing. (1981, p. 178)

Stephen Schiffer: Believing [is] the relation expressed by 'believes' in a sentence of the form '*x* believes that *S*'. The 'that'-clause ... is a referential singular term whose reference is a proposition. (1992, pp. 491 & 505)

Scott Soames: Propositions are objects of the attitudes ...; that is, these attitudes are relations to propositions. ... To believe that *S* is to believe the proposition that *S*. (1988, pp. 105–106)

Robert Stalnaker: The semantics of belief attributions seems ... very simple: the transitive verb *believe* expresses a relation between a person ... and a proposition denoted by the sentential complement. (1988, pp. 140–141)

RABR is intuitively appealing because it reflects the apparent logical form of belief sentences. In particular, it explains what appears to be the formal validity of inferences like the following:

			apparent logical form
I1.		Art believes everything that Bart says.	$(x)(Sbx \supset Bax)$
		Bart says that Nixon was a crook.	Sbp
	∴	Art believes that Nixon was a crook.	Bap
I2.		Art believes that Paderewski had musical talent.	Bap
		Bart believes that Paderewski had musical talent.	Bbp
	∴	There is something that Art and Bart both believe.	∴ $(\exists x)(Bax \& Bbx)$

Given RABR, these inferences have the indicated forms and are formally valid. However, there is a problem with its third tenet, the Specification Assumption. It turns out that these inferences do not have the indicated forms and are not formally valid.

In order to appreciate what is wrong with this assumption, we need to consider the kind of puzzle case, introduced by Kripke (1979), that arises without substitution.

(3) Peter believes that Paderewski had musical talent.

(4) Peter disbelieves that Paderewski had musical talent.

As Kripke puts the problem, Peter uses the name 'Paderewski' for what he takes to be two different individuals. However, as noted earlier with the substitution problem, it is inessential to the problem that the believer have any familiarity with the name in question or have any name at all for the object of belief. Uses of (3) and (4) could be prompted by Peter's reaction to two different photographs, for example. Whatever the details, the problem posed by (3) and (4) is to explain, given that Peter doesn't realize that Paderewski the statesman is Paderewski the pianist, how (3) and (4) can both be true (not that both would be uttered in the same context without qualification). They seem to have Peter believing and disbelieving the same thing. If the following inference is formally valid, that is, if its steps are correctedly represented by the forms on the right,

I3.		Peter believes that Paderewski had musical talent.	Bap
		Peter disbelieves that Paderewski had musical talent.	Dap
	∴	There is something that Peter both believes and disbelieves.	∴ $(\exists x)(Bax \& Dax)$

then (3) and (4) do have Peter believing and disbelieving the same thing. But this seems incorrect. After all, Peter is not being illogical – he does not believe contradictory things – he is merely ignorant. Moreover, his problem does not seem to be, as both the hidden-indexical and the neo-Russellian views would have it, that he believes and disbelieves the same proposition but under two different ways of taking that proposition. Intuitively, the problem concerns *what* he believes, not *how* he believes it. As used, (3) and (4) are plausibly understood to have Peter believing one thing and disbelieving something else. If that is correct, inference I3 does not have the indicated form and, contrary to linguistic appearance, is not formally valid. But then, since there is no relevant difference between I3 and inferences I1 and I2 above, linguistic appearances are misleading for those two inferences as well – they do not have the forms indicated for them and are not formally valid either. 'That'-clauses do not refer to terms of the relation expressed by 'believes' (or whatever the attitude verb).

Aside from the above considerations, there is some striking linguistic evidence against RABR, especially when extended to reports of other sorts of propositional attitude. It is supported by the apparent equivalence of (5) and (5p),

(5) The Joker believes that Batman will capture him.

(5p) The Joker believes the proposition that Batman will capture him.

but look what happens when we replace the verb 'believes' with 'thinks'. There is quite a difference in meaning between (5t),

(5t) Oscar thinks that Batman will capture him.

which entails belief, and (5tp),

(5tp) Oscar thinks the proposition that Batman will capture him.

which does not. And whereas replacing 'believes' in (5) with such other verbs as 'suspects', 'fears', 'expects' yields the unproblematic (5v),

(5v) The Joker suspects/fears/expects that Batman will capture him.

similar replacements in (5p) are nonsensical:

(5vp) The Joker suspects/fears/expects the proposition that Batman will capture him.

You can suspect (or fear or regret) that such-and-such, but you can't suspect (or fear or regret) a proposition (that such-and-such).

3. The descriptivist view

According to the view I wish to defend, (3) describes Peter as believing something and (4) describes him as disbelieving something but, because they do not have Peter believing and disbelieving the same thing, they can both be true. According to the "descriptivist" view and contrary to the Specification Assumption, the 'that'-clause in (3) does not specify which thing Peter believes, and the 'that'-clause in (4) does not specify which thing he disbelieves. So these needn't be the same thing. And there is no reason to suppose that *either* of these things is the proposition expressed by the 'that'-clause in (3) and (4), the proposition that Paderewski had musical talent. By symmetry, any reason to suppose that (3) says that Peter believes this proposition would be an equally good reason to suppose that (4) says that Peter disbelieves this proposition. But he does not believe and disbelieve the same proposition.

The lesson of the Paderewski case, then, is that 'that'-clauses are not content clauses. The Specification Assumption is false: even though their 'that'-clauses express propositions belief reports do not in general *specify* things that people believe (or disbelieve) – they merely *describe* or *characterize* them. A 'that'-clause is not a specifier (much less a proper name, as is sometimes casually suggested) of the thing believed but is merely a descriptor of it. A belief report can be true even if what the believer believes is more specific than the proposition expressed by the 'that'-clause used to characterize what he believes.

It is not clear how to make this precise or even that it should be made precise. According to the descriptivist view, the condition on the truth of a belief report is that the believer believe something which requires the truth of the proposition expressed by the 'that'-clause in the belief report. In order for (3) to be true, for example, Peter must believe something that requires the truth of 'that Paderewski had musical talent'. In other words, he must have a certain sort of that-Paderewski-had-musical-talent belief, a belief which requires that it be true that Paderewski had musical talent. However, the language of (3) does not specify precisely what belief this is. As will be suggested below, the further constraint imposed by the 'that'-clause on what belief the believer must have for a belief report to be true can vary with the context. Just as 'Adam bit a certain apple' does not specify which apple Adam bit, although it entails that there is a certain one that he bit, so 'Peter believes that Paderewski had musical talent' does not specify which sort of that-Paderewski-had-musical-talent belief he has, although it requires that there be a certain one that he has.

The basic idea of the descriptivist view may be brought out by the following puzzle. Consider Kripke, who, unlike Peter, realizes that Paderewski the statesman was the same person as Paderewski the pianist. Whereas both (3) and (4) above are true, (3k) is true and (4k) is false.

(3k) Kripke believes that Paderewski had musical talent.

(4k) Kripke disbelieves that Paderewski had musical talent.

But if, as the descriptivist view says, what Peter disbelieves is not the same as what Peter believes, then does (3k) have Kripke believing what Peter believes or believing what Peter disbelieves? There seems to be no reason to say that Kripke believes one rather than the other or that he believes both – he has but one relevant belief about Paderewski. Perhaps we should say this: what Kripke believes is consistent with the thing Peter believes and consistent with the (other) thing that Peter disbelieves, but he does not believe either of those things (since it is not clear what these "things" are, I am reluctant to call them "propositions").

The lesson of the Paderewski case, that 'that'-clauses do not necessarily specify belief contents, applies to substitution cases, such as (1) and (2) above. Contrary to linguistic appearances, due to the illusion created by the Specification Assumption, the following inference does not have the indicated form and is not formally valid,

I4.	The Joker believes that Bruce Wayne is a wimp.	$Bj\langle w, W\rangle$
	Batman is Bruce Wayne.	$b = w$
$\therefore$	The Joker believes that Batman is a wimp.	$\therefore Bj\langle b, W\rangle$

even assuming Direct Reference and Semantic Innocence. On those principles, the proposition expressed by the 'that'-clause in the argument's first premise and the one expressed by the 'that'-clause in its conclusion are identical: $\langle w, W\rangle = \langle b, W\rangle$. So it might seem that the first premise and the conclusion have the Joker believing the same thing. But this appearance is deceptive. Neither the first premise nor the conclusion have the Joker believing any specific thing – they merely characterize things he believes, and these need not be the same thing.

From the standpoint of the descriptivist view, there is a straightforward explanation why replacing one term with a coreferring term can affect the content of an entire belief report even though it does not affect the content of the 'that'-clause. This happens because the two belief reports do not characterize the same beliefs. That is, what the believer must believe in order for the second belief report to be true can be different from what he must believe for the first to be true. For example, if (2) is true, its truth might have nothing to do with the truth of (1).

(1) The Joker thinks that Bruce Wayne is a wimp.

(2) The Joker thinks that Batman is a wimp.

The Joker might come to believe that Batman is a wimp quite apart from the fact that he already believes that Bruce Wayne is a wimp. The belief that makes (2) true could be different from the belief that makes (1) true, even though the 'that'-clauses of both belief reports express the same singular proposition. Substitution of one coreferring term for another, even though it does not affect the proposition expressed by the 'that'-clause, can make for a difference in the belief being characterized.

4. The significance of substitution

The specific difference that a particular substitution makes is not determined by any difference in the semantic values of the two terms. That difference is not semantic but contextual. The same substitution can make one difference in one context, another difference in another context, and no difference in a third context. Whether a substitution makes any difference in a given context depends on what is being substituted for what. For example, if Batman were known by the Joker and everyone else as the Hero of Gotham, then substituting 'the Hero of Gotham' for 'Batman' in (2) would not make any difference even though substituting 'Bruce Wayne' for 'Batman' would.

If substitution (of coreferring terms) makes no semantic difference, how can it affect the content of a belief report? How can substitution turn a true belief report into a false one? Part of the answer is that the sentences used to make the belief reports, though semantically equivalent, are also *semantically incomplete*. That is, they do not express complete propositions, and to that extent they are like such sentences as

(5) Fred is ready.

and

(6) Jerry has finished.

Though syntactically well-formed (compare (6) with the virtually synonymous but ungrammatical 'Jerry has completed'), these sentences are semantically incomplete because of a missing argument. The hidden-indexical theory claims that belief reports are semantically incomplete for the same reason: a belief report not only reports the proposition believed but makes implicit "reference to a contextually determined mode of presentation" (Schiffer, 1977, p. 34); this is the argument missing from a belief sentence. However, lacking an argument is not the only way for a sentence to be semantically incomplete (for further discussion of this notion see Bach (1994)). On the descriptivist view, belief sentences are semantically incomplete for a different reason. Like words such as 'big' and 'short', a belief-predicate does not have a context-independent condition of satisfaction, so that a sentence containing it does not have a context-independent truth condition. A belief-predicate does not express, independently of context, a unique belief-property. So, for example, there is no unique property of believing that Batman is a wimp. Completion is achieved by the import of using of one term rather than another in the 'that'-clause, e.g., 'Batman' rather than 'Bruce Wayne'. This determines what it takes, relative to the context in which the belief report is made, for the believer to satisfy the belief-predicate. Using one term rather than another, coreferring term makes a contextually relevant difference concerning what the subject must believe for the belief report to be true. So, for example, uttering (2), 'The Joker thinks that Batman is a wimp', rather than (1), 'The Joker thinks that Bruce Wayne is a wimp', is not misleading (as the neo-Russellian theory would say) but downright false.

The difference that substitution makes can vary with the context. What is variable is whether the appropriate identity is presumed. A presumed identity licenses substitution. Substitution is blocked if it makes a contextually relevant difference, due either to the absence of or to the suspension of a presumption of identity. Ordinarily, there is no presumption of identity, and using one name rather than another name carries a presumption of nonidentity. In utterances of (1′) and (2′), for example,

(1′) The Joker thinks that Harvey Furber is a wimp.

(2′) The Joker thinks that Marvin Frubish is a wimp.

there is no presumption of identity between Harvey Furber and Marvin Frubish, who, for all we know, are one and the same guy. There is a suspension of a presumed identity in the case of the original (1) and (2). Its suspension explains why the truth of (1) and the falsity of (2) have no tendency to suggest that the Joker believes that someone both is and is not a wimp. The situation would be different if it were common knowledge that Bruce Wayne is Batman and presumed that the Joker realized this. But this is not presumed. So even if it came to be true that the Joker believed that Batman is a wimp, this would be so in virtue of a different belief on his part.

Now consider the situation among those of us who do realize that Bruce Wayne is Batman. For us, a belief which could be characterized as a that-Bruce-Wayne-is-a-wimp belief could equally be characterized as a that-Batman-is-a-wimp belief. If Val is such a person, one and the same belief on his part would make either of the following belief reports true:

(7) Val thinks that Bruce Wayne is a wimp.

(8) Val thinks that Batman is a wimp.

If Val thought that Bruce Wayne is a wimp and that Batman is not a wimp, he would be guilty of believing a contradiction, because in his case that would be tantamount to believing that Bruce Wayne both is and is not a wimp. He could not be merely a victim of ignorance, like the Joker. The presumption of identity, though maintained above (with respect to Val), would be suspended in the following iterated case.

(9) Val thinks that the Joker thinks that Bruce Wayne is a wimp.

(10) Val does not think that the Joker thinks that Batman is a wimp.

We would suspend the presumption of identity here, because we do not suppose that the Joker thinks that Bruce Wayne is Batman or, more to the point, that Val thinks that the Joker thinks that Bruce Wayne is Batman.

Substitution in a belief report makes for a difference in the belief described and thus is relevant to the content of the report. Why does substitution have no such effect in the case of simple sentences? If you utter "Bruce Wayne is a wimp", you thereby say, and express the belief, that Bruce Wayne is a wimp. But you are not saying that you are saying this or that you believe this. If you uttered "Batman is a wimp" instead, you would not be expressing the same belief, but the content of what you are saying would be the same, the singular proposition that Batman/Bruce Wayne is a wimp. For you are expressing your belief but not describing it. You are talking about Batman/Bruce Wayne, not your belief about him. The opacity of attitude reports, on the other hand, is due to the fact that they describe attitudes.

When substitution fails, as in the inference from (1) to (2), it fails not because 'that Batman is a wimp' refers to a different proposition than 'that Bruce Wayne is a wimp' but because it characterizes a different belief. But it can also characterize the same belief, namely when it is no news to anyone, including the believer, that Batman is Bruce Wayne. In that case, substitution preserves truth value. So sometimes it fails and sometimes it does not. This is so not because the name sometimes occurs "opaquely" and sometimes "transparently" or because the belief report may be either "de dicto" or "de re" (there is a difference between "de dicto" and "de re" *beliefs* (Bach, 1987, Chapter 1), but that, in my view, has nothing to do with the alleged difference between de dicto and de re belief reports).

There is no reason to assume that there is any specific sort of difference that substitution makes. In particular, it need not be a difference in associated mode of presentation. There might not be any unique mode of presentation (or even unique type of mode of presentation) associated with each of the terms in question. Associated mode of presentation may vary, perhaps in unpredictable ways, from one person to another and from one time to another for a given person. It may not be determinate enough, even relative to a given context of utterance, to be part of what is communicated. Even so, communication can still be successful. Nor need the difference that substitution makes concern which words the subject would use to express his belief. The subject may not even be familiar with the terms used to ascribe the beliefs in question. He may not even be familiar with synonyms of those terms or with translations of them in his own language. The use of different terms might mark differences in modes of referring to, and thinking of, the individuals in question without signalling just what those differences consist in. So, for example, a Batman/Bruce Wayne case could arise just from pointing to different pictures. Using a 'that'-clause containing one name rather than the other indicates, barring a presumption of identity, a difference in ascribed belief, but that is not sufficient to determine which particular belief the believer is being said to have.

Obviously there is no contextual effect of substitution in the Paderewski case, since there is no substitution. Here only the context can vary – the 'that'-clause is fixed. Utterances of (3) and (4)

(3) Peter believes that Paderewski had musical talent.

(4) Peter disbelieves that Paderewski had musical talent.

can both be true, even without any implication that Peter believes that someone both did and did not have musical talent, provided that what 'that Paderewski had musical talent' in (4) describes Peter as disbelieving is not the same thing as what in (3) it describes him as believing. How is this possible? If (3) and (4) were both uttered in what, broadly speaking, is the same context, there would have to be some immediate difference in the circumstances of their utterance, e.g., a demonstration first of one photograph and then of another. There would have to be some way for one and the same 'that'-clause to signal a difference between what Peter is being said to believe and what he is being said to disbelieve. This difference could be indicated by using the appositives 'the pianist' and 'the statesman' after the name 'Paderewski'. Using one appositive rather than the other would be sufficient, in the context, to differentiate one belief from the other, although both beliefs are such as to be true only if Paderewski had musical talent.

5. Is the descriptive view a hidden-indexical theory in disguise?

People have suggested to me that the descriptivist view is a notational variant of the hidden-indexical theory, or perhaps of the overt indexical theory (briefly mentioned earlier), but this is a misunderstanding. Both views, it is true, claim that belief sentences are semantically incomplete, hence that utterances of them need completion in context to convey a complete proposition. And both views claim that substitution, despite not affecting the semantic content of the 'that'-clause, can affect the content of the entire belief report (the specific difference that it makes in each case is determined contextually). But the resemblance ends there. The hidden-indexical theory claims that a belief report makes tacit reference to a way of taking the proposition expressed by the 'that'-clause; the descriptivist view does not. Indeed, the hidden-indexical theory claims that, contrary to linguistic appearances, the belief relation is not dyadic but triadic. The descriptivist view claims no such thing. It denies that belief reports make tacit reference to anything. In this way, it can maintain that the relation expressed by 'believes' is the dyadic relation it appears to be.

The descriptivist view is distinct from both the hidden- and the overt-indexical theories in that it denies that there is any reference to ways of taking propositions or ways of thinking of their constituents. Therefore, it cannot hold that the difference that substitution makes is a matter of which such ways are signalled by which terms. Then what difference does substitution make, according to the descriptivist view? The use of one term rather than another, e.g., 'Bruce Wayne' rather than 'Batman', in the 'that'-clause of a belief report signals a contextually relevant difference in belief, *whatever that is*. The semantics of belief reports is silent as to what the difference consists in. Maybe it does consist in differences in ways of taking the same proposition, but that is a matter of the theory of belief, not the theory of belief reports. The semantics of belief reports just says that there may be some such difference, signalled but not encoded by the difference in coreferential terms. As mentioned earlier, for a given substitution there can be one difference in one context, another difference in a another context, and no difference in a third. There is no hard and fast difference, for example, between believing that Batman is a wimp and believing that Bruce Wayne is wimp, and not always any difference at all.

Even so, it might seem that although the descriptivist view is not explicitly a hidden-indexical theory, still it cashes out into one. For what can the difference consist in between believing that Batman is a wimp and believing that Bruce Wayne is wimp? Surely there is a difference only if one does not believe that Bruce Wayne is Batman, and the easiest way not to believe that Bruce Wayne is Batman is to believe that Bruce Wayne is not Batman. But to do that, so the objection goes, requires thinking of Bruce Wayne/Batman in two different ways, and this is precisely the difference that is marked between (1) and (2), just as the hidden-indexical theory says. And it does not say that the distinct 'that'-clauses of (1) and (2) specify the difference, but only that they mark the difference. However, it also says that there is reference to the two different ways of thinking of Bruce Wayne/Batman or, to allow for indeterminacy of what those ways are, to two different types of ways of thinking of him. This is what the descriptivist theory denies. Unlike the hidden-indexical theory, it does not claim that the explanation of the difference enters into the content of the belief reports.

Finally, it might even seem that the descriptivist theory is really just a notational variant of the neo-Russellian theory. For it could be argued that everything I have said is consistent with the claim that belief reports do report relations to propositions. After all, if the 'that'-clause of a true belief report expresses a proposition, then the believer does bear a certain relation to that proposition. The trouble with this objection, however, is that the relation in question is not the belief relation. If it were, then Peter would bear the belief relation both to the proposition that Paderewski had musical talent and to the proposition that Paderewski did not have musical talent, in which case he would believe contradictory propositions. The descriptivist theory specifically denies this. Besides, because the relation in question would vary from one context to another, it could not be *the* belief relation.

6. Every case a Paderewski case

Substitution cases show that propositionally equivalent 'that'-clauses can characterize different beliefs – substitution can be proposition-preserving without being belief-preserving. Different beliefs can be characterized – they are not fully specified – by semantically equivalent but linguistically distinct 'that'-clauses. 'That'-clauses narrow down the beliefs they characterize to the degree circumstances require, but different 'that'-clauses, even semantically equivalent ones, do so differently. The Paderewski case, which involves no substitution, illustrates why 'that'-clauses do not individuate beliefs – the same 'that'-clause, as in (3) and (4), can be used to characterize a coherent belief-disbelief pair. And, as I now wish to show, every case is a Paderewski case, at least potentially.

For any 'that'-clause 'that *S*', there could be circumstances in which it is true that *A* believes that *S* and true that *A* disbelieves that *S* but without *A*'s being illogical. This is illustrated by what (3) and (4) say about Peter. Not every case is an actual Paderewski case, of course, but it is not on account of its 'that'-clause that a given belief report fails to be such a case. Moreover, if beliefs (belief types) are individuated by their contents, then no 'that'-clause is inherently capable of fully individuating a belief (type). So there is really nothing special about 'that Paderewski had musical talent' – it is a perfectly ordinary 'that'-clause. *Any* 'that'-clause could be used, given the right circumstances, to describe something that someone believes and to describe something that he disbelieves, and do so without imputing any incoherence to him. Similar puzzles arise with belief reports whose 'that'-clauses express general propositions rather than singular ones. For *any* 'that'-clause 'that *S*', there could be circumstances in which someone believes that *S* and disbelieves that *S* without being illogical. For it need not specify anything that he both believes and disbelieves.

A natural objection here is that such a 'that'-clause does not contain enough detail. Make it more specific in one way and you can say what Peter believes; make it more specific in another way and you can say what he disbelieves. Thus we could embellish (3) and say that Peter believes that Paderewski *the pianist* had musical talent and embellish (4) and say that he disbelieves that Paderewski *the statesman* had musical talent. But ultimately this strategem does not work. Consider the following variation on the original version of the Paderewski case. Suppose that Peter hears a recording of Paderewski playing Rachmaninov in Carnegie Hall. Peter likes what he hears. Then Peter hears a recording of Paderewski playing with a jazz combo at the Apollo Theatre. This time he hates what he hears. It is clear to us that Peter does not realize he has heard the same pianist twice. But here it won't do any good to say that Peter disbelieves that Paderewski the pianist had musical talent, because we could also have truly said that he believes that Paderewski the pianist had musical talent. We could say that Peter disbelieves that Paderewski the *jazz* pianist had musical talent and say too that he believes that Paderewski the *classical* pianist had musical talent. But this ploy won't ultimately work either. Suppose Peter hears a recording of an atrocious performance of Paderewski playing Mozart. It is clear to us that Peter does not realize that he has heard the same pianist a second time. We could say that Peter disbelieves that Paderewski the classical pianist had musical talent, but this would not distinguish what he disbelieves from what he believes. We would need to say that Peter disbelieves that Paderewski the classical pianist *playing Mozart* had musical talent, and that Peter believes that Paderewski the classical pianist *playing Rachmaninov* had musical talent. Well, you get the idea.

If every case is potentially a Paderewski case, then 'that'-clauses are not inherently capable of specifying the contents of beliefs fully. Any 'that'-clause that describes something someone believes could also describe something he coherently disbelieves. Then how are belief contents to be specified fully? That is a very good question, one which I cannot answer. As we just saw, the extended versions of the Paderewski case, which involve inserting additional material into the 'that'-clause, show that insufficient detail is not the problem – you can add all the detail you want but the problem doesn't go away. No matter how much material is inserted into it, a 'that'-clause does not determine belief content but merely narrows it down. So it seems that no belief report is inherently capable of specifying a belief fully. That is why I say that every case is potentially a Paderewski case. A belief report can always be tightened, if need be, by means of more verbiage, so as to meet any given threat that it is an actual Paderewski case, but any such elaboration will be open to further threats of the same sort.

Tightening a belief report can at least meet the threat that actually arises. According to the descriptivist view, such a tightening plays the role which, according to other theories, specifying a mode of presentation is supposed to play: it distinguishes one belief from another when the original 'that'-clause fails to do so. However, it does this not by specifying how what is believed is believed but by describing the belief more fully. That is, it narrows down the condition that must be met if the belief report is to be true. It narrows this condition down to the extent that is contextually relevant, that is, to the extent to which, in the context, different ways of expressing the proposition expressed by the original 'that'-clause would make a difference to what belief is being characterized.

Nothing is being said here about what beliefs are. Whatever they are, the claim is that nonsemantic differences between two referring terms in the 'that'-clauses of two otherwise identical belief reports signal contextually relevant differences in the described beliefs (beliefs whose possession by the subject make the belief reports true). The descriptivist view does not imply that there are two types of content. Although I agree with Loar's (1988) well-known argument, to which this paper is indebted, that 'that'-clauses do not express contents of the sort relevant to psychological explanation and relevant to capturing the subject's point of view, I want to deny that 'that'-clauses capture any sort of mental content. Rather, they abstract from mental contents. Mental contents are more specific than the 'that'-clauses used to characterize them. As I have urged, different 'that'-clauses, even semantically equivalent ones, merely differentiate mental contents, to the degree contextually required.

For all we know, beliefs are not realized by encodings of individual propositions – they could be abstractions from cognitive maps, for example, representations of possibly infinitely many propositions. That is why Jackson raises the question "whether we should think of the causes of behaviour as individual beliefs and desires, or as rich systems of belief and desire" (1996, p. 403). If the latter is correct, then they might be like maps, in which case there are "no natural ways of carving up maps at their representational joints", natural ways of itemizing what they say and correlating each item with the way they say it. Particular elements of a map (and of a picture – see Bach (1970)) play many representational roles at once, different ones in relation to different other elements. If systems of belief are like this, then, as Jackson writes,

> when Jones believes that snow is white, . . . inside Jones there is a structure that constitutes a rich system of belief that represents, among a great many things, that snow is white: Jones believes that snow is white by having a system of belief according to which snow is white. We can still talk of individual beliefs in the sense of aspects of the way heads represent things as being which can be captured in individual sentences, but there will be no underlying individual states that these belief sentences report. (Jackson, 1996, pp. 404–405.)

At present no one is in a position to know the truth about the nature of belief. So it is advisable for theories of belief reports to be neutral on the subject. We should not suppose, for example, that because we use 'that'-clauses to report beliefs, beliefs are couched in some sort of "language of thought". On the other hand, we can acknowledge that differences in semantically equivalent 'that'-clauses can make for differences in the beliefs reported, specifically differences in their logical properties. However, the logical properties of reported beliefs are not fully determined but are only delimited by the semantic contents of the 'that'-clauses used to report them. In saying this I am not implying that there are two *kinds* of content ("wide" and "narrow") but only that the contents of beliefs are more fine-grained than the contents of 'that'-clause used to report them. Nonsemantic differences in semantically equivalent 'that'-clauses can signal, even though they do not encode, logical differences in reported beliefs. The opacity of belief contexts does not have a semantic basis (aside from the semantic incompleteness of belief sentences).

There is also a linguistic reason for denying that the semantics of 'that'-clauses is the source of opacity. There are alternatives to the standard form of belief report ('*A* believes that *S*') which contain no embedded clauses but still give rise to the same phenomenon:

(1a) In the Joker's opinion/According to the Joker/From the Joker's point of view, Bruce Wayne is a wimp. [true]

(2a) In the Joker's opinion/According to the Joker/From the Joker's point of view, Batman is a wimp. [false]

So it has been only for the sake of discussion that I have played along with the widespread philosophers' myth that belief sentences must contain 'that'-clauses.

7. Loose ends

The descriptive view has been sketched and motivated here, but it has not been explained fully or defended against objections. A fuller exposition would offer a precise account of what it is for a 'that'-clause to describe or characterize a belief. It would consider puzzle cases involving general rather than singular terms, such as

(11) a. Lorena thinks that attorneys are rich.

b. Lorena thinks that lawyers are not rich.

(12) Byrd thinks that aviaries house airplanes.

It would take into consideration the fact that 'that'-clauses can themselves be semantically incomplete and fail to express full propositions, as in

(13) Dan thinks that Fred has arrived.

(14) John thinks that Jerry is late.

It would take up cases in which the described belief is explicitly more specific than the proposition expressed by the 'that'-clause, e.g.,

(15) Newt thinks that someone is following him, but I forget who.

It would have to reckon with cases involving 'that'-clauses which are necessarily false.

(16) Jenny thinks that Jerry is Jerry's father.

(17) Marla thinks that Donald's sloop is longer than it is.

(18) a. Albert thinks that $1024 > 1000$.

b. Albert thinks that $4^5 < 1000$.

Needless to say, there are many other sorts of puzzle cases. Dealing with them would require a fuller account of the various ways in which using one term rather than another in a 'that'-clause can affect the content of a belief report.

More needs to be said about the presumption of identity and its absence or suspension. In this regard, it might be objected that the descriptivist view gets caught in a circle when the 'that'-clause expresses an identity proposition, as in (19),

(19) The Joker thinks that Bruce Wayne is Batman.

This seems to pose a problem, because the descriptivist view says that substituting one coreferring term 'b' for another 'a' can affect the content of a belief report only if there is no presumed identity '$a = b$' in force. If the 'that'-clause expresses an identity, how can there be a presumption of identity or of nonidentity? What allows or, alternatively and more to the point in this case, what prevents the substitution? Presumably (19) is not being used to attribute a trivial belief in someone's self-identity, as (20) would be.

(20) The Joker believes that Batman is Batman.

What prevents the substitution is that the very use of two different names in a identity statement, or in the attribution of an identity belief, suspends any *presumption* of identity that might be in force. So the (short) reply to this objection is that with such belief reports there is no presumed identity – substitution always matters, precisely because identity is at issue. A longer reply would have to address Frege's puzzle about identity statements. Indeed, for Frege himself the problem of propositional attitude reports was subsidiary to the problem concerning the informativeness of identity statements.

Another objection points out that 'that'-clauses occur in contexts other than belief sentences, e.g., causal and modal contexts, and that there they are used to refer. However, the descriptivist view of belief reports can concede that in causal and modal statements 'that'-clauses *are* used to refer, but say that this is because actual and possible states of affairs are the subject matter of such statements, unlike that of propositional attitude reports. In causal and modal statements 'that *S*' is used elliptically for 'the fact/state of affairs that *S*', but it is *not* so used in belief and other attitude reports. Besides, as noted earlier, attitude reports do not require the use of sentences containing 'that'-clauses. So the opacity of attitude sentences cannot be due to any distinctive feature of 'that'-clauses. Rather, it stems from the fact that they are used to describe propositional attitudes.

The following theses summarize the descriptivist approach to belief reports.

Descriptivist Theses

1. 'That'-clauses don't refer, they describe ('that' is not a terrn-forming operator on sentences, and 'that'-clauses are not noun phrases).
2. 'That'-clauses generally do not specify complete contents of beliefs (belief-predicates do not individuate belief contents) – a belief report can be true even if the person does not believe the proposition expressed by its 'that'-clause.
3. Coherent belief/disbelief pairs can be described with the same 'that'-clause, or with semantically equivalent ones.
4. Belief reports do not distinguish the "how" from the "what" of belief. They make no reference to ways of taking propositions (or to representations or modes of presentation of their constituents).
5. Semantic content of a belief report: An utterance of '*A* believes that *S*' is true iff *A* believes a certain thing which requires the truth of the proposition that *S*.
6. Belief reports are semantically incomplete (not true or false independently of context) – they are sensitive to contextually variable conditions of difference of thing believed.

7. Substitution of coreferring terms in the 'that'-clause of a belief report can affect its content and change its truth value, but not because of anything encoded by the different terms.
8. Presumed identities license substitution; contextually relevant differences in semantically identical 'that'-clauses are due to the absence or suspension of a presumed identity.

My main aim has been to undercut the Specification Assumption, shared by the various theories of belief reports, which says that 'that'-clauses of belief reports specify the contents of beliefs being reported. My descriptivist view respects the anti-substitution intuition, which rightly resists free substitution of coreferential terms in belief contexts. Unlike the neo-Russellian theory, the descriptivist view does not try to explain this intuition away and, unlike the hidden-indexical view, it insists that the difference that substitution makes concerns what is believed, not how it is believed. Both the Fregean and the metalinguistic ways of explaining the difference that substitution makes implausibly attribute a reference shift to embedded terms. In my view, verbal differences in semantically identical belief reports generally make for differences in beliefs reported, but I have not gone into detail on just what these differences can consist in or on how variation in context, specifically in shared background information, can affect what the difference is in a given case. But much of what is missing here goes beyond the semantics of belief reports. To say that a belief report of the form '*A* believes that *S*' is true iff *A* believes a certain thing which requires the truth of the proposition that S is not to say how it is determined what that thing is.

Addendum

In an important paper that appeared after this paper was drafted, David Shier (1996) also rejects the Specification Assumption, although he calls it "Relational Analysis" (recall that what I call by that name includes two other theses along with the Specification Assumption). Focusing specifically on singular belief reports of the form '*S* believes that *n* is *G*', he proposes the "Quantified Relational Analysis", according to which a singular belief report is true just in case *S* believes some "finer-grained version" of the proposition expressed by the 'that'-clause, namely a proposition of the form, 'the *F* is *G*', where *n* is the *F*. Shier's primary motivation, as suggested by his title "Direct Reference for the Narrow Minded", is to reconcile direct reference with narrow individuation of beliefs. Like me, he agrees with Schiffer (1977) that a singular, object-involving proposition cannot comprise the complete content of a propositional attitude. By claiming that a singular 'that'-clause 'that *n* is *G*' "is used to *characterize*, though not to *specify*, the content of the belief" (1996, p. 227), Shier can deny that the singular 'that'-clause, although it expresses a singular proposition, individuates the belief being reported. The belief report can be true if *S* believes a finer-grained version of that proposition.

Although I am in general sympathy with Shier's position, my own view differs from his in several important respects. First, on Shier's view it is straightforward how to specify the complete content of a singular belief: you just replace 'that *n* is *G*' with 'that the *F* is *G*'. This requires that there be some determinate definite description which picks out the object in question and under which, if the belief report is true, the believer thinks of the object (it is unclear whether Shier requires that the belief reporter have this description in mind). So Shier assumes a descriptional theory of singular thought, according to which the contents of ostensibly singular thoughts are really general propositions, of the sort given by Russell's theory of descriptions (Shier's "Russellian individualism" does not invoke Fregean senses). Along with many others, I have argued against this view of singular thought. Contrary to that view, the objects of a singular thought are determined "relationally", not "satisfactionally". The object is thought of under what I call a "de re mode of presentation", not under a description (Bach, 1987, Chapter 1).

Second, Shier's formulation of QRA implicitly assumes that any general proposition, whose only singular terms are bound variables, *can* be the complete content of a propositional attitude. In effect, he is assuming that the substitution problem arises only with respect to terms for particulars and not terms for universals (property or kind terms). However, the same problem arises for the latter as well. For example, it might be true that Larry believes that Lee is a lawyer and false that Larry believes that Lee is an attorney.

Third, QRA says that a singular belief report is true just in case the believer believes *any* maximally fine-grained version of the proposition that n is G. In this respect, QRA is like the Salmon–Soames view – it denies the opacity of belief reports. It does this by appealing to Russellian descriptions rather than Fregean senses (in this respect calling the Salmon–Soames view "neo-Russellian" is rather misleading, since it invokes ways of taking propositions, i.e. modes of presentation of them). On QRA, if A believes that n is G then if $m = n$, A believes that m is G. For if the proposition that the F is G is a finer-grained version of the proposition that n is G, and A believes that the F is G, then, since $m =$ the F, A believes that m is G.

Shier does not attempt to explain away the anti-substitution intuition. It seems to me, however, that his Russellian individualism does not require him to reject opacity. Instead of holding that a belief report is true just in case the believer believes *any* maximally finer-grained version of the proposition that n is G, he could take a contextualist approach and claim that a singular belief report implicitly alludes to a certain contextually determined definite description, and says that A believes a contextually determined finer-grained version of the proposition that n is G. This would accommodate the anti-substitution intuition. Even so, I am reluctant to concede that it is literally true that *any* proposition of the form 'the F is G' is a finer-grained version of the proposition that n is G. For even if n is the F, n does not enter into the proposition that the F is G. Because that proposition does not have n as a constituent, it does not require the truth of the proposition that n is G. The proposition that the F is G is no more a version of the proposition that n is G than is the proposition that some F is G. Shier rightly says that the Paderewski puzzle "just evaporates" once it is understood that Peter is not being said to believe contradictory propositions, but, it seems to me, this cannot be because what he believes and what he disbelieves are different "versions" of the proposition that Paderewski had musical talent.

Acknowledgments

For comments on the previous draft of this paper, thanks to David Braun, Ray Elugardo, Jeff King, David Shier, and David Sosa. For comments on its more distant ancestors, thanks to Jonathan Berg, Mark Crimmins, Bob Fiengo, Mike Harnish, Ernie LePore, Brian Loar, Kirk Ludwig, Bob Matthews, Robert May, Stephan McCaffery, Brian McLaughlin, Stephen Schiffer, and Andrew Woodfield. Thanks also to members of audiences at the universities of Arizona, Barcelona, the Basque Country, California (Davis, Irvine, and Santa Cruz), London (Birbeck College), Maribor (Slovenia), and Rutgers, especially (in addition to many of those mentioned above) Ramon Cirera, Dave Chalmers, David Copp, Michael Jubien, Mike Martin, Colin McGinn, François Recanati, Stephen Neale, Terry Parsons, Paul Pietroski, Gabriel Segal, and Bill Taschek.

References

Bach, K. (1970), *Part of what a picture is*, British Journal of Aesthetics **10**, 119–237.
Bach, K. (1987), *Thought and Reference*, Oxford University Press, Oxford.
Bach, K. (1993), review of Crimmins (1992), Mind & Language **8**, 431–441.
Bach, K. (1994), *Conversational impliciture*, Mind & Language **9**, 124–162.
Burge, T. (1980), *The content of propositional attitudes*, Noûs **14**, 53–60.
Crimmins, M. (1992), *Talk about Belief*, MIT Press, Cambridge, MA.
Crimmins, M. and Perry, J. (1989), *The Prince and the Phone Booth*, Journal of Philosophy **86**, 685–711.
Fodor, J. (1981), *Propositional attitudes*, Representations, MIT Press, Cambridge, MA.
Frege, G. (1892), *On sense and reference*, Translations of the Philosophical Writings of Gottlob Frege, P. Geach and M. Black, eds, Blackwell, Oxford, 1966.
Jackson, F. (1996), *Mental causation*, Mind **105**, 377–413.
Kripke, S. (1979), *A puzzle about belief*, Meaning and Use, A. Margalit, ed., Reidel, Dordrecht.
Loar, B. (1988), *Social content and psychological content*, Contents of Thought, R.H. Grimm and D.D. Merrill, eds, University of Arizona Press, Tucson.
Recanati, F. (1993), *Direct Reference: From Language to Thought*, Blackwell, Oxford.

Richard, M. (1990), *Propositional Attitudes: An Essay on Thoughts and How We Ascribe Them*, Cambridge University Press, Cambridge.

Salmon, N. (1986), *Frege's Puzzle*, MIT Press, Cambridge, MA.

Salmon, N. (1989), *Illogical belief*, Philosophical Perspectives **3**, 243–285.

Schiffer, S. (1977), *Naming and knowing*, Midwest Studies in Philosophy **2**, 28–41.

Schiffer, S. (1987), *The 'Fido' – Fido theory of belief*, Philosophical Perspectives **1**, 455–480.

Schiffer, S. (1992), *Belief ascription*, Journal of Philosophy **89**, 490–521.

Shier, D. (1996), *Direct reference for the narrow minded*, Pacific Philosophical Quarterly **77**, 225–248.

Soames, S. (1987), *Direct reference, propositional attitudes, and semantic content*, Philosophical Topics **15**, 47–87.

Soames, S. (1988), *Substitutivity*, On Being and Saying: Essays in Honor of Richard Cartwright, J.J. Thomson, ed., MIT Press, Cambridge, MA.

Stalnaker, R. (1988), *Belief attribution and context*, Contents of Thought, R.H. Grimm and D.D. Merrill, eds, University of Arizona Press, Tucson.

CHAPTER 8

Attitude Ascriptions, Context and Interpretive Resemblance

Anne Bezuidenhout

Contents

PRAGMATICS OF PROPOSITIONAL ATTITUDE REPORTS
Current Research in the Semantics/Pragmatics Interface, Vol. 4
Edited by K.M. Jaszczolt

This paper sketches a view about the pragmatics of attitude reports. That is, it attempts to give an account of those aspects of meaning that go beyond what is semantically encoded, and that depend on features of the conversational context in order to be understood.

Philosophical discussions still tend to assume that when one talks of the pragmatics of attitude reports one is talking about something like the need to appeal to Gricean conversational implicatures to account for aspects of meaning that go beyond what is licensed by the semantics of attitude reports. For instance, Salmon (1989) appeals to Gricean implicatures in order to defend his direct reference account of attitude reports, and in order to explain away our intuitions that substitutions within the scope of attitude verbs can alter truth-values.

Another way in which pragmatic considerations have entered the philosophical discussion of attitude reports is through the suggestion that there is a hidden indexical component to attitude ascriptions. See Crimmins (1992). Once again, the underlying semantics is taken to be a direct reference semantics, and the idea of a hidden indexical component is then invoked to account for intuitions that modes of presentation play a role in attitude reports. They become the referents of the hidden indexical component, and pragmatic considerations similar to those that would be invoked in any account of indexicals are appealed to in the explanation of the workings of attitude reports.

The picture sketched in this paper appeals to neither Gricean conversational implicatures nor to a hidden indexical component. Instead, it relies on ideas that have been extensively discussed in the literature on Relevance Theory (RT). The notion of interpretive resemblance plays an especially crucial role, as does the distinction between conceptual and procedural information. These and other relevance theoretical notions used below will be explained as they are introduced.

This pragmatic account will be elaborated in Section 2, after a brief detour through semantics in Section 1. Section 2 focuses on what I call standard attitude reports; ones involving the that-clause construction. The account offered here for standard attitude reports can be extended in natural ways to deal with non-standard attitude reports and non-standard uses of standard attitude reports. These sorts of attitude reports are discussed in Sections 3 and 4 respectively. In Section 5, an objection by Recanati that the sort of account offered here fails to respect the principle of semantic innocence will be considered. See Recanati (1997, 1998). His own account, which he alleges *is* semantically innocent, will also be examined. It will be argued that Recanati's account does not have any obvious advantages over the account offered here, at least with respect to the pragmatic issues that are the central focus of this paper.

1. Semantics

Although this paper is focused on the pragmatics of attitude reports, it is not possible to talk about pragmatic issues while being entirely neutral as to the semantics of attitude reports. So I begin with a few remarks about the semantic view presupposed in this paper. This view cannot be defended here, although I have attempted a partial defense elsewhere (Bezuidenhout 1996, 1997a). My semantic view may not be the only one compatible with the pragmatic picture sketched here. But it does mesh nicely with the pragmatic perspective I am adopting, which is largely inspired by work in relevance theory, as well as work by certain neo-Griceans. See Recanati (1991), Bach (1994), Sperber and Wilson (1995), Carston (1997). And in any case, it is simply easier to talk about the pragmatic aspects of attitude reports while having some semantic story in view.

In this paper I will be assuming the by now fairly mainstream view that that-clauses are (complex) singular terms referring to propositions. However, I'll be assuming that the propositions referred to by that-clauses are fine-grained ones, containing modes of presentation of objects and properties, rather than simply the bare objects or properties themselves. This Fregean assumption is *not* generally accepted. Most who treat that-clauses as referring terms prefer to think of the referents of such clauses as singular (Russellian) propositions, since most philosophers of language wish to accept something like a direct reference semantics.

Frege's own view is that in attitude contexts the sentences embedded in that-clauses shift their referents, and refer to their customary senses in place of their customary referents. Frege in other words accepts a thesis of *semantic deviance*. Words inside of attitude contexts have different referents from the ones they have outside of attitude contexts. Davidson (1984) urges philosophers to return to a pre-Fregean *semantic innocence* and to recognize that it is "plainly incredible that the words 'The Earth moves', uttered after the words 'Galileo said that', mean anything different, or refer to anything else, than is their wont when they come in different environments". (p. 108)

More recently it has been argued that one does not have to accept Frege's reference-shifting hypothesis just because one treats that-clauses as terms. In other words, that-clauses can be treated as terms without loss of semantic innocence. See Crimmins and Perry (1989), Pietroski (1996). The claim is that the embedded content sentence still has its normal semantic function – i.e. it expresses a proposition and refers to a truth-value. It is the complete that-clause, not the embedded sentence, that refers to a proposition. Recanati (1997, 1998) has argued vigorously against this view. He writes:

> . . . if, in order to protect innocence, we draw a sharp distinction between the embedded sentence (which expresses a proposition) and the 'that'-clause (which names it), *we run the risk of making the former disappear from the logical scene*. For the relevant semantic unit is the complete 'that'-clause. At the level

> of logical form the sentence 'John believes that *S*' has the form *aRb* – it consists of a two-place predicate and two singular terms. The embedded sentence plays a role only via the 'that'-clause in which it occurs. What role? Arguably a *pre-semantic* role analogous to that of the demonstration which accompanies a demonstrative. If that is right, then semantically the complexity of the 'that'-clause matters no more that the pragmatic complexity of a demonstrative-cum-demonstration or the pictorial complexity of a quotation. (Recanati, 1997, p. 17. His emphases.)

Recanati argues that the only way to have a truly semantically innocent view is to treat 'believes that' and other attitude verbs as sentence forming operators which take a term and a sentence to form a sentence. Only in this way can we say that a sentence *S* plays the same semantic role, whether it occurs in isolation or embedded in an attitude report. Below I will say more about Recanati's alternative view, and ask whether it really has the virtues he claims for it. For the time being, I will continue to assume the mainstream view that that-clauses have the function of referring to propositional contents.

As the quotation from Recanati makes clear, the mainstream view commits one to the idea that attitude reports express a relationship between a person and the proposition (Fregean or Russellian, depending on one's view) that gives the content of the ascribed attitude. The sentence embedded in the that-clause (which I will call the content sentence) plays a role in picking out this proposition, in virtue of the fact that it itself expresses a certain proposition.

Two questions naturally arise at this point. What is the relationship between the proposition expressed by the content sentence and the content of the ascribed attitude? Secondly, is the proposition expressed by the content sentence the one that it would express for the speaker of the report or for the subject of the attitude? There are two possible answers to the first question. Either the relationship between the proposition expressed by the content sentence and the content of the ascribed attitude is one of *identity*, or it is one of *resemblance*. Devitt (1996, pp. 197–198) argues in favor of the first alternative, but the second alternative is the one that will be defended in this paper. That is, it will be argued that the content of the ascribed attitude need only *resemble* the proposition expressed by the content sentence. Strict identity is not required, and in some cases cannot be achieved, for instance when a subject's mode of presentation involves a perspective that cannot be adopted by another person. Yet this impossibility of literally adopting the subjective perspectives of others does not prevent us from ascribing (and sometimes truly ascribing) attitudes to others.

With respect to the second question, there are again two possible answers. Either the proposition expressed by the content sentence is the one that it would express for the speaker, or it is the one that it would express for the subject of the attitude. The latter alternative seems ruled out however, by the consideration that the subject may not speak the language to which the content sentence belongs, or may speak no language at all, in which case the content sentence would express no proposition for the subject. Yet clearly we can ascribe attitudes to people who do not speak our language, or to creatures, such as higher primates or very young human infants, who speak no language at all.

So, the ascribed attitude is one whose content *resembles* the proposition that would be expressed by the content sentence from the point of view of the *speaker* of the attitude report. The naïve suggestion is therefore that the semantic rule for attitude reports of the form '*S* believes that *p*' can be given by means of a clause in a truth theory along the following lines:

(1) '*S* believes that *p*' is true if and only if *S* believes something similar to *p*.

However, Larson and Ludlow (1993) following Segal (1989) have raised a cogent objection to any account that attempts to build the notion of similarity or resemblance into the truth-conditions of attitude reports in the way suggested by (1). The problem with any such suggestion can be made vivid by the following analogy. Suppose there is a group of language speakers for whom the predicate '*x* kicks *y*' means what in English we would express by '*x* kicks something similar to *y*'. In other words, in this language, call it English*, if John is similar to Peter and Betty kicks John, one can truly say 'Betty kicks Peter'. Now, how is a semanticist who is a monolingual speaker of English* to represent these semantic facts about English* 'kicks'? One might think that the appropriate clause in a truth definition would be the following:

(2) '*x* kicks *y*' is true if and only if *x* kicks something similar to *y*.

But this will not do, as the word 'kicks' used on the right hand side of the biconditional is the English word 'kicks', and thus is not a word available to the semanticist. The semanticist could of course introduce a new technical notion 'kicks+' into his language (which would in fact coincide with English 'kicks'), and then analyze English* 'kicks' in terms of this new relation as follows:

(3) '*x* kicks *y*' is true if and only if *x* kicks+ something similar to *y*.

But a much simpler alternative is to offer the following definition, in which the term mentioned on the left-hand side of the biconditional is used on the right-hand side:

(4) '*x* kicks *y*' if and only if *x* kicks *y*.

Segal's argument is that any attempt to analyze '*S* believes that *p*' along the lines of (1) would run into the same problem. The similarity theorist is in a position similar to that of the monolingual semanticist of English*. In (1) the word 'believes' used on the right-hand side of the biconditional cannot be the same as the one mentioned on the left-hand side. The similarity theorist could introduce a new notion 'believes+' into the language, and then offer a definition along the following lines:

(5) '*S* believes that *p*' is true if and only if *S* believes+ something similar to *p*.

The problem now is to say what this new relation 'believes+' could be. Segal despairs of being able to give any such account, and concludes that the simplest solution to the problem is to dispense with the foreign notion 'believes+' and the notion of similarity, and to offer a definition in which the word 'believes' mentioned on the left-hand side of the definition is used on the right-hand side, as follows:

(6) '*S* believes that *p*' is true if and only if *S* believes that *p*.

Larson and Ludlow (1993) endorse Segal's conclusion, and say that "... similarity or same-saying ... is fundamentally a matter of *usage* and not content, and that the correct account of these phenomena falls outside the domain of semantics proper and into pragmatics." (p. 339. Their emphasis.) However, it may be that although the notion of resemblance cannot be a part of the truth-conditional content of an attitude ascription, it does nevertheless play a semantic role. Only if one has an overly narrow conception of semantics as limited to truth-conditional semantics is one forced to conclude that the notion of similarity has no semantic role to play.

A distinction has been made within RT between procedural and conceptual information. See Blakemore (1987, 1988), Wilson and Sperber (1993). Blakemore's original suggestion was that discourse particles such as 'however', 'yet', 'so' etc. encode procedures, in the sense that they give instructions as to how to inferentially process the propositions expressed by the sentences making up a discourse, constraining the contextual effects that are derivable, and hence contributing to the relevance of the discourse. Since then many sorts of expressions have been said to semantically encode procedures. See Nicolle (1995, 1998) for more details.

Moreover, Wilson and Sperber (1993, pp. 20–21) suggest that encoded procedural information can constrain not only the derivation of implicatures, which is a process involving inferences over propositions, but also the inferential processing of the *sub*-propositional elements (concepts) needed for the construction of propositions (or as Sperber and Wilson say, of propositional forms).[1] For instance, they suggest that what philosophers have called the *character* of an indexical can be thought of as a procedural rule for determining the referent of the indexical in

[1] A proposition on my view is something whose constituents are concepts or modes of presentation, and hence is something that could be constructed in the course of pragmatic processing. When Sperber and Wilson talk of propositions, they appear to be talking about Russellian propositions, which are not psychological in nature. This is presumably why they talk of the construction of propositional *forms*, rather than of propositions. Propositional forms can be thought of as modes of presentation of Russellian propositions.

context. Hence it contributes to the process hearers must go through to understand what proposition is expressed by an utterance in which such an indexical occurs.[2]

The *procedural information* associated with an expression does not become a part of the propositional contents of the utterances containing the expression, and hence it is not part of the truth-evaluable contents of those utterances. Its job is to give instructions to the performance system as to how conceptual content is to be pragmatically processed. On the other hand, semantically encoded *conceptual information* (suitably pragmatically processed) *will* become a part of the propositional contents of utterances containing expressions which encode such conceptual information. Hence semantically encoded conceptual information is potentially truth-conditionally relevant.

According to this view, some expressions semantically encode procedures (e.g., 'I'), and some encode concepts (e.g., 'horse'), but it may also be that some expressions semantically encode *both* sorts of information. That is, one part of the semantic information they encode will contribute to the propositional contents of utterances containing those expressions, while another part encodes instructions for the inferential processing either of sub-propositional constituents or of complete propositions. For example, the deictically used pronoun 'he' may encode procedural information to the effect that the referent is some highly accessible individual, and also encode the conceptual information that the entity is 3rd person, masculine, singular. See Nicolle (1995, p. 50).[3]

I would like to propose that English that-clauses encode procedural information. An attitude ascription in English of the form 'S ϕ's that p' that is uttered in context C encodes the following procedure:

(7) Assign a content to S's attitude ϕ that resembles in contextually appropriate ways the content that would be expressed by the speaker in C were she to sincerely utter the sentence p,

where S is replaced by an expression – either a singular referring expression such as 'Jack Spratt' or a quantifier expression such as 'Some children' – that picks out

[2] Kaplan (1989, p. 505) says that the indexical 'I' is associated with the character or meaning rule 'the speaker or writer {of the token expression}'. Hence the procedure would be to search the context for the speaker/writer.

[3] Actually, things may be more complex than Nicolle suggests. Nunberg (1993) makes a distinction between the index and the interpretation/referent of an indexical or a deictically used pronoun. Index and interpretation can in principle come apart. This would happen in cases of deferred uses of pronouns. For example, one could utter: 'He {pointing to the man Michael Creighton} is always a good read', intending to say that Michael Creighton's books are always a good read. Here the gender information associated with 'he', which Nicolle identifies as conceptual rather than procedural, does not become a part of the interpretation of the utterance. Its role seems to be to help the hearer to locate the index. Further pragmatic processing then gets the hearer from the contextually indicated object (the man) to the intended referent (the books). This suggests that in such cases gender information is procedural rather than conceptual. A more detailed discussion and critique of Nunberg's views can be found in (Bezuidenhout, 1997b).

the subject(s) of the attitude, ϕ is replaced by a mental attitude verb, and p by a sentence of English. The net result is that the listener will understand the speaker to have said that S's attitude ϕ has the content q, where q is a content resembling the content of the sentence p in appropriate ways.

In other words, we are to think of that-clauses as terms associated with a procedural rule which helps the hearer (when it is supplemented with contextually available *non*-linguistic information) to determine the contents of the ascribed attitudes. One could think of this procedural rule as what Recanati has called a *linguistic* mode of presentation (Recanati, 1993). But this mode of presentation does not become a part of the proposition expressed by the attitude report. It is truth-conditionally irrelevant. Instead, what becomes a part of the proposition expressed by the attitude report is what Recanati calls a *psychological* mode of presentation. This psychological mode of presentation of the content of the reported attitude is a pragmatically processed version of the conceptual information encoded in the content sentence, arrived at by conforming to the interpretive resemblance constraint procedurally encoded by the that-clause.

Nunberg (1993) makes a distinction between the index and the referent/interpretation of an indexical or a deictically used expression. He argues that what Kaplan has called the character of an indexical, and which Kaplan assumes determines the *referent* of the indexical, in fact merely determines the *index* of the indexical. Sometimes this coincides with the intended referent. But sometimes it comes apart. For instance, in the case of the first person plural pronoun ‘we’, the index is the speaker of the token expression, but the referent will be some contextually determined group to which the speaker belongs. Similarly, with deictically used pronouns, the accompanying demonstration (which Kaplan assumes determines the referent of the expression) merely determines the index. Sometimes this coincides with the intended referent. But sometimes it comes apart from the referent, as in cases of deferred reference. In such a case the demonstrated object is the index, and the referent is some object which is contextually related to the index. Determining the referent is therefore a pragmatic process which requires the hearer to move from index to referent.

Nunberg also puts his distinction to work to give an account of the distinction between referential and attributive uses of referring terms. But here I would like to apply his distinction to my account of attitude reports. One could think of the proposition expressed by the content sentence as akin to what Nunberg calls the index of an indexical or deictically used expression. The referent is one which resembles it, and to get to the intended referent one must rely on pragmatic processes of the sort that will be described in the next section, operating under the constraint of interpretive resemblance.

One could think of the interpretive process as a two-step affair. The hearer has to figure out what proposition the content sentence expresses for the speaker in context. This process calls for the ordinary sorts of interpretive processes that are used to understand what speakers say by uttering sentences in context, processes such as the ones of enrichment or loosening that will be explained below. Once the hearer has recovered a complete propositional representation in this way, a second stage of processing will require further adjustments to arrive at a content that resembles this one in contextually appropriate ways. Actually, we will see that the process is more seamless than this suggests, as the need to satisfy the interpretive resemblance constraint will result in suitable applications of enrichment and loosening that directly yield a representation of the ascribed content.[4]

In the following sections, I will attempt to show *how* the listener's recovery of a semantic representation along the lines suggested in (7) above, together with contextually available *non*-linguistic information, enables the listener to infer what the content is that the speaker intends to ascribe to the subject of the attitude report. In other words, an attempt will be made to show the way in which listeners use context to interpret the speaker's ascription, and thereby to understand how the speaker in turn is interpreting the subject of the ascription.

2. Pragmatic processes involved in understanding attitude ascriptions

The main point I'll be arguing for in this section is that that-clauses are *context sensitive* singular terms, and thus what proposition is picked out by a that-clause can vary from context to context, even though the sentence embedded in the that-clause remains the same.[5] One consequence of this, I will try to argue, is that a sentence containing a term that is conventionally associated with one mode of presentation of an object or property can be embedded in a that-clause in a way that allows the speaker to ascribe quite another mode of presentation to the subject of the propositional attitude.

I will begin by looking at several examples of standard that-clause ascriptions. For example, suppose Lucy and Ricky are strolling through the streets of the city that is now once again named 'St. Petersburg'. But suppose this event takes place

---

4 Nunberg (1993) suggests that the sort of pragmatic processing that gets one from the character to the index and then from there to the interpretation/referent is a two-stage process. Bezuidenhout (1997b) is critical of this separation of the process into two stages, and argues that the processing is more seamless than Nunberg suggests. Similarly in the case of propositional attitude interpretation, I would suggest that the process that gets one from the linguistic mode of presentation (which encodes the procedural rule, plus some conceptual elements) to the proposition expressed by the content sentence, and then to the ascribed content need not be separated into two stages. The processing is all of a piece, and needn't involve a stage at which the full content of the embedded sentence is entertained, before there is a move away to a content which resembles it.

5 Why think that there is always a definite proposition that is picked out by a that-clause? Couldn't it be that what is picked out is a *set* of propositions? Or a propositional *type*? Or some general *property* of a proposition? Many singular terms may be used either referentially or attributively. See Bezuidenhout (1997b) for a defense of this claim. This may be true of that-clauses as well as any other referring term. For the time being I'll focus on cases in which that-clauses are referentially used to pick out a single proposition. In Section 4 I will return to other possible uses of that-clauses.

back in the Communist era and the city is still called 'Leningrad'. As they are strolling through the streets Ricky says to Lucy:[6]

(8) It is not hard to see why Pushkin believed that Leningrad is the most beautiful city in Russia.

Now, let us suppose, Lucy knows that it is Leningrad she and Ricky are strolling through. She is not confused about where they are at the moment. Moreover, it is manifest to both her and Ricky as they stroll though the city that there are buildings of a certain architectural design, streets arranged in certain ways, parks and gardens laid out in certain ways. This information will be a part of Lucy's encyclopedic information about the city of Leningrad. Her encyclopedic entry for the city of Leningrad will also contain a lot of other information. For instance, it will contain the information that the city is called 'Leningrad'. Lucy may also know that the city was once called 'St. Petersburg', which of course was what it was called in Pushkin's day. Other information she may have is that the sewer system is antiquated, that the inhabitants are friendly, that the queues for food are long, and so on.

But this other information is irrelevant to interpreting Ricky's remark about Pushkin's belief. All that Lucy need focus on is the mutually manifest information about the buildings and the general layout of the city, which is part of her encyclopedic knowledge of Leningrad. This information will allow Lucy to interpret Ricky as saying that Pushkin believed that Leningrad qua city with such-and-such buildings and lay-out is the most beautiful city in Russia. Moreover, since Ricky begins his remark with the words "Its not hard to see why...", Lucy will infer that Ricky *endorses* Pushkin's belief that Leningrad is the most beautiful city in Russia. In fact, Ricky's reason for invoking Pushkin's name may be an appeal to authority, intended to provide some justification for his own aesthetic judgment about the city.

Even though Ricky uses the name 'Leningrad', he can invoke a mode of presentation of the city which differs from the one either he or Lucy associates with the name. This mode that differs from either of theirs is the one that he is ascribing to Pushkin. What happens when Ricky uses the name 'Leningrad' is that he invokes Lucy's encyclopedic entry for that city. The procedurally encoded information that is retrieved as a result of processing Ricky's attitude ascription will instruct Lucy to look for a mode of presentation of the city resembling hers in certain ways, and the information that the city contains buildings of a certain architectural style is singled out from her encyclopedic entry as relevant, given what is mutually manifest in the conversational context. Thus she understands what Ricky is saying Pushkin believed about the city by altering her own conception of the city in relevant ways.

[6] In this paper I talk of speakers and hearers, though what I'm saying is meant to apply equally to writers and readers. In other words, I am concerned with attitude reports both in written and in oral communication.

The process of pragmatic adjustment in this case is one which is akin to the process of *loosening* that relevance theorists have claimed goes on when a listener understands a speaker's loose use of a certain term. For example, suppose Lucy and Ricky are looking for a challenging and exciting route to follow on their planned cycling trip, and Ricky proposes that they travel through Holland. If Lucy replies: 'Holland is flat', she does not mean that the surface area of Holland is completely level, but simply that there aren't any significant hills or terrain that would present much challenge for a cyclist.

According to this relevance-theoretical account, what happens when a listener interprets a speaker's loose use is that the lexical concepts in the listener's lexical entry for 'flat (surface)' provide input to a pragmatic process of loosening, where some of the relevant information associated with those lexical concepts is used, along with other contextually available information, to construct an *ad hoc* concept, which then becomes a constituent of the proposition that the listener will recover as the content of the speaker's utterance in the context. See Carston (1997). The proposition Ricky understands Lucy to have expressed is therefore the proposition that Holland does not have any hills of significant size. Of course Lucy also conversationally implicates that they should not put Holland on their itinerary for their cycling trip.

Similarly, when Ricky utters (8), Lucy does not understand him to have said that Pushkin had any thoughts involving the information 'is called "Leningrad" '.[7] Rather, given other information available to Lucy in the conversational context, she is able to discard certain elements of her encyclopedic information about the city to arrive at a conception of the city that Pushkin might have had. Of course, not only is the information 'is called "Leningrad" ' likely to be discarded, but also other bits of information that are not relevant to the present context. Via a process of pragmatic loosening, she arrives at a conception of Leningrad/St. Petersburg that resembles hers (and Ricky's) in certain ways.

To say the speaker or the hearer's conception resembles Pushkin's in certain ways does not entail that either must share Pushkin's belief about the beauty of the city in order for the ascription to be made or understood. As already noted, because of the preamble 'It's not hard to see why. . .", (8) does suggest that Ricky is endorsing Pushkin's belief. But perhaps Lucy hates the architectural style of Leningrad's buildings, preferring the clean lines of modern architecture. This does not prevent her from understanding the attribution. In this situation, the interpretation process will be more or less as described above. It is just that extra inferencing is required on Lucy's part.

Lucy will still need to access her encyclopedic entry for 'Leningrad', with its information about the city's name, the architectural style of the buildings, the city's

[7] As noted above, in Pushkin's day, the city was called 'St. Petersburg', and so the mode under which Pushkin knew the city would have included the encyclopedic information that the city's name was 'St. Petersburg'. More precisely, it would have contained information about the Russian version of this name. Moreover, being literate, Pushkin would have known how to render this in Cyrillic script.

layout and so on. In addition though, one bit of non-linguistic information that is mutually manifest to her and Ricky in their current conversational context is that different people have different architectural preferences. So, the conception Lucy attributes to Pushkin resembles hers in containing information to the effect that the city has many buildings of such-and-such an architectural style, but then she *adds* the information that this is a pleasing architectural style to the attributed conception. This addition is an enrichment. In other words, in addition to the pragmatic process of *loosening*, elements of what Sperber and Wilson call *enrichment* play a role.

It is recognized in the literature on relevance theory that to retrieve the proposition expressed by a speaker, the hearer will sometimes need to engage in both enrichment and loosening processes. Carston (1997) gives the example of understanding the expression ‘plastic duck’. Presumably to arrive at the conception of a plastic duck one first loosens one’s conception of a duck, focusing only on certain shape features, and excluding features such as animacy, ability to fly and so on. This conception is still too broad, however, as its extension will include both real and plastic ducks. So this loosened conception will have to be narrowed or enriched, by addition of features such as being composed of plastic.

Of course, there are also cases which call just for a process of *enrichment*. In cases requiring enrichment, the lexical concepts that are constituents of the logical form (LF) of an utterance must be contextually enriched.[8] Inferential processes integrate lexical information with non-linguistic information that is available either from perception or memory. Sometimes this enrichment is required because the underlying lexical concepts are semantically underdetermined, and supplementation with contextual information is needed for any complete content to be expressed at all. In such cases the contextual information saturates or completes the underlying concepts, so the processes involved can be called *saturation* or *completion* (Recanati, 1993, Chapter 14; Bach, 1994). Recanati also distinguishes a sort of enrichment that he calls *free enrichment*, because the contextual supplementation is not needed for a complete thought to be expressed, but it is needed if the listener is to be able to recover the proposition expressed by the speaker on the particular occasion.[9] Recanati (ibid.) has in addition suggested that there is a pragmatic process of *transfer*, in which the listener has to move from a concept of one sort (e.g., the

[8] Here I am assuming that the initial stages of utterance processing involve a process of *decoding*, the result of which is that the listener recovers a representation of the logical form of the utterance, in the linguists’ sense of ‘logical form’. This LF representation is the output of the grammar module at the conceptual-intentional interface. See Chomsky (1995, pp. 19–20).

[9] This process of free enrichment is similar to the pragmatic process Bach (1994) calls *expansion*. The difference is that Bach thinks that the result of such expansion processes is the retrieval of an *impliciture*, rather than what relevance theorists call an *explicature*. Bach argues that the result of expansion processes is the retrieval of a proposition which is only implicit in what is said, and that it is a mistake to claim that such a proposition lies on the explicit side of what is communicated, as one must hold if one regards it as an explicature. See Vicente Cruz (1998) for an argument in support of the relevance theoretical position and against Bach’s introduction of the category of implicitures.

mode of presentation of an individual – an individual concept) to one of a different sort (e.g., the mode of presentation of a property – a general concept).[10] All these pragmatic processes are at work in utterance interpretation generally, so they must also be at work in the particular case of the interpretation of attitude reports.

An example of the way in which loosening (or loosening plus enrichment) may be at work in the interpretation of attitude reports has already been discussed. Thus a question arises as to whether the process of enrichment (by itself) or of transfer may similarly be involved in the interpretation of propositional attitude reports. It will be argued that they do. In fact, two classic examples, which have been much discussed in the philosophical literature, can serve as illustrations.

Firstly, consider the following elaboration on Mark Richard's Steamroller Case. See Richard (1990, pp. 117–118). Mr. X is talking to Gracie over the telephone. Mr. X looks out his window, and sees a steamroller bearing down on a woman in a phone booth. Unbeknownst to him, the woman in the phone booth is Gracie. He waves frantically at the woman in the booth, in an attempt to warn her of the impending danger. But he keeps talking calmly into the telephone. George is standing in the booth with Gracie. He says to her:

(9) The man at the window believes that you are in danger.

Also, George can hear that the man on the other end of the telephone sounds quite calm. So he says to Gracie:

(10) The man on the telephone believes that you are not in danger.

This variant of Richard's steamroller example is essentially the one discussed by Devitt (1996, p. 219). Devitt claims that (9) and (10) 'seem to ascribe contradictory beliefs' to Mr. X, who of course is both the man to whom Gracie is speaking and the man waving from the window. This is a problem, says Devitt, because Mr. X is surely not irrational.[11] Devitt locates the problem in the fact that what he calls the *general demonstrative mode*, associated with the two occurrences of the pronoun 'you' in the that-clauses of (9) and (10), is not fine-grained enough to distinguish between the two different *specific demonstrative modes* under which Mr. X is acquainted with Gracie.

Devitt believes that it is a feature of our language that we have no *standard* way in which to distinguish Mr. X's more specific demonstrative modes. It is of course possible to ascribe beliefs to Mr. X in such a way that the appearance of inconsistency disappears. But such ascriptions, says Devitt, would be *non*-standard. For

[10] Throughout this paper, when I talk about concepts, I mean concepts in the *non*-Fregean sense of conceptions or modes of presentation of something. Frege treated concepts as the *referents* of predicates, rather than as senses or modes of presentation of things.

[11] Of course, George is unaware that the man waving from the window is one and the same as the man to whom Gracie is speaking over the phone. So from George's point of view there is no inconsistency between (9) and (10). I presume that Devitt means that the appearance of inconsistency is an appearance *for us*, who know the facts of the situation.

instance, George could have uttered the following two sentences, in which there is no appearance of inconsistency:

(9*) The man at the window believes that you, *qua* person he sees out his window, are in danger.

(10*) The man on the telephone believes that you, *qua* person he is talking to over the phone, are not in danger.

However, despite the fact that Devitt thinks that (9) and (10) usually ascribe a *general* demonstrative mode to one of Mr. X's mental tokens, and despite the fact that Devitt thinks that there is no standard way of ascribing specific demonstrative modes, he does concede that (9) and (10) *could* be used in certain contexts to ascribe *specific* demonstrative modes to Mr. X. This is because the *qua* clauses which are explicit in (9*) and (10*) might in effect be supplied by the context, rather than being explicitly stated. Of course, if (9) and (10) were used in this way, then such ascriptions would be context dependent, because the speaker (George) would be relying on the listener (Gracie) to retrieve certain information from the context in order to figure out what concepts or modes of presentation he intended to ascribe.

What Devitt thinks might on rare occasions happen, I would argue is what in fact typically happens. The pronoun 'you' in the that-clauses of (9) and (10) may indeed be associated with a general demonstrative mode of presentation of the addressee, but that is not the mode that the speaker is attributing to the subject of the attitude. What Devitt calls the general demonstrative mode associated with 'you' is in effect what Kaplan would call the character associated with the pronoun, and in this case would be something like 'the addressee in the context'. We have already seen above that relevance theorists treat the character of an indexical or of a deictically used pronoun as *procedurally* encoded information, which gives instructions to the hearer as to which object in the context is the referent of the indexical or pronoun. In the case of 'he' or 'she' there is arguably also some encoded *conceptual* information associated with the expression, namely gender information. But 'you' lacks such encoded conceptual information. Rather, the listener will use contextually available *non*-linguistic information, under the guidance of the encoded procedural information 'the addressee in the context', to construct an *ad hoc* concept or mode of presentation of the addressee. The process here is essentially one of enrichment. It is this enriched conception (what Devitt calls the *specific* mode of presentation) which will be understood to have been attributed by the speaker to the subject of the attitude. Thus Gracie will in effect understand George to have attributed (9*) and (10*) by his utterances of (9) and (10).

Turning now to cases in which the pragmatic process of *transfer* is used, we can illustrate the workings of this process by means of an example first discussed by Stephen Schiffer, and elaborated in (Devitt, 1996, pp. 145–147). Suppose Poirot, the famous detective, stumbles across the badly mutilated corpse of Smith. Contemplating the body of Smith, and the terrible wounds inflicted on the body, he utters the following:

(11) The murderer of Smith is insane.

Here the description is being used attributively, as Poirot is saying that the murderer of Smith, whoever he or she is, is insane. Poirot has as yet no idea who the murderer is. He says this simply because he believes no sane person could inflict such savage wounds on someone. A reporter interviews Poirot, and his remark (11) is quoted on the front page of the daily newspaper the following day. The moll of a local gangster reads the report in the newspaper. She happens to know that the gangster, whose name is 'Big Felix', is Smith's murderer. The moll turns to one of Felix's gang members and utters the following:

(12) Poirot believes that Smith's murderer is insane.

Devitt claims that the moll, given what she knows, could equally well have uttered:

(13) Poirot believes that Big Felix is inane.

He takes this as evidence that the attribution in (12) should be given what he calls a *simply transparent* reading, as opposed to what he calls opaque and rapport transparent readings. It is simply transparent, according to Devitt, because any expression which from the moll's point of view is co-denoting or co-referring with 'Smith's murderer' can be substituted for that expression in (12) without altering its truth-value. Devitt's view is problematic for two reasons.

Firstly, as Goble (1997) has argued, it is far from clear that all such substitutions are allowable. Suppose that Big Felix is also the mayor of the city. In his role as mayor he is known to Poirot, and in this capacity Poirot thinks of him as an upright citizen, capable neither of gangsterism nor murder. Even though the moll of course knows Big Felix in all his guises, it seems as though the moll could *not* truly utter:

(14) Poirot believes that the mayor is insane.

Secondly, the idea of simply transparent attitude reports can be challenged. What Devitt calls simply transparent readings of attitude reports are what others have called *de re* attitude reports. Despite the fact that the distinction between *de dicto* and *de re* reports is fairly well entrenched in the philosophy of language, and despite the fact that philosophers have traditionally thought it obvious that many reports are to be interpreted as *de re* reports, Crimmins (1995) has argued that *de re* attitude reports are not nearly as common as they are generally thought to be. He argues that modes of presentation are almost always in play, even though in some cases the modes may be identified only by their type, or by some property they share with other modes, and not in a singularly identifying manner.[12] Something

[12] For a critique of Crimmins' views and a reaffirmation of the traditional view, see Reimer (1995).

like this view (freed of its association with the hidden indexical account advocated by Crimmins), is the view that I would like to advocate.

Let us go back to the report (13) which Devitt alleges Big Felix's moll can without infelicity assert to one of the gang members. Devitt considers only what the moll knows, and seems to assume that simply because she knows that Big Felix is Smith's murderer, the substitution of 'Big Felix' for 'Smith's murderer' in (12) is licensed. But this is not necessarily so. The moll needs to be sensitive to what is *mutually* manifest to her and her hearer, the gang member. What information do the two need to share in order for (13) to be properly understood by the gang member? It seems that the gang member is going to have to know pretty much what the moll knows about Big Felix.

Assume that the gangster knows who Poirot is. Suppose also that it is mutually manifest that Poirot knows Big Felix only under his mayoral guise, and that Poirot would never think that Big Felix, qua mayor, is insane. Also, assume that the gangster can see that the moll's remark is prompted by something she has read in the newspaper. So something must have been reported in the newspaper which would have prompted Poirot to conclude that Big Felix, under some guise other than his mayoral one, is insane. It is mutually manifest to the moll and the gangster that newspapers report on sensational murders. If the gangster knows that Big Felix killed Smith, and knows about the brutal mutilation of the corpse, then he will understand the moll to have said that Poirot thinks that Big Felix, qua murderer of Smith, is insane.

If I am right about the sort of pragmatic processing that the gangster must go through to correctly interpret the moll's report (13), the process will involve the pragmatic process of *transfer*. The gangster will not end up attributing a singular belief about Big Felix to Poirot, but a general belief involving a salient property of Big Felix's, namely the property of being the murderer of Smith. In other words, on the assumption that the moll and the gangster share all the relevant information about Big Felix with one another, the moll will in effect have ascribed the belief reported in (12) by her utterance of (13).

On the other hand, suppose that the gangster does *not* know that Big Felix is Smith's murderer. Then the moll's report will be rather difficult to interpret. Perhaps, based on the mutually manifest information that newspapers tend to report sensational events, and on the mutually manifest information that Poirot is a detective, the gangster may infer that Big Felix is somehow implicated in a crime. But why should this lead anyone to the judgment that Big Felix is insane? Perhaps some additional inferential processing might get the gangster to the point of concluding that Big Felix has done something crazy that has made the authorities think he is crazy. But, don't forget that it is mutually manifest to the moll and the gangster that Poirot only knows Big Felix under his mayoral guise, so the gangster will have to conclude that somehow Big Felix, qua mayor, is implicated in some sort of crime that has led the authorities to think that he is insane. If the gangster gets to this conclusion, he will have to extinguish his previous belief that Poirot would never think that the mayor is insane. Clearly, this chain of inference is leading the gangster down the wrong path, and the moll should have anticipated this. She should only utter (13) if it is mutually manifest that the gangster knows as much about Big Felix as she does.

Having shown that the interpretation of attitude reports may involve any one (and sometimes more than one) of the pragmatic processes of loosening, enrichment and transfer, I turn in the next section to showing how the above account of the interpretation of standard attitude reports can be extended to non-standard reports.

3. Non-standard ascriptions

There are various *non-standard* forms of attitude ascriptions.[13] Consider for instance ascriptions of the following sort, which Recanati (1997) calls *adverbial metarepresentations*:

(15) The Bulls are a great team, according to Jim.

(16) In the opinion of the man I consulted at the brokerage firm, I should buy stocks in Amazon.com.

In cases like these, although there is no that-clause, it is plausible to say that the procedural rule (7) is invoked by the fact that the parenthetical clause clearly signals that someone's attitude is being characterized. Thus the pragmatic processing involved will be essentially like the processing already described for the standard cases.

However, there are also situations in which there is *no overt indication* in the sentences used to ascribe mental contents that an ascription is being made. There is neither an overt that-clause nor an overt adverbial construction, although it is clear from the context that an ascription is being made. Consider the following examples:

(17) Lucy: I asked my broker what stocks he thinks I should buy.
Ricky: And?
Lucy: I should buy Amazon.com stocks.

(18) Sue was mulling over what had happened at the meeting. That dreadful bore Harry would have to be dealt with somehow. Perhaps a little

[13] These are only non-standard in the sense that philosophical discussions rarely pay any attention to them. They are not non-standard in the sense that they rarely occur in ordinary discourse. On the contrary, these ways of ascribing beliefs and other attitudes are probably more widespread than ascriptions using the that-clause construction.

accident could be arranged. Meetings would be so much more pleasant without Harry's long-winded and irrelevant lectures about what the group should do.

In (17), although Lucy never utters the sentence 'My broker thinks that I should buy Amazon.com stocks', Lucy's first utterance and her reply to Ricky's prompt are tantamount to such an ascription. In (18), the first sentence of this discourse says that Sue is engaging in some mental activity, but it doesn't explicitly say what the content of her speculations is. The following sentences specify the contents of several mental states; Sue's belief that Harry is a bore, her reasons for thinking that Harry is a bore, her desire to do something that would make it the case that Harry doesn't attend any more meetings, and her consideration of some way to realize this goal.

Clearly, some sort of pragmatic processing must be involved in cases like (17) and (18), as there are no expressions whose semantic contribution can explain how these utterances can be interpreted as attitude reports. It must be that the procedural information which has become conventionally associated with the that-clause construction (given in (7) above) can be invoked in other situations as well, even if there is no grammatical construction which signals the need to use this procedural rule. Here clues from the context about the speaker's intentions will have to enable this rule to be invoked. Like all procedural rules, (7) works to constrain the assumptions that will be accessed in the course of processing the speaker's utterance. It constrains the contextual effects that will be derived from processing the utterance, and hence the relevance of the utterance.

Exchanges like those in (17) have been extensively discussed by Sperber and Wilson (1995). They have discussed cases like these in the context of explaining their concept of *interpretive resemblance*. Suppose the broker actually uttered the words 'You should buy Amazon.com stocks'. Lucy could have reported the broker's opinion by echoing the actual words he used to express his opinion. Then Lucy's utterance would have resembled the broker's as closely as possible, by being a token of the very same syntactic and semantic type. Ricky of course would have had to figure out that the 'you' in Lucy's utterance was an echoed 'you', and not meant to refer to Ricky. But this would have been clear from the context, especially if Lucy had somehow altered her tone of voice or in some other way signaled that she was adopting the broker's point of view.

As it is, Lucy utters a sentence which doesn't exactly match the one the broker used. She has made suitable adjustments between the second- and first-person points of view, uttering instead 'I should buy Amazon.com stocks'. Lucy's utterance still interpretively resembles the broker's utterance (and hence resembles the opinion to which his utterance gives expression), because her utterance has some of the same logical and contextual implications as his.[14] Ricky will be able to

[14] Sperber and Wilson would say that Lucy's utterance interpretively resembles the broker's because it has the *same propositional form as* his. However, they are assuming that the propositions expressed

make some of the same inferences on the basis of processing Lucy's utterance as he could have made had he directly processed the broker's utterance.

Moreover, Lucy could even have uttered a sentence like 'I should buy some sort of Internet stock'. In this case her utterance would have shared fewer logical and contextual implications with the broker's, but it still would have interpretively resembled the broker's utterance (and hence his belief) to some degree. What sort of license the speaker takes is determined by various sorts of contextual factors. It will be determined by what can be presumed to be mutually manifest to speaker and hearer, by the intentions of the speaker (for instance, is the speaker attempting to seriously report on someone's attitude, or is she trying to ironically distance herself from the views of the person whose attitude is being reported?), and so on.

Turning now to examples like (18), it should be clear that this is a very common way of characterizing the beliefs of a character in a work of fiction. The narrator takes up the point of view of the subject, and reports on the subject's attitudes by, as it were, giving direct expression to these attitudes. The narrator talks in the voice of the other. But it is not only in fiction that mental attitudes are reported in this way. The following sort of exchange should seem very commonplace:

(19) Lucy: Did Charles find anyone to be the object of his affections while he was on vacation?
Ricky: Yes. The most perfect, the most ravishingly beautiful, woman in the whole world, by the name of Dorothy!

Here Ricky is not being disloyal to Lucy, by claiming that Dorothy is the most perfect woman in the world. He is characterizing Charles' attitude towards Dorothy, and at the same time conveying his own mocking attitude towards Charles' infatuation with Dorothy. Charles may not even have used words such as 'perfect' and 'ravishingly beautiful' to describe Dorothy. He may simply have gone on at length about all the qualities he perceived her to have, and Ricky is communicating that the net effect is that Charles thinks of Dorothy as a paragon of virtue and beauty. Here again Ricky's utterance satisfies the interpretive resemblance constraint. The content of Ricky's utterance interpretively resembles the content of Charles' thoughts about Dorothy, and this is why it can be used to report on the content of Charles' attitude.

Example (19) is very similar to cases of irony that are discussed by Sperber and Wilson. See Sperber and Wilson (1991). They treat ironical utterances as cases of interpretive use, in which the speaker echoes the contents of the utterances or opinions of an individual or group of individuals, in such a way as to communicate

---

by the broker's and Lucy's utterances are Russellian propositions. In this paper I have been advocating the view that the proposition expressed by an utterance in context is something more fine-grained than a Russellian proposition. A process of enrichment will be involved in the recovery of this proposition. In the broker's case, it will involve a mode of presentation of Lucy, and not simply Lucy herself, bare of any mode of presentation. On the other hand, the proposition expressed by Lucy's utterance will involve a mode of *self*-presentation of Lucy.

something about the speaker's own attitude towards the echoed contents.[15] Thus one person might utter the words 'What a lovely day for a picnic'. Later in the day, while on the picnic, it may begin to rain. Someone else, echoing the first person's words, might utter the sentence 'Lovely day for a picnic indeed'. Here the second speaker is being ironical, and is indicating that he rejects the opinion expressed earlier by the first speaker.

Of course not all cases of echoic use are cases of irony. The speaker may intend to endorse or sympathize with the echoed content. Suppose that when the two people described above go on their picnic the weather does indeed prove to be wonderful. Then the second speaker's utterance will echo the first speaker's utterance, but in such a case it will be understood that the second speaker emphatically endorses the first speaker's opinion.

One might therefore argue that what I have classified as non-standard attitude reports are better classified as cases of irony, or more generally as cases of echoic use. Something like this is suggested by Recanati (1997). He suggests that cases of irony involve 'a form of pretense or mimicry' (p. 35). Commenting on the picnic example just described, he says:

> the ironist ... playfully (simulatively) describes the world as it would have been had the meteorological prediction been correct. The point of the ironist is to show how much the 'world' thus described differs from the actual world. (p. 36.)

But Recanati also wants to maintain that there is a crucial difference between what he calls metarepresentations (to cover both the '*S* believes that *p*' and the 'According to *S*, *p*' forms of belief attribution) and simulations. Recanati (1997, pp. 52–54) discusses the contrast he sees between the following examples:

(20) John is totally paranoid. Everybody spies on him or wants to kill him, including his own mother.

(21) John believes that he is being persecuted.

The former Recanati says is a typical example of free indirect speech, whereas the latter is a metarepresentation. Free indirect speech, according to Recanati, involves an act of mental simulation. In (20) for example, an imaginary world (John's paranoid world) is first mentioned, and then the speaker takes up the perspective of that imaginary world. Now Recanati denies that 'John is totally paranoid' is a metarepresentation, because although it is about a representation (the-world-according-to-John) and that representation has a content, 'John is totally para-

15 Actually, there are also cases in which some feature other than the content of a previous speaker's utterance can be echoed. One could echo someone's pronunciation of a word, in order to communicate that one thinks the person's pronunciation is deviant. For example, one could utter the sentence: 'He's going to Harvard' {pronouncing the final word hɔ.^{ə}vəd} to convey disapproval of the snobbish way the person pronounces 'Harvard'.

noid' does not actually display the content of the-world-according-to-John. Recanati also denies that the second sentence in (20) is a metarepresentation, even an elliptical one. Rather, he calls it a pretend assertion. The imaginary world that is mentioned in the first part of (20) is simulatively assumed in the pretend assertion that follows it.

So, neither of the parts of (20) by themselves is a metarepresentation. But does it follow that (20) as a whole is not a metarepresentation either? Why deny that it is a metarepresentation simply because there is no explicit that-clause or adverbial construction like 'according to John'? The same procedural rule (7) could be invoked by the utterance of (20) as would have been invoked had it contained an explicit grammatical marker of interpretive use. Via pragmatic processes of the sort described in the previous section, the hearer will arrive at a content which interpretively resembles the one expressed by the content sentence, viz. the second sentence in (20). This is the content that the hearer will understand the speaker to have attributed to John.

All the cases I've discussed so far involve some sort of interpretive use, and I do not see why only the cases which explicitly signal this interpretive use, either through the presence of the that-clause construction or the adverbial form, deserve the title 'attitude report'. Blass (1990) discusses cases of languages, such as Sissala, that have an interpretive use marker. Sissala uses the sentence-final particle rɛ́ (or one of its variants) to indicate that the speaker's utterance is meant to resemble the utterance or the opinion of another, or perhaps of a group of others. Often the speaker will in addition succeed in conveying his own attitude towards the echoed utterance or opinion.[16] Rɛ́ also sometimes introduces a complement clause, and in these cases it functions like the English that-clause construction. When rɛ́ introduces a complement clause there will be an explicit attitude or speech act verb in the sentence. But in cases in which it is used as a particle, there need be no explicit attitude or speech act verb. Blass gives the following instances from her data (here I simply cite Blass' English glosses):

(22) Whatever small thing you learn, tomorrow you will eat its fruit.

(23) We have become immortal.

In (22) the speaker is giving voice to a piece of traditional wisdom, and the interpretive use marker signals that the expressed content is being attributed to someone, in this case to people in the culture in general, rather than to any particular individual or group of individuals. The speaker also communicates that he

[16] Other researchers have argued that this marker, and similar markers in other languages, should be treated as *hearsay* markers. A hearsay marker indicates that the speaker is reporting on something that she has learned through the testimony of others. It may also communicate that the speaker's evidence for the reported fact is less secure than had she learned the fact first hand. Blass convincingly argues against this evidential interpretation, and against that claim that rɛ́ is confined to a use as a hearsay marker. It is better classified as a general marker of interpretive use.

endorses this piece of wisdom. The speaker's appeal to this traditional wisdom is presumably meant to lend the weight of authority to his own opinion.

The original context for (23) was a conversation between a group of people about sacrificial meat from Mecca which had been given to the Sissala people during a time of famine. The group had just eaten some of this meat, and the speaker of (23) clearly intended the utterance ironically. This is signaled by the interpretive use marker. Here the opinion that the speaker is echoing is what the speaker takes to be the Muslim belief that sacrificial animals have divine, life-saving powers. The speaker also communicates that he does not endorse this opinion.

If the same particle is used to introduce the complement of a speech act or propositional attitude verb as is used to signal interpretive use in contexts where there is no explicit speech act or propositional attitude verb, then Recanati's distinction between metarepresentations and other cases of interpretive use seems to evaporate. In some languages, such as Sissala, we will not be able to draw Recanati's contrast in such a sharp way. Of course, it is still true that in English there is no interpretive use marker comparable to the Sissala sentence-final particle rɛ̃. What speakers of Sissala can achieve by (partly) grammatical means speakers of English must achieve by (purely) pragmatic means.

4. Non-singular uses of that-clauses

This section is simply to fulfill a promissory note made above. It can be skipped by those who are eager to get to the next section, which attempts to squarely face Recanati's objection that an account like the one offered above violates semantic innocence.

Earlier I noted that any singular term can potentially be used both referentially and attributively. If that-clauses are treated as singular terms, which refer to a proposition which resembles the proposition expressed by the embedded content sentence, it may be that there are occasions on which a that-clause is used attributively, not to pick out a particular proposition, but rather some general feature of a proposition, or some propositional type.

I do indeed think that this is the case. The following example is meant to illustrate such an attributive use of the standard that-clause form. It is also intended to illustrate the sort of pragmatic processing involved in such a case. Suppose that, unbeknownst to Smith's murderer, a blind tramp was hiding in the warehouse where the murder took place. The tramp has now come forward to the police, claiming that he thinks he can identify the murderer, if he has an opportunity to hear his voice and smell him again. Poirot's investigation has turned up various leads, and Big Felix (a.k.a. the mayor) is one of the prime suspects. Poirot arranges for a special police line-up. Big Felix, as well as others whom the police have chosen because they have similar sounding voices, are asked to shower and then put on identical, specially laundered trousers and shirts. Each in turn is asked to stand in front of a screen and say a series of scripted lines. The tramp is to signal to Poirot if he thinks any of these men is the man he smelled and heard on the night of the murder. The tramp picks out Big Felix from the line-up. Afterwards, one of the detectives points to Big Felix and says to another detective:

(24) The tramp thinks that he is the man from the warehouse.

The detectives of course can see Big Felix, and they also know him under various other guises – e.g., as the man they brought in for questioning, as the mayor of the city and so on. None of these guises, let us suppose, is one under which the tramp knows Big Felix. He knows him only under some sort of olfactory/auditory guise. This is mutually manifest to the two detectives, who know the tramp is blind, as they have been involved in setting up the elaborate police line-up that their boss, Poirot, had ordered.

The detectives will not suppose that the tramp's conception of Big Felix resembles their own visual or mayoral conceptions of Big Felix. The detectives, like the tramp, also have some sort of olfactory/auditory mode of presentation of Big Felix, but their modes of presentation are not fine-grained enough to help them tell Big Felix apart from the other men in the line-up. They are in fact pretty astounded at the tramp's ability to distinguish people by these means, and they have no idea what it would be like to have such an ability. The tramp's conception of Big Felix resembles their own merely in that it shares the property of being olfactory/auditory in nature, but they cannot characterize it in any more specific way than this.

So, when the hearer processes the speaker's attitude report, the interpretive resemblance constraint will force the hearer to focus simply on this general property of the tramp's conception, and the hearer will therefore understand the speaker to have said that the tramp believes that Big Felix, under some olfactory/auditory guise or other, is the man from the warehouse.

Here is a second example in which the that-clause must be interpreted as referring to a propositional type, rather than to a specific proposition. This example is loosely based on an example used for another purpose by Sperber and Wilson (1995). Suppose George and Gracie have just entered their hotel room at the seaside village where they'll be spending their vacation. The room is stuffy, so George goes over to open the doors leading onto the balcony. He steps out onto the balcony. Then turning towards Gracie he breathes in deeply, sighs contentedly, and makes a sweeping gesture, taking in the panoramic view from their balcony. What is he thinking?

Sperber and Wilson are of course interested in a slightly different question, namely what is he trying to communicate to Gracie? With regard to their very similar example, they conclude that the gesture *weakly* communicates a *range* of propositions. In the current example we might say that George is attempting to make mutually manifest such things as the tangy smell of the air, the raucous cries of the gulls wheeling in the air, the dazzling sunshine reflecting off the ocean, the sound of the waves pounding on the rocks at the bottom of the cliff on which the hotel is perched, and so on. So, to return to my question: what is George thinking? He is thinking about all these things and many more, in some implicit way.

Now, suppose Gracie sits down to write a letter to a friend back home. The friend was the one who suggested this village and this hotel, and George was at first reluctant to come on this vacation, not trusting Gracie's friend to be able to pick a good vacation spot. Gracie wants to let her friend know that George has come around. She writes the following sentence:

(25) George thinks that our view is wonderful.

The friend has stayed in this hotel before, and so she has a conception of what the view is like from various locations in the hotel, but she does not know exactly which room Gracie and George are staying in, and so she cannot know precisely what the view from their room is like. Is it the view over the ocean, or do they perhaps have a room overlooking the hotel gardens and the village? This is mutually manifest to Gracie and her friend. The friend will therefore assume that George's conception resembles her own merely in being some sort of sensory gestalt. So, when the friend processes Gracie's attitude report, the interpretive resemblance constraint will lead her to understand Gracie to have said that George believes that the view from their room, presented by means of some sort of sensory gestalt, is wonderful.

5. Semantic innocence and metarepresentations

In this section, I examine a critique of the assumption that that-clauses are referring expressions raised by Recanati (1997, 1998). Recanati argues that any such account violates semantic innocence, and he argues that only an account which respects a principle he calls the Principle of Iconicity can be semantically innocent. He argues that his treatment of 'believes that' as a sentential operator is one such account. However, I will argue that it is unclear whether Recanati's account has advantages over the view defended in this paper, especially if one pays attention to the *context-sensitivity* of belief reports.

In Section 1 above, a long passage from Recanati was quoted, expressing the heart of his objection to any view which treats that-clauses as referring terms. His claim is that on any such view the embedded content sentence disappears from the logical scene, playing at most a pre-semantic role, akin to the demonstration accompanying a demonstrative. Its role is simply to express a proposition for the that-clause to refer to.[17] The overall logical form of an attitude report will be

[17] Of course on my interpretive resemblance view, the that-clause does not refer to a proposition *identical* to the one expressed by the content sentence, but to a proposition which *resembles* it in contextually appropriate ways.

'*aRb*'. But, says Recanati, "If a sentence *S* expresses a certain proposition *P*, then, within a truly innocent framework, *that proposition must be semantically a part of the proposition expressed by the complex sentence in which S occurs* (unless *S* occurs within quotation marks)." (Recanati, 1997, p. 7. His emphases.) He goes on to say that this means that, if we want a truly innocent account, we must respect the *Principle of Iconicity*:

> (PI) Attitude reports and other metarepresentations contain the object-representation not only syntactically (in the sense that dS contains S), but also semantically: the proposition Q expressed by dS 'contains' as a part the proposition P expressed by S – and that is why one cannot entertain Q without entertaining P. (Ibid., p. 9.)

First we need to be clear about the way in which my view, which treats that-clauses as referring terms, violates (PI). One might think that it is possible to respect (PI) while maintaining that that-clauses refer to propositions. The claim would be that this is possible if one treats that-clauses as directly referring terms. Since the content of a directly referring expression is its referent, it looks as though one can hold that the proposition expressed by the content sentence will be a part of the proposition expressed by the attitude report. What the that-clause contributes to the content of the attitude report is simply the proposition it refers to, namely the proposition expressed by the content sentence.

Recanati argues that this strategy will not work, as it requires us to hold that the content of a term (the that-clause) is the same as the content of a sentence (the embedded content sentence), despite the fact that they have different referents (the proposition expressed by the content sentence and a truth-value respectively), and despite the fact that these expressions belong to very different semantic categories (term and sentence respectively). See Recanati (1997), pp. 18–20. But it is not important to me whether one accepts Recanati's critique of the direct reference approach, for the approach is not one that I would want to adopt in the first place. My (anti direct-reference) view commits me to saying that it is not the proposition expressed by the content sentence itself that is a part of the proposition expressed by the attitude report, but merely a *mode of presentation* of the expressed proposition. So my account certainly violates (PI).

Recanati thinks that to satisfy (PI) we must therefore say that a belief report is simply a display of the reported content. We report the content of an attitude by displaying/expressing that very content, and so what is expressed by the report contains the displayed content as a constituent. This is why we can't entertain the report without entertaining the displayed content. He argues that the only sort of semantic account compatible with this view is one which treats 'believes that' as an operator that takes a term and a sentence to form another sentence. His argument depends on stressing the analogy between modal operators and the 'believes that' and 'according to' constructions. The proposition expressed by the sentence *p* is a part of the proposition expressed by the sentence formed by attaching a necessity or possibility operator in front of the sentence p. Similarly, argues Recanati, the proposition expressed by the sentence p is a part of the proposition expressed by the sentence formed by attaching 'believes that' or 'according to' to a term-sentence pair thus: BelievesThat$\langle S, p \rangle$.

However, even though Recanati's account may seem to respect (PI), and even though we may accept (PI) as a requirement that any satisfactory *semantic* analysis of attitude reports must satisfy, it is not clear that Recanati's account can deal with the sort of *pragmatic* features of attitude reports which have been the focus of this paper.

In order to explain what is involved in entertaining (and presumably also in understanding) a metarepresentation, Recanati develops an account which appeals to the idea of mentally simulating the world as it is from the perspective of the subject of the attitude. A metarepresentation however is not merely a mental simulation of the subject's belief world. It results from *reflection on* this simulation. When one simulatively takes up an imaginary perspective, one merely makes pretend assertions; i.e. assertions within the scope of a pretense. A metarepresentation on the other hand is an act of simulation within the scope of a serious assertion. A metarepresentation of the form 'S believes that p' seriously asserts that it is a fact {in the real world} that in S's belief-world it is a fact that p.

So metarepresentations are reflections on simulations. To understand what this means, we need to understand two notions that Recanati introduces, namely *reflection* and *projection*. As he understands these, they are both *cognitive processes*.

About reflection he says: "If the subject comes to *reflect on* the situation which the representation concerns and makes it explicit, the representation, hence the fact which it expresses or articulates, becomes more complex." (Recanati, 1997, p. 48. His emphases.) What Recanati calls a fact is a structured entity, essentially what was earlier called a Russellian proposition. But he also introduces the notion of a *global* or *Austinian proposition* (Ibid., p. 47). Utterances state or are *about* facts, but they also *concern* situations. The global proposition represents both the fact and the situation. For example, suppose Recanati utters 'It is raining' in Paris at some time t, intending to communicate that it is raining {in Paris} at that time. The fact this states (that it is raining at t) and the situation it concerns (Paris) can be represented by the global proposition:

(26) $\{\text{Paris}\} \models \langle\langle \text{Rain}(t) \rangle\rangle$

Now if Recanati were to reflect on his situation and make it explicit, he might utter the sentence 'It is raining in Paris'. He is now stating a fact which concerns a wider situation, in the sense that implicitly he is contrasting what is happening in Paris with what is happening elsewhere, say in Europe. This new fact and its different, wider situation might be represented by the following global proposition:

(27) $\{\text{Europe}\} \models \langle\langle \text{Paris} \models \text{Rain}(t) \rangle\rangle$

The cognitive movement from (26) to (27) is what Recanati calls *reflection*. See Recanati (1997, pp. 47–49). Projection on the other hand is a process operating in the opposite direction. It is involved in cases where a situation is first mentioned, and then the speaker projects herself into the situation, and states something with respect to that situation. An example would be:

(28) Berkeley is a nice place. There are bookstores and coffee shops everywhere.

This might be represented by the following pair of global propositions:

(29) {USA} $\models$ ⟨⟨Berkeley is a nice place⟩⟩

(30) {Berkeley} $\models$ ⟨⟨There are bookstores and coffee shops everywhere⟩⟩

The cognitive movement from (29) to (30) is an instance of *projection*. The way in which this distinction between reflection and projection applies to attitude reports can be illustrated by two earlier examples, repeated here for convenience:

(20) John is totally paranoid. Everybody spies on him or wants to kill him, including his own mother.

(21) John believes that he is being persecuted.

As noted in Section 3, Recanati thinks that (20) and (21) are essentially different, and that only (21) is a metarepresentation. (20) is an instance of what he calls free indirect speech. It is now possible to say more specifically wherein lies the difference that Recanati sees. (20) he would say involves the cognitive process of *projection*, whereas (21) is a case of *reflection*. We could represent (20) by the following pair of global propositions:

(31) {Real world} $\models$ ⟨⟨John is paranoid⟩⟩

(32) {John's paranoid world} $\models$ ⟨⟨Everybody spies on John etc. ⟩⟩

On the other hand, (21) could be represented by the following global proposition:

(33) {Real world} $\models$ ⟨⟨John's paranoid world $\models$ John is being persecuted⟩⟩

The idea presumably is that the movement from (31) to (32) involves the cognitive process of projection, whereas (33) is a case of reflection. However, there are a number of problems with these claims.

Firstly, Recanati's claim about reflection seemed to be that it involves a cognitive movement in which one reflects on a situation and makes it explicit, thereby articulating a more complex fact. This was illustrated by the movement from (26) to (27). But then (33) cannot by itself be a case of the cognitive *process* of reflection. Rather, it would have to be the *end result* of reflection. For there to be a process here, one must first entertain a representation, which is then reflected on. The beginning point for the process of reflection which ends in (33) could be represented by the global proposition below. The process of reflection would then be the movement from (34) to (33):

(34) {John's paranoid world} $\models$ ⟨⟨John is being persecuted⟩⟩

Perhaps Recanati would say that because (34) is contained in (33) as a proper part, (34) does not need to be entertained separately. But then he should likewise have to say that in entertaining (27) one is engaging in a process of reflection, even if one never separately entertains the proposition (26). The trouble with this is that it is hard then to see why one would think that the fact one is stating in uttering 'It is raining in Paris' has the sort of articulation (27) represents it as having. Why should one see this fact as articulated into a simpler fact and a situation? One reason might be that one at first entertains a thought about this simpler fact, but on reflection sees that it implicitly concerns a particular situation, which one now is able to make explicit. In other words, it seems that there must be a movement from (26) to (27) for the articulation in (27) to make sense. Otherwise, one might just as well have conceived of ⟨⟨ Rain-in-Paris (t)⟩⟩ as the simple fact one it stating in uttering 'It is raining in Paris'. Then the global proposition representing this fact and the situation it concerns would be:

(35) {Europe} $\models$ ⟨⟨Rain-in-Paris (t)⟩⟩

Analogous reasoning would suggest that the articulation in (33) makes sense only if one first articulates a simpler fact that reflection shows implicitly concerns a particular situation, which one is then able to make explicit. Otherwise, one might very well think of the fact expressed by an utterance of 'John believes that he is being persecuted' as the fact ⟨⟨ John is being persecuted-in-his-world ⟩⟩, and the global proposition representing this and its implicit situation would be:

(36) {Real world} $\models$ ⟨⟨John is being persecuted-in-his-world⟩⟩

There is even some justification for this way of representing things, as we could have reported John's belief that he is being persecuted by uttering the following sentence:

(37) John is being "persecuted".[18]

[18] Of course, the way in which the pragmatic view defended in Sections 2 to 4 would deal with (37) is to see it as involving an *interpretive use*. The hearer will take the speaker to be echoing John's own opinion that he is being persecuted, while simultaneously communicating the speaker's belief that John is crazy, and that John is not really being persecuted. The interpretive resemblance constraint would not require that John have actually used the words 'I am being persecuted' to describe his situation. Perhaps John expressed his belief by uttering the sentence 'Everybody is spying on me and wants to kill me, including my own mother'. Nevertheless, what the speaker expresses interpretively resembles the content of John's belief, in virtue of sharing some of its logical and contextual implications.

The main conclusion to be drawn from these considerations is that for the articulation in (33) to make sense, there must be a process which begins with the entertaining of the fact that John is being persecuted, which is represented in (34). A process of reflection then makes explicit that this fact is relative to or concerns John's paranoid world, a fact which is made explicit in (33). Although Recanati talks in terms of facts, situations and global propositions, and in terms of a process of reflection, the picture that emerges of the processing involved in entertaining (or, I am assuming, in understanding) attitude reports is very similar to the sorts of pragmatic processes described in the earlier sections of this paper.

Suppose a speaker utters '*S* believes that *p*'. For the hearer to understand the speaker's utterance, there must be what can be thought of as a two-step process which begins with entertaining the proposition expressed by the content sentence of the attitude report. A process of reflection then makes the situation against which this proposition is entertained explicit, and thus results the understanding that can be represented by a global proposition of the form:

(38) $\{\text{Real world}\} \models \langle\langle S\text{'s belief world} \models p\rangle\rangle$

Recanati talks of the process of reflection being one which makes a situation explicit or which articulates a fact. This could be construed as very similar to the sorts of pragmatic processes (such as enrichment and loosening) that relevance theorists argue are involved in the recovery of the *explicature* of a speaker's utterance. In relevance theory terms, the explicature is the proposition expressed by an utterance, and it must be recovered via an inferential process that uses both encoded semantic information and contextually available *non*-linguistic information. Critics of RT, such as (Bach, 1994), have argued that relevance theorists are committed to saying that what belongs to an utterance's explicature is explicit in the utterance, and that this is problematic because much of the content relevance theorists have argued belongs to the utterance's explicature goes beyond anything that is explicitly encoded in the utterance. However, rather than think of the explicature as what is explicit, one should think of the explicature as *what is arrived at by explicating* (i.e. what is arrived at by drawing out or articulating, in Recanati's sense of making more complex) the encoded meaning against a background of currently accessible contextual information.

Take the earlier example in which Recanati utters 'It's raining' at time *t*, intending to communicate that it is raining in Paris at *t*. Relevance theorists would say that mutually manifest information available in the context enables the hearer to enrich the semantically encoded information 'Rain at *t*' to arrive at the explicature that it is raining in Paris at *t*. Had the context been different, Recanati's utterance might have expressed a different proposition. For example, suppose that Recanati is talking to a friend, and mentions that he has just minutes ago spoken on the phone to his wife, who has taken their children to the seaside for the day. The friend asks whether they have good weather at the seaside, and Recanati replies 'It is raining'. Although Recanati utters this in Paris at *t*, the friend will understand

Recanati to have expressed the proposition that it is raining at the seaside at t, not that it is raining in Paris at t.

Recanati's cognitive process of reflection, which takes one from (26) to (27),

(26) $\{\text{Paris}\} \models \langle\langle \text{Rain } (t) \rangle\rangle$

(27) $\{\text{Europe}\} \models \langle\langle \text{Paris} \models \text{Rain } (t) \rangle\rangle$

seems very similar to the RT process of enrichment, which takes one from the encoded semantic information, together with contextually available non-linguistic information, to the explicature. However, although there are clearly parallels between Recanati's views and those defended in the earlier sections of this paper, there are also ways in which Recanati's views are less developed. For instance, Recanati says nothing about what might trigger the cognitive process of reflection or the opposite process of projection. How in the course of interpreting a speaker's utterances, and especially his or her attitude reports, does the hearer know to engage in projection or reflection?

Another reason that Recanati's view is undeveloped is that it says nothing about how a hearer understands what proposition is expressed by the content sentence in an attitude report. In earlier work, Recanati has shown how context-dependent utterance interpretation is. See Recanati (1991, 1993). The same sentence uttered in different contexts can express very different propositions. Thus the context can potentially make a difference to what proposition is expressed by the content sentence of an attitude report. In (Recanati, 1997) this layer of complexity is left out, and there is the suggestion that the constituents of the proposition expressed by the content sentence correspond one-to-one to the terms in the sentence. Thus no accommodation is made for phenomena, such as semantic underdetermination, that Recanati himself has drawn our attention to in earlier work of his.

Another issue that is not explicitly addressed by Recanati concerns the relationship between the proposition expressed by the content sentence of an attitude report and the content of the ascribed attitude. Are they identical, or do they merely resemble one another? One can infer from Recanati's claim that an attitude report *displays* the content of the attitude it reports, and from his commitment to the Principle of Iconicity, that he is committed to *identifying* the content of the attitude report with the proposition expressed by the content sentence. This is problematic, as it has the consequence that many attitude reports are false. Suppose for instance that John is disposed to expresses his paranoia by uttering sentences such as 'Everybody is spying on me and wants to kill me, including my own mother', but not the sentence 'I am being persecuted'. According to the view defended in earlier sections, we can still truly report John's belief by uttering:

(21) John believes that he is being persecuted.

This is because the proposition expressed by the content sentence need only interpretively resemble the content of John's belief. But unless the property of being persecuted is a constituent of John's paranoid world, Recanati's view commits him to saying that the report in (21) is false. From a pragmatic point of view this is simply too strict, as it is clear that we are often satisfied with less than strict identity of content. Moreover, there are going to be cases where strict identity is not possible, namely in those situations in which we cannot literally adopt the perspective of another, although we can adopt a perspective that resembles it is appropriate ways.

A final worry that I want to raise about Recanati's view concerns his sharp distinction between attitude reports (and metarepresentations in general) and what he calls cases of free indirect speech. As mentioned in Section 3 above, there are pragmatic reasons for seeing these cases as on a par. If I am right, they both involve the notion of interpretive resemblance. The mere fact that in one case the interpretive use is signaled grammatically and in the other it must be contextually indicated is not a sufficient reason for distinguishing these cases. We also saw that there are some languages, such as Sissala, in which both sorts of cases are grammatically marked with the same marker. In Sissala the marker is rɛ́ (and its variants). This suggests that, cognitively speaking, interpreting attitude reports is similar to interpreting free indirect speech, and the pragmatic account developed in Section 3 has the virtue of seeing the same sorts of processes in operation in both cases.

The worries raised in this section are meant to show that even if we concede to Recanati that the Principle of Iconicity is a constraint that any semantically innocent account must satisfy, and that therefore the *semantic* view outlined in Section 1 must be rejected, it is by no means clear that Recanati's account of the processes of reflection and projection involved in entertaining attitude reports is to be preferred to the *pragmatic* account of attitude reports defended in Sections 2 to 4. In fact, I have given reasons for thinking that although there are ways in which Recanati's account of the cognitive processes involved in entertaining attitude reports has suggestive parallels to the pragmatic processes described in earlier sections, Recanati's account is also less developed, and less able to deal with the pragmatic factors influencing the understanding of attitude reports. Thus one could say that the ultimate conclusion of this paper is that any satisfactory account of attitude reports is going to have to combine Recanati's semantic insights with the pragmatic insights of Relevance Theory.

References

Bach, K. (1994), *Conversational implicitures*, Mind and Language **9**, 124–162.

Bezuidenhout, A. (1996), *Pragmatics and singular reference*, Mind and Language **11** (2), 133–159.

Bezuidenhout, A. (1997a), *The communication of de re thoughts*, Nous **31** (2), 197–225.

Bezuidenhout, A. (1997b), *Pragmatics, semantic underdetermination and the referential/attributive distinction*, Mind **106** (423), 375–409.

Blakemore, D. (1987), *Semantic Constraints on Relevance*, Blackwell, Oxford.

Blakemore, D. (1988), *"So" as a constraint on relevance*, Mental Representations: The Interface Between Language and Reality, R.M. Kempson, ed., Cambridge University Press, Cambridge, 183–195.

Blass, R. (1990), *Relevance Relations in Discourse: A Study with Special Reference to Sissala*, Cambridge University Press, Cambridge.
Carston, R. (1997), *Enrichment and loosening: Complementary processes in deriving the proposition expressed?*, Linguistische Berichte, 103–127.
Chomsky, N. (1995), *Language and nature*, Mind **104**, 1–61.
Crimmins, M. (1992), *Talk About Beliefs*, MIT Press, Cambridge, MA.
Crimmins, M. (1995), *Notional specificity*, Mind & Language **10** (4), 464–477.
Crimmins, M. and Perry, J. (1989), *The prince and the phone booth*, Journal of Philosophy **86**, 685–711.
Davidson, D. (1984), *On saying that*, Inquiries into Truth and Interpretation, Clarendon Press, Oxford, 93–108.
Devitt, M. (1996), *Coming to Our Senses: A Naturalistic Program for Semantic Localism*, Cambridge University Press, Cambridge.
Goble, L. (1997), *Translucent beliefs*, The Maribor Papers in Naturalized Semantics, D. Jutronic, ed., University of Maribor, Maribor, 285–296.
Kaplan, D. (1989), *Demonstratives: An essay on the semantics, logic, metaphysics, and epistemology of demonstratives and other indexicals*, Themes from Kaplan. J. Almog, J. Perry and H. Wettstein, eds, Oxford University Press, New York, 481–563.
Larson, R.K. and Ludlow, P. (1993), *Interpreted logical forms*, Synthese **95**, 305–355.
Nicolle, S. (1995), *Conceptual and procedural encoding: Criteria for the identification of linguistically encoded procedural information*, University of Hertfordshire Relevance Theory Workshop, Peter Thomas and Associates, Hatfield Peverel, UK.
Nicolle, S. (1998), *A relevance theory perspective on grammaticalization*, Cognitive Linguistics **9** (1), 1–35.
Nunberg, G. (1993), *Indexicality and deixis*, Linguistics and Philosophy **16**, 1–43.
Pietroski, P.M. (1996), *Fregean innocence*, Mind & Language **11** (4), 338–370.
Recanati, F. (1991), *The pragmatics of what is said*, Pragmatics: A Reader, S. Davis, ed., Oxford University Press, New York, 97–120.
Recanati, F. (1993), *Direct Reference: From Language to Thought*, Blackwell, Oxford.
Recanati, F. (1997), *The Iconicity of Metarepresentations*, Centre de Recherche en Epistemologie Appliquee, Paris.
Recanati, F. (1998), *Opacity and the attitudes*, Knowledge, Language, and Logic: Questions for Quine, A. Orenstein and P. Kotatko, eds, Kluwer, Dordrecht.
Reimer, M. (1995), *A defense of* de re *belief reports*, Mind & Language **10** (4), 446–463.
Richard, M. (1990), *Propositional Attitudes: An Essay on Thoughts and How We Ascribe Them*, Cambridge University Press, Cambridge.
Salmon, N. (1989), *Illogical belief*, Philosophical Perspectives: Philosophy of Mind and Action Theory, Vol. 3, J. Tomberlin, ed., Atascadero, Ridgeview, 243–285.
Segal, G. (1989), *A preference for sense and reference*, Journal of Philosophy **86**, 73–89.
Sperber, D. and Wilson, D. (1991), *Irony and the use-mention distinction*, Pragmatics: A Reader, S. Davis, ed., Oxford University Press, New York, 550–563.
Sperber, D. and Wilson, D. (1995), *Relevance: Communication and Cognition*, Blackwell, Oxford.
Vicente Cruz, B. (1998), *Against blurring the explicit/implicit distinction*, Revista Alicantina de Esudios Ingleses **11**, 241–258.
Wilson, D. and Sperber, D. (1993), *Linguistic form and relevance*, Lingua **90**, 1–25.

CHAPTER 9

The Default-Based Context-Dependence of Belief Reports

K.M. Jaszczolt

Contents

PRAGMATICS OF PROPOSITIONAL ATTITUDE REPORTS
Current Research in the Semantics/Pragmatics Interface, Vol. 4
Edited by K.M. Jaszczolt

0. Introduction

In this paper I put together three ideas that I introduced in my earlier publications on the subject of propositional attitudes (e.g., Jaszczolt, 1997, 1998a, 1998b, 1998c, forthcoming), namely that

(1) belief reports allow for three different readings which I call *de re*, *de dicto*$_1$ and *de dicto proper*;

(2) the *de re* reading is the default one, guaranteed by the Default Semantics based on the default referential intention and subsequently on the intentionality of mental states; and

(3) the departures from the default are guided by the context and in particular by the degree of the referential intention present.[1]

Hence, all the three readings can be placed on a scale of 'degrees of intentionality', translatable into degrees of fineness of grain of the mode of presentation of the referent.

This proposal amounts to a mild version of context-dependence of attitude ascriptions. The default reading does not rely on the intrusion of contextual information to the propositional representation as far as the identity of the referent is concerned. Naturally, it may rely on pragmatic processes in some other respects if the enrichment of the logical form is required before the truth-conditional representation of what is said can be reached.[2] The departures from the default, i.e. the readings *de dicto*$_1$ and *de dicto proper*, corresponding respectively to the belief *de re* about someone else (i.e. a referential mistake) and a belief *de dicto*, to be introduced in detail in the following section, rely on the intrusion of the identifying information about the referent to the propositional representation.

I suggest that context-dependence works best when paired with semantic defaults. Otherwise, in its heavy version, it becomes a wastebasket for various kinds of embellishments to the logical form and loses its appeal through losing its explanatory power concerning the effort the hearer exerts in processing a belief report.

1. *De re, de dicto*$_1$, and *de dicto proper*

There are many interrelated problems with belief reports, both theoretical and practical. Among the latter there is the circumstance that the reporter may not have adequate evidence for belief attribution, or, taken from the recipient's perspective, the hearer of the report may be in possession of some evidence that such a lack of evidence took place on the part of the reporter. The reporter can be referentially

[1] I consider intentions to be constitutive parts of context.

[2] See Bach (1994) on the expansion of a minimal proposition and the completion of a propositional radical.

mistaken or have no sufficient knowledge to individuate the referent of his or her own report. Similar problems may affect the holder of the belief or the hearer of the report. Let us, for now, confine the discussion to the believer's set of beliefs, or the believer's 'belief box'. Theoretical problems that pertain in one way or another to the issue of the compositionality of belief sentences (see, e.g., Schiffer, 1992, 1993, 1994, 1995, 1996, and this volume) are best seen as stemming out of the practical difficulty with reporting on beliefs and interpreting such reports. Unfortunately, the theoretical and the practical have been regarded as disjoint at least since Quine's quantifying in (1956), which made propositional attitudes fall victim to frequently vacuous theoretical debates. The revival of the interest in the pragmatic contribution to the semantic representation of a sentence brought with it an interest in the mode of presentation that in some way or other contributes to the proposition, though not necessarily to its content (for its various statuses and guises see, e.g., Schiffer, (1977, 1992, 1995, 1996), Crimmins and Perry (1989), Crimmins (1992), Kaplan (1989), Richard (1990, 1995), Forbes (1990, 1997), Recanati (1993), Salmon (1986)[3]). The mode of presentation, especially when seen as the believer-dependent (and hence non-Fregean, *pace* Forbes's *logophor*[4]) way of thinking about the referent, constitutes a bridge between the theory and practice of belief ascription and I shall use it in my classification of the readings that a belief report can assume.

Let us for this purpose use Quine's famous character Bernard J. Ortcutt, extrapolating from the rest of his scenario. A speaker, John, utters (1) about his colleague Ralph.

(1) Ralph believes that Ortcutt is a spy.

The circumstances leading to this report may be thought up endlessly. Let us look at three possibilities.

Situation A: Ralph walks along the beach with John, spots a man wearing a brown hat and utters (2) to John.

(2) The man in the brown hat is a spy.

Let us assume that the man in the brown hat is called Bernard J. Ortcutt and John thinks (or assumes) that Ralph knows it. Here the report in (1) is *de re* and corresponds to a *de re* thought on the part of the holder of the belief.

Situation B: As in A, except that Ralph thinks, unbeknownst to John, that the man in the brown hat is Mr Smith. Here the report in (1) corresponds to a belief *de re about someone else*, i.e. a referential mistake, and can be called *de dicto*$_1$ due to its opacity.

[3] For a discussion see, e.g., Donnellan (1990), Clapp (1995), Soames (1987, 1995), Ludlow (1995, 1996).

[4] See footnote 14.

Situation C: As in A, except that Ralph does not know who the man wearing a brown hat is, unbeknownst to John. Here the report in (1) is *de dicto proper*: it corresponds to a *de dicto* belief.

In this way we obtain a tri-partite distinction on the level of belief reports: *de re*, *de dicto*$_1$, and *de dicto proper*. This distinction corresponds to the two-way distinction on the level of beliefs, viz. *de re/de dicto*, albeit with a sub-case of *de re about someone else* (see Jaszczolt (1997, p. 320) for a tabular presentation). The novelty of this categorization lies in the hybrid *de dicto*$_1$ that pertains to a *de re* belief but is nevertheless classified as *de dicto* as it involves a referential mistake.[5]

The situations A to C can be even more plausibly distinguished with reference to the reporter's set of beliefs. If we imagine that the man in the brown hat is Mr Smith and John takes him to be Ortcutt, we obtain *de dicto*$_1$. If we imagine that Ralph utters (3) and John, ignorant about the identity of the named individual, reports on it using (1), we obtain *de dicto proper*.

(3) Bernard J. Ortcutt is a spy,

perhaps the latter with some sacrifice of the Gricean or neo-Gricean conversational heuristics according to which it is rational to say as much as necessary (see, e.g., Levinson, 1987, 1995). In fact, when John realizes his inadequate referential information, he is more likely to utter (1a) or one of its variants.

(1a) Ralph believes that somebody whom he calls Ortcutt is a spy.

Similarly, in Situations B and C, if we took away the qualification 'unbeknownst to John', we would be most likely to obtain different reports, to the effect as in (1b) and (1c) respectively.

(1b) Ralph believes that Smith is a spy, although he mistakenly calls him Ortcutt.

---

5 On the level of beliefs, a relevant distinction has been drawn in anthropological research. Dan Sperber distinguishes a type of belief that is held without having a full understanding of its content. He calls it a representational belief with semi-propositional content (Sperber 1985, pp. 56–60) or, in another categorization, it is classified under the so-called 'reflective beliefs', opposed to intuitively grasped beliefs (Sperber, 1996, p. 89, 1997). These beliefs, ill-understood by their holders, are called by Recanati (1997, p. 84) 'quasi-beliefs'. The idea is that sometimes a representation contains some uninterpreted symbol and is, so to speak, 'semi-propositional', some of its material is 'put in quotes', stored for future understanding.

It is easy to extend this underdetermination to referential underdetermination of the *de dicto* beliefs. Following Recanati, however, this underdetermination of the propositional content will be regarded as epistemic rather than semantic, in agreement with my claim discussed later on in this paper that there is no separate level of underdetermined semantic representation but instead intentions intrude into the semantic form to produce the correct interpretation. Cf.:

> "Sperber's claim concerning semi-propositionality can (...) be construed as a claim concerning the epistemical state of the user, rather than a claim about semantic content." Recanati (1997, p. 93).

(1c) Ralph believes that somebody called Ortcutt is a spy but he does not know who he is.

Other scenarios, such as saying 'Ortcutt' while pointing at Smith due to poor eyesight rather than a lasting confusion, fall easily under the same pattern.

All in all, whatever the situations leading to *de re*, de *dicto*$_1$ and *de dicto proper* may be, the fact is that three such interpretations of a belief report are possible and it would be short-sighted to subsume them under a binary distinction *de re /de dicto* which is more suitable for beliefs (although even there it appears to be contentious) than for sentences ascribing them. If we wish the theory to proceed alongside the practical problems with reporting on beliefs, we have to represent these three readings in our semantics. In Discourse Representation Theory (Kamp and Reyle, 1993), these options of interpretation of (1) can be summarized as in Figure 1.

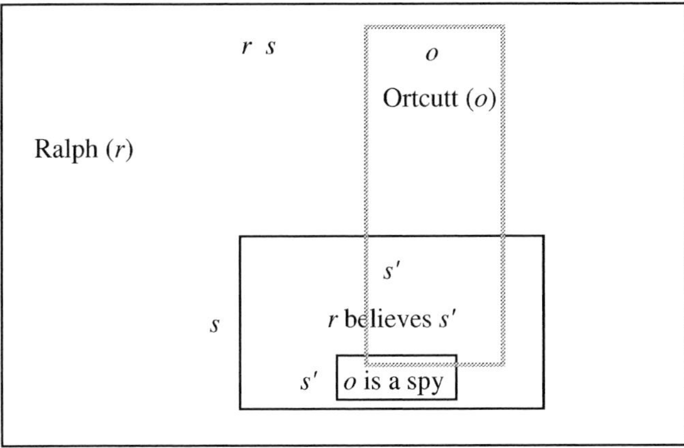

Fig. 1. (Adapted from Jaszczolt (1998c, p. 16).)

The broken line marks the possibilities of placement of the discourse referent '*o*' standing for the individual called Ortcutt. I have translated here the three readings of a belief report into three levels of embedding of the discourse referent. These degrees of depth of embedding signal that there is some gradation or scale involved. This scale is what I turn to next.

2. Referential intention

Utterances come with various types of intentions. In the case of sentences involving expressions used to refer[6] such as proper names, definite descriptions and pro-

[6] The term 'referring expression' is deliberately avoided here as it is usually used more restrictively (but see Bach (1987b, pp. 55–56) and footnote 13 below).

nouns (after reference resolution), the differences of interpretation correspond to the differences in the referential intention. The term 'referential intention' was proposed by Bach (e.g., 1987a, pp. 51–52) but was not developed further.[7] The presence or absence, and even the *degree* of the referential intention indicate the degree of referentiality with which the whole utterance has to be interpreted. For example, instead of the celebrated referential-attributive distinction (Donnellan, 1966), we obtain degrees of referring properties. By simple inheritance, these degrees apply to belief reports. Instead of *de re* and *de dicto*, we have, so to speak, 'degrees of being *de re*'. Now, the most over-arching of intentions is the communicative intention. This intention has to be recognized by the hearer in order to be fulfilled (cf. Bach and Harnish, 1979, p. 15; Bach, 1987a, p. 142). Referring is a component of the communicative intention, or, in other words, the referential intention is embedded in the communicative one. Arguments for finer-grained distinctions, such as that into the communicative and informative intention (of Sperber and Wilson, 1986) will not be attended to as they are tangential to the present discussion.[8]

On some occasions, speakers do not refer to any particular individual but instead talk about an event or a state as a whole. Referential intention will then be weaker than in the case of referring to parts of such a state or event (cf. Jaszczolt, 1998b, p. 102). Since referring to states and events is always present, even when the speaker refers specifically to their parts, we can say that in the case of referring only to an eventuality (state or event[9]), the referential intention is absent. Now, the case of a referential mistake is the 'middle' case. The referential intention is weakened through targeting a 'wrong' individual. This can be measured through the contribution this intention makes to the overall communicative intention. A misfired referential intention does not make the communicative intention 'stronger': it does not add to the strength of intending to communicate, neither does it help the recognition of this intention or the informativeness of the message.

The strengths of referential and communicative intentions are not an unsupported postulate. They are a result of the intentionality of mental states. According to the respectable phenomenological tradition, acts of consciousness are directed toward objects. Intentionality amounts to 'aboutness', 'direction' or 'orientation' to objects (cf. Brentano, 1874; Husserl, 1900-01; Jaszczolt, 1996). So, intentionality and referential intention are joined by their common orientation to objects. This *intending an object* can be externalized in language in the form of conveying a referential intention. It is important to realize that it is so because language is one of the vehicles of thought (cf. Dummett, 1991, pp. 322–323; Jaszczolt, 1996), *not*

[7] Cf. also: "... what is said, to the extent that it is not fixed by linguistic meaning, is determined by speaker intention, which itself can include the intention to refer to what one is demonstrating." Bach (1992, p. 140).

[8] See Jaszczolt (1998a) for a more detailed analysis.

[9] The term 'eventuality' is due to Emmon Bach (see Bach (1981, p. 69) and Kamp and Reyle (1993, p. 509)).

because, for example, of some enigmatic inheritance of conditions of satisfaction of speech acts from mental states as Searle (1983) has it.

Now, by analogy, intentionality would also have to allow for degrees. And, indeed, it does. Although a belief is always intentional at the 'intending' or 'directing', 'firing' level, in practice this intentionality may become dispersed when the object of the belief does not correspond to the socially recognized object named by the referring term which the linguistic vehicle uses for this 'firing' at an object.[10] If John *intends* Smith in using the term 'Ortcutt', then the intentionality is weaker. In a corresponding utterance, the referential intention is weakened due to the referential mistake. If John does not mean anyone in particular in his utterance, i.e. his mental file labelled 'Ortcutt' is empty, then intentionality sets off as normal but does not reach anyone. As a result, there is no referential intention accompanying his utterance.

The question remains, if we uphold these interpretive options, do we have to subscribe either to semantic ambiguity or to semantic underdetermination (see, e.g., van Deemter and Peters, 1996). Neither of the options is methodologically satisfactory: the first is unparsimonious, while the other places too heavy a burden on context-dependence and postulates a level of underspecified semantic representation with extremely doubtful psychological reality. In other words, there is no evidence that communicators indeed go through the stage of an underspecified representation in recovering the meaning of the utterance. Postulating such a level amounts to multiplying levels of sense beyond necessity.[11] Fortunately, neither underspecification nor ambiguity has to ensue if we admit the common-sensical idea of default interpretations.

3. Semantic defaults

Default meanings become increasingly better acknowledged in linguistic semantics and pragmatics, on the level of word meaning (e.g., Lascarides and Copestake 1998), sentence and utterance meaning (Levinson, 1995), and meaning in discourse (e.g., Lascarides and Oberlander, 1993). Default interpretations, dubbed 'jumping to conclusions' because we know when to 'think twice', have also been acknowledged by Kent Bach (1984). To sum up, the general idea is that reasoning utilizes generalizations and stereotypes of everyday life, things are taken for granted, and default meanings ensue, unless the hearer has some evidence that a departure from this default (in the form of a marked interpretation) is present.

In the case of the three readings of belief reports, i.e. *de re*, *de dicto*$_I$ and *de dicto proper*, it is also plausible to expect such defaults. In other words, we would presume not only that the hearer of a sentence of the form (4) arrives at an un-

[10] For relevant diagrams see Jaszczolt (1997).

[11] See Jaszczolt (1999, forthcoming) for my Parsimony of Levels principle.

marked, default interpretation, but also that sentences of this form have the default semantics.

(4) *A* believes that *B* ϕs.

Speakers tend to talk about known individuals or objects. This intuition is supported by the property of intentionality of mental states, their orientation at an object. Since all beliefs are intentional, directed at an object, or *about* an object of some sort and status, the referential intention is assumed by the communicators to be present in its strongest, undisturbed form, unless contextual clues point towards a departure from this standard. This is a rule that is part of human rational communicative behaviour. Now, if the communicative intention contains such an unimpeded referential intention, the speaker's belief is taken to be *de re*. And this is the default interpretation of the instantiations of (4), guaranteed by the intentionality of the underlying mental state. To repeat, the weakened form of intentionality (and the weakened referential intention) are only recovered when there are contextual clues that a referential mistake has been involved. Similarly, the total dispersion of intentionality (and the absence of the referential intention) are recovered when the context signals that this is the case, i.e. nobody (or nothing) has been referred to. These correspond to our *de dicto*$_1$ and *de dicto proper*, respectively.

On this picture, the referential intention *intrudes* into the semantic interpretation or, in other words, it interacts with the logical form of the expression, producing the default semantic representation and two principled context-dependent departures from the default. I have provided multiple arguments for the Default *De Re* principle (e.g., Jaszczolt, 1996, 1997, 1998a, 1998c, forthcoming) and will not repeat them here. It is perhaps necessary to point out that this proposal solves many difficulties and confusions present in the current literature on the subject, such as the need to choose between ambiguity and underspecification, or the logical form problem of attitude reports that is founded on the *un*founded assumption that the adicity (also known as 'arity', the number of required arguments) of the belief predicate has to be preserved. There will be more about the latter in the following section. Also, the problem with direct reference as opposed to contextual (or token-) reference[12] is side-stepped in that my account begins with the practical problem of reference assignment in which the strength of the referential intention does not pick and choose between directly referring and 'sometimes referring', i.e. contextually referring expressions: it affects them all equally.[13] But this is another strand of argument that will not be further pursued here.

[12] Cf.: "...descriptions can only be 'token-referential', whereas proper names and demonstrative expressions are 'type-referential'." Recanati (1993, p. 31).

[13] See also Saul (1997a) on the context-dependence and the lack of substitutivity of proper names, even in simple sentences. *Nota bene*, Bach (1987b, pp. 55–56) offers a common-sensical definition of a referring expression as an expression *standardly* used to refer to an individual. This class comprises proper names, definite descriptions and pronouns (including demonstrative).

4. The hidden-indexical theories and types of modes of presentation

Stephen Schiffer (e.g., 1977, 1992) proposes that if the semantics of natural languages is compositional, then belief reports of the type (4) have a logical form which includes a type of mode of presentation. This is a version of the hidden-indexical theory. Believing is construed as a three-place relation $\mathrm{Bel}(x, p, m)$ among the believer, the structured proposition, and the mode of presentation (henceforth: MoP) under which the believer believes this proposition. This MoP is determined by the MoPs of the constituent objects and properties of the proposition. So, sentence (5) has the logical form in (6), where Φ^* is "an implicitly referred to and contextually determined type of mode of presentation" (Schiffer, 1992, p. 503).

(5) Ralph believes that Fido is a dog.

(6) $(\exists m)\ (\Phi^* m\ \&\ B(\text{Ralph}, \langle \text{Fido}, \text{doghood} \rangle, m))$

Crimmins and Perry's (1989) and Crimmins's (1992) notion (an unarticulated constituent of the proposition) and Kaplan's (1989) character (a way of thinking about an individual) fit into the same general category of solutions.[14]

Now, Schiffer is committed to belief as a three-place relation. And yet it seems that this constraint on the adicity of the belief predicate is unnecessary and, indeed, harmful.[15] Considering that the degree to which the way the referent is thought of by the believer (or the reporter) is of varying importance to the semantics of the belief report, and considering that this gradation culminates in the total irrelevance of this MoP, flexibility between $\mathrm{Bel}(x, p, m)$ and $\mathrm{Bel}(x, p)$ would be useful to retain. Schiffer defines MoP functionally: it is "... whatever can play a role in determining a propositional mode of presentation", where the latter is "... whatever can play the role defined by the mode-of-presentation place in the belief relation" (Schiffer, 1995, p. 108). It seems then that when this role need not be fulfilled, we can revert to belief as a two-place relation. After all, no particular MoP may be intended, or none may be sufficiently salient to be recovered by the hearer. Moreover, the speaker may make reference to several contextually salient MoPs or types of MoPs (see Schiffer, 1995, p. 113). Types of MoPs allow for degrees from referring to a particular MoP to believing a proposition under some unspecified MoP. Similarly, the relevance of MoPs to the semantics allows for degrees. In the case of a *de re* belief ascribed in a *de re* report, the MoP need not be considered. There are normally many MoPs involved, all salient enough to convey the fact that the speaker is talking about a particular, identified individual. In the case of a referential mistake, i.e. *de dicto*$_I$ report, it is the type of MoP that is relevant rather than

[14] See also Forbes's (1990, 1997) modes of self-presentation ('logophors') as in (i)

(i) Lois has always believed *that Superman can fly*, so-labelled

(from Forbes (1997, p. 109)) and Saul's (1997b) criticism from the position of direct reference theory.

[15] On the adicity problem see also Ludlow (1995, 1996).

the MoP itself. In other words, MoP is relevant to the semantics only insofar as it performs the task of the clarification of the referential mistake. Finally, in the case of the *de dicto* belief rendered by the *de dicto* report, MoP matters a great deal because substitutivity tends to hold only if the original way of thinking about the referent is preserved. It has to be remembered that Schiffer's types of MoPs were introduced so as to avoid the need for particular MoPs pertaining to individuals and properties. Instead, he proposes a third argument for the belief predicate. It is determined functionally, preserves the Russellian proposition and yet accounts for context-sensitivity of reports. But it seems that we do not need as finely-grained a device as Schiffer's types of MoPs. Although in the default, *de re* case epistemically relevant MoPs may be mutually salient to the interlocutors, they are irrelevant from the semantic point of view in that preserving MoPs is unnecessary for the report to be successful. All we seem to need is three stages of the 'fineness of grain' of the information contained in types of MoPs: 'zero' for *de re*; enough to resolve the referential mistake in *de* $dicto_1$, and going the whole hog into as much of the type of MoP or the MoP itself as is in fact there, in the case of *de dicto proper*.[16] As the difference between the possible MoPs of the proposition pertains only to the differences in referring, i.e. MoPs of the referent rather than the properties of the propositions, I conclude without any further investigation into the MoPs of the latter, that $\mathrm{Bel}(x, p, m)$ may safely become $\mathrm{Bel}(x, p)$ in the transparent, default *de re* cases. Knowledge of language would account for other differences in MoPs but, for the present purpose, it can be safely assumed as shared.

In postulating three *meta*-types of MoPs I do not claim that these types have any privileged epistemic status. I merely adhere to the postulate that types of MoPs are functional notions and hence we distinguish only these aspects of the MoPs that are relevant for the semantics of belief reports. And these are the aspects that give us, for example, the three levels of embedding of the discourse referent standing for Ortcutt in Figure 1.

I have been discussing here Schiffer's meaning intention problem. But it seems that the meaning intention problem (cf., e.g., Schiffer, 1996) leads directly to a solution to the problem of the logical form of belief reports. We can retain m in the logical form, assigning to it a function of a legitimate argument, but the fineness of grain of the relevant type of MoP that may adopt the value zero for default *de re* allows us to change the adicity of the belief predicate.

We can go further than that. Since intentions themselves allow for degrees and they can interact with the semantic representation, we may not need the conjecture that speakers refer implicitly to MoPs, characters, notions, senses, and the like. All these may appear to be merely figures of discourse that help us grasp what degrees of intentions do.[17]

---

[16] See also Jaszczolt (1998a, p. 33) on the proposal of *meta*-types of MoPs.

[17] This claim was first put forward in Jaszczolt (1998a, p. 40).

5. Default-based context-dependence

There are two traditions in the philosophy of language, called by Recanati (1994, pp. 156–157) contextualism and anti-contextualism. According to the first, contextual information is normally necessary to ascribe the truth-conditional content to a sentence. In other words, natural language sentences express a complete thought only when taken in the context of their utterance. For example, according to contextualism, the meaning of the English 'and' differs from the meaning of the truth-functional conjunction in first-order logic in that it can adopt the temporal or consequential sense. Anti-contextualism relegates such contextual information to the position of implicatures, i.e. information separate from the propositional form, or separate from what is said. All that is allowed on the level of propositional form is reference assignment to indexical expressions, where the latter constitute a strictly defined category. According to anti-contextualism, there are context-independent, 'eternal' sentences, i.e. sentences whose truth conditions can be formed without reference to the context of utterance.

The default-based account of attitude reports seems to sit mid-way between the two positions delineated by Recanati. On the one hand, it is anti-contextualist in that its normal, default case is the proposition being expressed by a sentence independently of the context of the utterance. In other words, the *de re* reading is *assumed*, taken for granted. On the other hand, the propositional content, or what is said, can depend on the context of the utterance when the default is not the case. This is how we obtain the readings *de dicto*$_1$ and *de dicto proper*. One does not have to resort to conversational implicature or semantic ambiguity in order to explain their occurrence. The context, in the form of the intentions in communication, contributes to the semantic representation in a dynamic manner and produces the propositional representation. Now, since semantic defaults are independently supported by the intentionality of mental states, they constitute a firm ground on which we can build the rest of the picture. And these defaults do not need context. Context-sensitivity proposed by Recanati's contextualism (see, e.g., 1994, p. 157) is too strong. Instead, a weak version has to be adopted according to which context 'intrudes' in the semantic representation when the default meaning is not the case.[18]

Devitt (1996, p. 197) postulates mild context-dependence of meaning but his version, on the other hand, seems to be too restrictive. He suggests that the more different meanings there are to a *that*-clause, the more difficult the interpretation. The reason is, presumably, that the interpretation becomes more heavily context-dependent. While this may be so in the case when the referring terms are indexicals or are otherwise clearly context-dependent, it does not seem to work as a general

[18] This weak contextualism should not be confused with Recanati's (1994, p. 166) 'Methodological Contextualism' which still adheres to the difference in principle between the linguistic meaning of a sentence and *what is said*. For a discussion of the (by now technical) term 'what is said' see, e.g., Recanati (1989).

rule. Devitt (1996, p. 199) says that the meaning of a token utterance tends to depend to a large extent on the conventional meaning of the type. The context guides the hearer towards the departures from this type. However, in the case of the three readings of belief reports, *de re*, *de dicto*$_I$ and *de dicto proper*, it is incorrect to talk about departures from the *literal* meaning. Instead, there are departures form the *default* meaning. The degree of context-dependence should not be thought of as 'additions' to the meaning of the sentence-type as Devitt has it, but rather as additions to (or, rather, departures from) the default meaning. This difference is essential for the theory of belief reports. Moreover, the number of meanings the sentence has need not affect the degree of difficulty of its interpretation. Since utterance interpretation is incremental, contextual clues are utilized as they become relevant. In other words, it is not the case that the hearer chooses one interpretation from the range of options where all the options are equally salient. Since Devitt favours Quine's ambiguity of attitude reports, he is bound by this psychologically unappealing view.[19] Context does not 'disambiguate' expressions. Instead, it contributes to their interpretation in a dynamic way.

There are some advantages to Devitt's view, though. Firstly, it represents mild context-dependence. Secondly, Devitt allows for MoPs to take the value zero, while the hidden-indexical theory shuns this move.[20] In other words, the speaker may have no particular mode in mind. But instead of semantic ambiguity, what is needed here is a Default Semantics and departures from the default, as introduced in Section 3.[21]

In response to Devitt, Bezuidenhout (1997) argues for heavy context-dependence of the meaning of attitude reports. Belief reports are said to be semantically underdetermined and the missing components of meaning are supplied by pragmatic information that includes the speaker's MoP of the referent. This contextual enrichment is a pervasive feature of belief reports. She founds this heavy context-dependence on Sperber and Wilson's view that pragmatic enrichment is non-modular, has access to other beliefs in the interpreter's 'belief box', and is always needed when the semantic representation alone does not suffice because there is nothing else that could bridge the gap. In other words, there are no default interpretations that would take the hearer beyond the logical form, there are only pragmatic processes that enrich it to the full proposition and pragmatic processes that lead to implicatures (cf., e.g., Carston, 1988, 1998). However, as I have argued with reference to the hidden-indexical theory, sometimes the meaning

[19] Devitt postulates an ambiguity of a 'special sort' in attitude reports. He is non-committal as to whether the ambiguity is syntactic or lexical (cf. 1996, p. 200, footnote 61). Since Devitt adheres to the transparent-opaque distinction, he cannot take into account the *degrees* of opacity. On the other hand, he can account for the true sense of transparency by saying that *no* MoP has to be present then (cf. p. 217).

[20] Albeit to a lesser and lesser extent according to Devitt's judgement (1996, p. 202, footnote 63). Cf. also footnote 19 above.

[21] And mainly in Jaszczolt (forthcoming).

goes through to the hearer without the contextual information such as MoP being known. Sometimes the MoP is assumed to be shared between the interlocutors and this assumption suffices. In fact, it seems that it is only in the cases when something goes wrong in the process of interpretation that the MoP and other contextual clues have to be resorted to. In view of the obvious fact that the default-based semantics is more parsimonious and is independently supported by my account of the referential intention and intentionality, I conclude that heavy context-dependence places too great a burden on the hearer in that it models a hearer as undertaking the enrichment of the sentence meaning on too many occasions of utterance interpretation.

Now, Discourse Representation Theory (Kamp and Reyle, 1993) subscribes to mild contextualism in that the truth-conditional representation may, but need not, contain the output of many types of pragmatic processes. For example, processes such as reference resolution (here mainly indexical resolution), as well as lexical and syntactic disambiguation, the completion of a propositional radical or the expansion of a minimal proposition (in Bach's (1994) sense) may contribute to the truth-conditional representation and their effects enter the discourse representation structure. It has to be remembered, however, that reference resolution may not be required. Whether it is required or not depends on whether the default *de re* goes through or has to be overridden. The presence of the default interpretation of belief reports and the principled departures from the default set clear constraints on the role of context in semantics. Contextual information is utilized in the dynamic manner, in the process of constructing a propositional representation but this process of constructing a propositional representation need not be set in context. In other words, although context has to be established before the interpretation takes place, it need not play an active role because the simple default meaning may go through. This picture seems to be compatible with Levinson's (1995) suggestion of the conventional, utterance-type meaning, called the third, middle level of meaning:

> "This third layer is a level of systematic pragmatic inference based *not* on direct computations about speaker-intentions, but rather on *general expectations about how language is normally used*." Levinson (1995, p. 93).

My version of contextualism for belief reports is similarly constrained by default interpretations.

6. Conclusions

Most common-sensically stated, the pivotal problem with attitudes is this:

> "The challenge is to develop a theory in which Russellian truth conditions are assigned to attitude ascriptions in certain contexts, thereby capturing the intu-

itions motivating Russellianism, while non-Russellian truth conditions are assigned to ascriptions in other contexts, thereby vindicating the Fregean intuition that substitution of coreferential singular terms is not always guaranteed to preserve truth value." Soames (1995, p. 524).

Soames sides with the view that sentences express annotated propositions (see Richard, 1990, 1995).[22] I hope to have gone further to show *when* Russellian truth conditions hold and when we have to resort to neo-Fregean solutions.

Soames (1995, p. 540) explicates the follow-up to this problem as follows:

"... in some contexts the information semantically expressed, and pragmatically conveyed, by belief ascriptions is purely Russellian, requiring only that the agent believe the singular, Russellian proposition expressed by the content clause of the ascription. The participants in the debate also agree that in other contexts additional information is conveyed regarding which representations the agent uses to express his belief. The fundamental question at issue is whether this additional information is part of the proposition semantically expressed by the belief ascription, or is only pragmatically implicated by it."

In suggesting that intentions allow for degrees and that they contribute directly to the logical form, I have taken on a contextualist stance in the debate. But by arguing for default *de re* interpretations, I have also confined contextualism to the role of a player *only* in marked interpretations.

A brief disclaimer is required at this point. I have not attempted to provide all the necessary steps of the arguments for default *de re* and degrees of intentions in this paper. Instead, I have summarized here the proposals developed in more detail elsewhere in order to attempt a first approximation at a more global picture of the semantics, pragmatics, and psychology of belief ascriptions. Naturally, there will be many postulates here that require further support and they have to be taken as such. Mark Richard concludes his book as follows:

"... among the contextual factors that can affect what a sentence strictly and literally says, are the intentions, expectations, and other intentional states of its [sic] participants." Richard (1990, p. 265).

I have proposed here a principled account of the relevant types and degrees of intentions and allocated it a place alongside the default semantics of belief reports.

Acknowledgment

I would like to thank Stephen Schiffer and Ken Turner for discussing with me some ideas pertaining to this paper and Walter de Gruyter for giving me permission

[22] Cf.: "*x believes that S* says (quite roughly) that *x* has a belief which is 'well rendered' or acceptably translated by *S*; since contextually variable information about what makes for a good translation helps determine the extension of 'believes', the verb is contextually sensitive." Richard (1995, p. 551).

to adapt Figure 1 that originally appeared in my article (1998c) in *Theoretical Linguistics*.

References

Bach, E. (1981), *On time, tense, and aspect: An essay in English metaphysics*, Radical Pragmatics, P. Cole, ed., Academic Press, New York, 63–81.

Bach, K. (1984), *Default reasoning: Jumping to conclusions and knowing when to think twice*, Pacific Philosophical Quarterly **65**, 37–58.

Bach, K. (1987a), *On communicative intentions: A reply to Recanati*, Mind and Language **2**, 141–154.

Bach, K. (1987b), *Thought and Reference*, Clarendon Press, Oxford.

Bach, K. (1992), *Intentions and demonstrations*, Analysis **52**, 140–146.

Bach, K. (1994), *Semantic slack: What is said and more*, Tsohatzidis, ed., 267–291.

Bach, K. and Harnish, R.M. (1979), *Linguistic Communication and Speech Acts*, MIT Press, Cambridge, MA.

Bezuidenhout, A. (1997), *How context-dependent are attitude ascriptions?*, The Maribor Papers in Naturalized Semantics, D. Jutronic, ed., University of Maribor, Maribor, 269–284.

Brentano, F. (1874), *Psychology from an Empirical Standpoint*, Transl. A.C. Rancurello, D.B. Terrell and L.L. McAlister (1973), Routledge and Kegan Paul, London.

Carston, R. (1988), *Implicature, explicature, and truth-theoretic semantics*, Mental Representations: The Interface Between Language and Reality, R.M. Kempson, ed., Cambridge University Press, Cambridge, 155–181.

Carston, R. (1998), *Postscript (1995)* to Carston 1988, Pragmatics: Critical Concepts, Vol. 4, A. Kasher, ed., Routledge, London, 464–479.

Clapp, L. (1995), *How to be direct and innocent: A criticism of Crimmins and Perry's theory of attitude ascriptions*, Linguistics and Philosophy **18**, 529–565.

Crimmins, M. (1992), *Talk about Beliefs*, MIT Press, Cambridge, MA.

Crimmins, M. and Perry, J. (1989), *The prince and the phone booth: Reporting puzzling beliefs*, Journal of Philosophy **86**, 685–711.

Devitt, M. (1996), *Coming to Our Senses: A Naturalistic Program for Semantic Localism*, Cambridge University Press, Cambridge.

Donnellan, K. (1966), *Reference and definite descriptions*, Philosophical Review **75**, 281–304.

Donnellan, K. (1990), *Belief and the identity of reference*, Propositional Attitudes: The Role of Content in Logic, Language, and Mind, C.A. Anderson and J. Owens, eds, CSLI, Stanford, 201–214.

Dummett, M. (1991), *The relative priority of thought and language*, Frege and Other Philosophers, Clarendon Press, Oxford, 315–324.

Forbes, G. (1990), *The indispensability of Sinn*, Philosophical Review **99**, 535–563.

Forbes, G. (1997), *How much substitutivity?*, Analysis **57**, 109–113.

Husserl, E. (1900-01), *Logical Investigations*, Transl. J.N. Findlay (1970), Routledge and Kegan Paul, London.

Jaszczolt, K.M. (1996), *Reported speech, vehicles of thought, and the horizon*, Lingua e Stile **31**, 113–133.

Jaszczolt, K.M. (1997), *The 'default de re' principle for the interpretation of belief utterances*, Journal of Pragmatics **28**, 315–336.

Jaszczolt, K.M. (1998a), *Reports on beliefs: Default interpretations and default intentions*, Journal of Literary Semantics **27**, 31–42.

Jaszczolt, K.M. (1998b), *Referring in discourse: Referential intention and the "taking for granted" principle*, Journal of Literary Semantics **27**, 96–109.

Jaszczolt, K.M. (1998c), *Discourse about beliefs*, Theoretical Linguistics **24**, 1–28.

Jaszczolt, K.M. (1999), *Default semantics, pragmatics, and intentions*, The Semantics/Pragmatics Interface from Different Points of View, K. Turner, ed., Elsevier Science, Oxford, 199–232.

Jaszczolt, K.M. (forthcoming), *Discourse, Beliefs, and Intentions: Semantic Defaults and Propositional Attitude Ascription*, Elsevier Science, Oxford.

Kamp, H. and Reyle, U. (1993), *From Discourse to Logic: Introduction to Modeltheoretic Semantics of Natural Language, Formal Logic and Discourse Representation Theory*, Kluwer, Dordrecht.

Kaplan, D. (1989), *Demonstratives: An essay on the semantics, logic, metaphysics, and epistemology of demonstratives and other indexicals*, Themes from Kaplan, J. Almog, J. Perry and H. Wettstein, eds, Oxford University Press, New York, 481–563.

Lascarides, A. and Copestake, A. (1998), *Pragmatics and word meaning*, Journal of Linguistics **34**, 387–414.

Lascarides, A. and Oberlander, J. (1993), *Temporal coherence and defeasible knowledge*, Theoretical Linguistics **19**, 1–37.

Levinson, S.C. (1987), *Minimization and conversational inference*, The Pragmatic Perspective. Selected Papers from the 1985 International Pragmatics Conference, J. Verschueren and M. Bertuccelli-Papi, eds, J. Benjamins, Amsterdam, 61–129.

Levinson, S.C. (1995), *Three levels of meaning*, Grammar and Meaning. Essays in Honour of Sir John Lyons, F.R. Palmer, ed., Cambridge University Press, Cambridge, 90–115.

Ludlow, P. (1995), *Logical form and the hidden-indexical theory: A reply to Schiffer*, Journal of Philosophy **92**, 102–107.

Ludlow, P. (1996), *The adicity of "Believes" and the hidden indexical theory*, Analysis **56**, 97–101.

Quine, W.V.O. (1956), *Quantifiers and propositional attitudes*, Journal of Philosophy **53**. Reprinted in A. Marras, ed. (1972), Intentionality, Mind and Language, University of Illinois Press, Urbana, 402–414.

Recanati, F. (1989), *The pragmatics of what is said*, Mind and Language **4**. Reprinted in S. Davis, ed. (1991), Pragmatics: A Reader, Oxford University Press, Oxford, 97–120.

Recanati, F. (1993), *Direct Reference: From Language to Thought*, Blackwell, Oxford.

Recanati, F. (1994), *Contextualism and anti-contextualism in the philosophy of language*, Tsohatzidis, ed., 156–166.

Recanati, F. (1997), *Can we believe what we do not understand?*, Mind and Language **12**, 84–100.

Richard, M. (1990), *Propositional Attitudes: An Essay on Thoughts and How We Ascribe Them*, Cambridge University Press, Cambridge.

Richard, M. (1995), *Defective contexts, accommodation, and normalization*, Canadian Journal of Philosophy **25**, 551–570.

Salmon, N. (1986), *Frege's Puzzle*, MIT Press, Cambridge, MA.

Saul, J.M. (1997a), *Substitution and simple sentences*, Analysis **57**, 102–108.

Saul, J.M. (1997b), *Reply to Forbes*, Analysis **57**, 114–118.

Schiffer, S. (1977), *Naming and knowing*, Midwest Studies in Philosophy **2**. Reprinted in P.A. French, T.E. Uehling and H.K. Wettstein, eds (1979), Contemporary Perspectives in the Philosophy of Language, University of Minnesota Press, Minneapolis, 61–74.

Schiffer, S. (1992), *Belief ascription*, Journal of Philosophy **89**, 499–521.

Schiffer, S. (1993), *Actual-language relations*, Language and Logic, Philosophical Perspectives Series 7, J.E. Tomberlin, ed., Ridgeview, Atascadero, CA, 231–258.

Schiffer, S. (1994), *A paradox of meaning*, Noûs **28**, 279–324.

Schiffer, S. (1995), *Descriptions, indexicals, and belief reports: Some dilemmas (but not the ones you expect)*, Mind **104**, 107–131.

Schiffer, S. (1996), *The hidden-indexical theory's logical-form problem: A rejoinder*, Analysis **56**, 92–97.

Searle, J.R. (1983), *Intentionality: An Essay in the Philosophy of Mind*, Cambridge University Press, Cambridge.

Soames, S. (1987), *Direct reference, propositional attitudes, and semantic content*, Philosophical Topics **15**. Reprinted in N. Salmon and S. Soames, eds (1988), Propositions and Attitudes, Oxford University Press, Oxford, 197–239.

Soames, S. (1995), *Beyond singular propositions?*, Canadian Journal of Philosophy **25**, 515–549.

Sperber, D. (1985), *Apparently irrational beliefs*, On Anthropological Knowledge, Cambridge University Press, Cambridge, 35–63.

Sperber, D. (1996), *Explaining Culture: A Naturalistic Approach*, Blackwell, Oxford.

Sperber, D. (1997), *Intuitive and reflective beliefs*, Mind and Language **12**, 67–83.

Sperber, D. and Wilson, D. (1986), *Relevance: Communication and Cognition*, Blackwell, Oxford. Reprinted in 1995. Second edition.

Tsohatzidis, S.L. (ed.) (1994), *Foundations of Speech Act Theory: Philosophical and Linguistic Perspectives*, Routledge, London.

van Deemter, K. and Peters, S. (eds) (1996), *Semantic Ambiguity and Underspecification*, CSLI Publications, Stanford.

CHAPTER 10

The Background of Propositional Attitudes and Reports Thereof

David Woodruff Smith

Contents

PRAGMATICS OF PROPOSITIONAL ATTITUDE REPORTS
Current Research in the Semantics/Pragmatics Interface, Vol. 4
Edited by K.M. Jaszczolt

0. Meaning, use, and background

Propositional attitudes – beliefs, desires, phantasies, volitions, etc. – rest on a background of basic beliefs and practices (among other things).

Speech acts are a type of action, or intentional bodily movement, and they too rest on such a background.

Reports of propositional attitudes are a type of speech act, and they too rest on such a background.

In short, our intentional activities – including our attitudes, speech, and reports-of-attitudes – form a nexus in which each attitude or action depends on a background. This background includes basic propositions and rules-of-practice that define our *Lebenswelt* or life-world.

Analysis of this background clarifies the intuitions behind two very different conceptions of meaning in language: meaning as content of thought or intentional activity (from Aristotle to Frege, Bolzano, Husserl) and meaning as use-of-words (Peirce to Wittgenstein and even Derrida). Thereby we clarify the boundary between the sense and use of words and so the boundary between semantics and pragmatics. To this end, we shall study the role of background in propositional attitudes themselves and in our reports of attitudes, where attitudes and attitude reports are intimately linked.[1]

1. Language and intentionality

Here I want to take a path less travelled in recent linguistic theory and philosophy of language, the intentionalist path.

For the later Wittgenstein, it may seem, language has a life of its own, uninvolved with the mental life of its users – if indeed there is mind beyond language games. For the intentionalist philosopher, however, language is ever involved with intentional activities of mind, indeed consciousness. An act of speech or writing involves an intentional mental act of expressing a meaning and intending to convey it to others and thereby to affect others in a variety of ways. The meaning expressed is itself an intentional content, a content of thought (perception, emotion, etc.). Words and sentences in a language are forms of expression, literally spatiotemporal forms of the behaviors of speakers or writers: as we say, types of token sounds of speech or token marks of writing. But speech or writing behavior is an abstracted aspect of the *action* of speaking or writing, which is intervolved with thinking and other forms of experience. The action itself uses the form of

[1] A cognate study is my essay, "Background Ideas", published in Italian as "Idee di sfondo" (1999). There I pursue the notion of background in a general theory of intentionality. Here I pursue implications for the pragmatics of propositional attitude reports. Some sections below rework materials developed in full in the cognate essay (not otherwise available in English).

expression it manifests in behavior in order to express and convey to others an intentional content, a content entertained in appropriate attitudes.

Intentionality – in the philosopher's technical idiom coined by Husserl – is a property of mental "acts" or states: not only "acts" of intending-to-do-something in purposeful bodily action; but also "acts" of thinking, perceiving, imagining, wishing, etc. Intentionality consists in a mental act or attitude's "intending" or being "directed" toward something: in colloquial terms, being "of" or "about" something, representing something. I want to approach language within the framework of intentionality theory, assessing reports of propositional attitudes within the same framework that we use in analyzing attitudes themselves.

The intentionalist account of language has roots tracing back to Aristotle and the Stoic logicians. It was articulated by Husserl early in the 20th century, combining a theory of reference via sense (compare Frege) and a theory of speech acts (compare Austin and Searle) with a *bona fide* theory of intentionality.[2] In recent years, amid the emergence of cognitive science, John Searle has rediscovered not only consciousness, but intentionality and social reality, on the heels of speech acts.[3]

Issues of intentionality have been often bracketed in formal semantics/pragmatics (Tarski, Montague, Kaplan et al.) and in reference theory (Putnam, Kripke, Kaplan, et al.). These are the issues I want to press here: about language-about-thought. Drawing on Searle, Wittgenstein, and Husserl, I want to pursue the implications of the concept of "background" for the interpretation of reports of propositional attitudes. I want to show how both propositional attitudes and our reports thereof depend on deep background assumptions at work in both our attitudes and our reports of them.

Before we get down to work, however, we need to lay out certain concepts, terms, and distinctions – part of the theoretical background on which I shall draw (noting the recursion on "background").

Let us keep constantly in mind the distinction among an assertion, a propositional attitude, and a report of a propositional attitude. An *assertion* is a speech act performed by uttering a declarative *sentence* '*p*', thereby expressing a *proposition* "[that] *p*". A *propositional attitude* is a mental act or state such as *a*'s thinking, judging, or believing that *p*. Its form is propositional because its content is a proposition "*p*", which is expressible by a declarative sentence '*p*'. The term 'proposition' has been used differently in alternative theories, and I shall adapt the usage of

[2] Husserl coined the term 'intentionality' ('Intentionalität' in German) for what Brentano called the "directedness" of mental phenomena (drawing on the Medieval notion of "intentio"), or what cognitive scientists today call mental representation. Husserl was the first to get straight many of the important features of intentionality: we can think of things that do not exist, we can think about an object only under a concept (a "sense" or "noema"), and the object of a thought always transcends that concept through which we think about it. On that basis Husserl gave an account of language, of sense and reference or "intention". See Husserl, *Logical Investigations* (1900-01) and *Ideas* I (1913), and Smith and McIntyre, *Husserl and Intentionality* (1982).

[3] See Searle, *Speech Acts* (1969), *Intentionality* (1983), *The Rediscovery of the Mind* (1992), and *The Construction of Social Reality* (1995).

Bolzano and Husserl so that 'proposition' (*Satz*) means the propositional content of an act of judging or believing, expressible as the meaning or sense (*Sinn*) of a declarative sentence and akin to what Frege called a "thought".[4] Not all intentional acts or attitudes are propositional, but here let us focus on those that are. (Seeing a sunset does not have the form of seeing "that the sun is setting".) Also, there are differences between occurrent "acts" and dispositional "attitudes", but let us pass over the differences here. Now, a *sentence reporting* a propositional attitude is a sentence such as '*a* believes that *p*', used to report to someone a propositional attitude. And a *speech act of reporting* a propositional attitude is performed by uttering such a sentence and thereby reporting a propositional attitude to someone. Let us define an *attitude report* as either a sentence reporting a propositional attitude or a speech act of reporting one (which involves uttering a token of the attitude-reporting sentence).

Thus, we distinguish:

(a) the propositional attitude: Russell believes that Wittgenstein is clever,

(b) the sentence reporting the propositional attitude: 'Russell believes that Wittgenstein is clever',

(c) the speech act of reporting the propositional attitude: David asserts, 'Russell believes that Wittgenstein is clever'.

By a propositional attitude report, we shall usually mean a reporting sentence as in (b), assuming that sentences are used in speech acts as in (c).

We must distinguish intentionality from intensionality, as these phenomena have often been conflated. A propositional attitude is said to be *intentional* (spelled with a 't') in that it is of or about something: Russell's belief in this case is about Wittgenstein (and his cleverness). By contrast, a propositional attitude sentence is said to be *intensional* (spelled with an '*s*') in that the logic of expressions following (here) 'believes that' is not extensional: terms in the context 'Russell believes that ___' do not obey the usual laws of substitutivity and existential generalization. That is, the following inferences are invalid:

(i) Russell believes that Wittgenstein is clever.
Wittgenstein = the author of the *Tractatus*.
Therefore, Russell believes that the author of the *Tractatus* is clever.

(ii) Russell believes that Wittgenstein is clever.
Therefore, there exists someone such that Russell believes that s/he is clever.

---

[4] In Frege, 'thought' (*Gedanke*) means the sense (*Sinn*) expressed by a declarative sentence or clause. In Russell 'proposition' means either a declarative sentence or what it asserts or expresses, in effect a putative state of affairs consisting of, say, an object's having a property. More recently, David Kaplan has popularized a neo-Russellian notion of proposition, defined semi-formally as an ordered pair consisting of a property and an object, or an *n*-tuple consisting of a relation and *n* objects. Sometimes a proposition is defined, in model-theoretic or possible-worlds semantics, as a function from models or possible worlds to truth-values, its value at a world being its truth or falsity in that world.

Thus, intentionality is a property of attitudes themselves, studied in philosophy of mind and phenomenology; while intensionality is a property of sentences reporting attitudes (or of such linguistic contexts), studied in philosophy of language, logic, and linguistics.[5]

In logico-linguistic theory (following Carnap following Charles Morris following C.S. Peirce): *Syntax* studies the forms of sentences, while *semantics* studies the meanings of sentences, and *pragmatics* studies the uses of sentences. The boundary between semantics and pragmatics is however quite unclear. Thus, the meaning of an indexical is defined, from Peirce to Kaplan, in terms of its context of use; yet for Wittgenstein, the meaning of an expression just is its use, namely, in appropriate contexts.[6] Now, the notion of "background" helps to distinguish meaning, context, and use, as we shall see.

Phenomenology is traditionally defined (following Husserl) as the study of consciousness, or conscious experience, beginning with structures of intentionality. In effect, phenomenology is the *theory of intentionality*: the study of the "meaning" or "sense" (*Sinn*) in mental acts or attitudes, including propositional attitudes, and the "use" and context of such intentional acts. Cognitive science has recently widened to include "consciousness studies", embracing not only phenomenological structures, but also neural bases of consciousness, and puzzling over phenomena such as intentionality, qualia, blindsight, and subjectivity (the "hard" problem of consciousness).[7] Now, attitude reports are forms-of-language in which we report intentional states-of-consciousness in others and sometimes ourselves. These forms of language are our public window on our private experiences or attitudes. And so the pragmatics of attitude reports is an indirect approach to the practice of phenomenology, to phenomenological reflections expressed in everyday language. Remember that we use basically the same forms of sentence to report the attitudes held by ourselves or by others. At the same time, phenomenology or intentionality theory provides a wide philosophical framework within which to address issues of semantics and pragmatics and the boundary between them.

As we explore the background of propositional attitudes and attitude reports, we shall find remarkable implications for the ontological status of propositions. Like words in Wittgensteinian language-games, propositions themselves appear to be entities with a life of their own in the background of our propositional attitudes and attitude reports. As such, propositions are abstract entities that are nonetheless dependent on consciousness, language, and social practice. But then they cannot have their being in a Platonic heaven, as traditionally claimed (glossing Bolzano, Frege, and the early Husserl).

---

[5] The differences are explained in detail in Smith and McIntyre, *Husserl and Intentionality* (1982).

[6] The history of theories of indexical terms and the emerging notion of context of use is insightfully tracked in Joseph Tougas, *Context* (1998).

[7] An anthology selecting from the literature of consciousness-studies is the recent volume, *The Nature of Consciousness*, edited by Block, Flanagan, and Güzeldere (1997).

2. Background assumptions at work in propositional attitude reports

Quine's Ortcutt case is a familiar touchstone in the semantics and pragmatics of propositional attitude reports.[8] Ralph is walking on the beach with a friend and sees a man in a brown hat of whom he says, 'That man is a spy.' His friend recognizes the man as community leader Bernard J. Ortcutt and later reports, 'Ralph believes that Ortcutt is a spy.' Ralph's assertion presupposes his perception and his 1950's concern about spies. The friend's report presupposes his own observation of Ralph's speech behavior and perceptual situation. Our interpretation of this belief report calls upon these background assumptions of Ralph and friend respectively.

But still deeper background assumptions are involved in propositional attitudes and reports thereof. Consider Mia and Edward. Mia says to Edward, 'I am your mother.' Edward later says, 'Mia thinks that she is my mother.'

Here are two assertions: the first gives voice to a propositional attitude, the second reports that attitude. How shall we interpret these assertions? What is the meaning of each? What is the meaning of the uttered sentence? What is the speaker's meaning? What is assumed and implied in each speech act?

At the level of pure semantics, the answers seem straightforward. The semantics of the indexical personal pronouns specifies that 'I' refers to the speaker and 'you' to the hearer. Given the lexical meaning of 'mother', the meaning expressed by Mia's utterance is the proposition that Mia is the mother of Edward. And the meaning expressed by Edward's utterance is the proposition that Mia thinks that Mia is the mother of Edward. Here we follow a semantics of 'I' modelled roughly on David Kaplan's logic of demonstratives.[9] Because context of utterance influences reference in a systematic and rule-governed way, we speak here with Kaplan of a semantics rather than a pragmatics of 'I'. But let us enrich the semantics. Within an intentionalist theory of language, let us assume an ontology of both propositions and states-of-affairs, and let us recognize properly indexical contents in propositions.[10] Then the proposition expressed by Mia is "I am your mother", which represents the state of affairs that Mia is the woman who gave birth to Edward. And the proposition expressed by Edward is "Mia thinks that she is my

---

[8] See Quine, "Quantifiers and Propositional Attitudes" (1956). Quine's puzzle concerned the interpretation of *de re* reports of beliefs, such as 'Ralph believes of someone that he is a spy', expressed in the form of quantifying-in, '$\exists x$(Ralph believes that x is a spy)'. Hintikka's semantics for propositional attitude ascriptions interpreted such quantifiers in terms of two types of individuation: see Hintikka, "Semantics for Propositional Attitudes" (1969). An intentionalist semantic interpretation drawing on both Quine and Hintikka is outlined in D.W. Smith, "The Ortcutt Connection" (1981b). A pragmatic interpretation drawing on different dimensions of discourse in the context of the speech act is recently developed in Jaszczolt, "Reported speech, vehicles of thought, and the horizon" (1996). Husserlian tools are used in both of the latter studies.

[9] See David Kaplan, "Demonstratives" (1989).

[10] See D.W. Smith, "Indexical Sense and Reference" (1981). Compare Husserl, *Logical Investigations* (1900-01), I, §26, VI, §5; on Husserl *vis-á-vis* Kaplan on indexicals, see Smith, "Husserl on Perception and Demonstrative Reference" (1982).

mother", which represents the state of affairs that Edward has a thought or belief with that content, which represents the state of affairs that Mia thinks she is the woman who gave birth to Edward.

Yet there is more to the meaning of these assertions, Mia's and Edward's. The wider context of these speech acts elicits a more complex account of their meaning, and that is how the phenomenon of background manifests itself.

The Case of Mia 1

Mia is indeed the mother of Edward, a small child. She has just told him to go to bed, and he has said, defiantly, 'I won't! I don't have to do what you tell me to.' She says, 'Oh, yes, you do!' Pausing, she adds, 'I am your mother.' Her intent is clear to any parent, and such is the pragmatic force of her utterance (what J.L. Austin called its perlocutionary force). The force of her speech act depends on psychological assumptions about the power and authority of parent over child, as well as cultural assumptions about the role of a parent (without servants, the parents put the children to bed). These factors are not specified in the semantics of the sentence Mia uttered, but they clearly play a role in the pragmatics of her utterance. Her meaning, in one clear version, is: "I have the authority to send you to bed." Here we take pragmatics to address the psychological background that helps to give her utterance this force.

Later, in his room, Edward mutters to himself, 'Mia thinks that she is my mother.' Feeling ornery, he uses his mother's proper name, distancing himself, and his meaning is in effect: "Mia thinks that she is my queen." This is the proposition expressed as Edward uses the given sentence – not literally, but figuratively – against a background understanding of the roles of parents and royalty. As psychology enters the pragmatics of this attitude report, the meaning expressed depends on assumptions about family life in our era and the life of royals in a by-gone era (known to Edward through story books).

Thus, the meanings – speaker's meanings – of these assertions by Mia and Edward, the intentional contents expressed thereby, depend on background assumptions about our psychology and our culture, quite basic assumptions about our all-too-human world.

The Case of Mia 2

Mia is a child of six, Edward is her father. Mia says, 'I am your mother.' Later, Edward says to his wife, 'Mia thinks that she is my mother.' Her assertion is not true, she did not give birth to Edward. His assertion reports a false belief. Right? Well, the context changes everything.

This family are practicing Buddhists who believe in reincarnation. What Mia means – the proposition she expresses – is: "In a past life I was your mother." And the belief Edward ascribes to her is her thinking that in a past life she was his mother (their roles of parent and child were reversed in that life); that is, the belief his report ascribes to Mia carries the content "In a past life I was your mother." Notice how the indexical pronouns work. In Mia's statement 'I' refers to the speaker (Mia) and 'you' or 'your' to the hearer (Edward). But Mia's use of the pronouns carries the assumption that the same individuals had past lives in which they played different roles than in this life. The meaning of Mia's assertion – speaker's meaning – depends on this background metaphysical assumption. And the meaning of Edward's report, the proposition "Mia thinks...", depends on a similar assumption, which he shares with Mia. (Indeed, the metaphysical assumptions are still more complex: classical Buddhist ontology says there is no substantial self but there is a continuity between one life and another. In modern European philosophy, Hume held such a view about the self, but within one life, without reincarnation. How deep into this metaphysics do Mia's and Edward's background assumptions reach?)

In the Case of Mia 1, the speakers' meanings depend on background assumptions about psychology and culture. In the Case of Mia 2, the speakers' meanings depend still further on background assumptions about the metaphysical nature of the self.

Enter we, the intentionalist linguistic theorists. How do our semantic and/or pragmatic interpretations depend on background assumptions about the nature of the world? In Case 1, we share with Mia and Edward the psychological and cultural assumptions at work in their beliefs and assertions, and we make use of these assumptions in interpreting their speech acts. We are all in the same linguistic-cultural community, and we all more or less share the same background attitudes, though children are in the process of learning these attitudes. In Case 2, however, our interpretations of Mia's and Edward's speech and attitudes depend on our understanding of their metaphysical assumptions about reincarnation, which we need not share; we consider their attitudes as well as our own in interpreting their assertions. This is the problem of cultural pluralism, increasingly familiar in modern political life.

Before us lies the general problem of background: How do intentional activities – from beliefs to speech acts to attitude reports to theorizing about these – depend on background assumptions about the world? Such assumptions include propositional attitudes, usually tacit beliefs. But intentional attitudes and reports thereof depend on still other background conditions. What are these conditions, and how does intentionality depend on them? That is the problem of "the background", and that is the theoretical context within which I propose to view speech acts and attitude reports along with other intentional activities.

As we map the roles of content and background in intentionality, we are charting the boundaries between "meaning" and "use" for intentional activities. But as we turn to the interpretation of attitude reports, we are exploring the boundary between semantics and pragmatics. The differences between the two Mia cases above show what roles background plays in both an attitude and a report of the same attitude.

3. The background of intentionality

As we home in on the concept of background, we need first to review some basic terms concerning intentionality. A mental act or attitude of thought, perception, volition, etc. – more especially, a propositional attitude – is *intentional* in that it "intends" or represents something. Further, a bodily *action* is intentional insofar as it is initiated by a volition or intention to do such-and-such: a proper part of an action is thus an intentional mental act or attitude of intending-to-do-such-and-such.[11] And a *speech act* of assertion in saying '*p*' is a special type of action: part of the assertion (*pace* Austin, Grice, Searle) is the intention to do such-and-such by uttering '*p*', specifically (and among other things), to convey a certain thought or feeling, to communicate the proposition "*p*". An attitude report in uttering the sentence '*a* believes that *p*' then includes the intention to convey the proposition "*a* believes that *p*". Here we stress that an action involves an intentional "act" or attitude as a proper part. We reserve the term 'action' for intentional bodily movements, including speech acts. The traditional Husserlian term 'act' we reserve for an intentional mental state or attitude (including the volition or intention that is part of an action). Here I stress the term 'attitude', as in 'propositional attitude', occasionally adverting to 'act' and evoking the Husserlian idiom.

Now, according to the theory of background, a mental act such as a propositional attitude can represent or intend something only against a *background* of other states including *inter alia* beliefs, emotions, and even bodily skills (non-intentional capacities). Similar views along these lines have been argued, convincingly and in very different idioms, by the likes of Husserl, Heidegger, Wittgenstein, and most recently John Searle.[12] Assertions, propositional attitudes, and attitude reports, we here observe, all depend on relevant background conditions.

To bring out the background, consider a mundane propositional attitude.[13] Reflecting on a recent earthquake,

> I think that the earth does not normally roll beneath me as I walk.

The content of this thought is the proposition "the earth does not normally roll beneath me as I walk". But there are a great many collateral propositions I would also seem to hold in belief:

---

[11] On intentionality in action, see D. W. Smith, "Consciousness in Action" (1992), and Searle, *Intentionality* (1983).

[12] See: Searle, *Intentionality* (1983), Chapter 5, *The Rediscovery of the Mind* (1992), Chapter 8, and *The Construction of Social Reality* (1995), Chapter 6; Wittgenstein, *On Certainty* (1972); Husserl, *Ideas* I (1913), *Ideas* II (1952), and the *Crisis* (1970).

[13] This example is a variation on an example recounted by Searle in *The Rediscovery of the Mind* (1992), pp. 184–185. In Searle's example a European philosopher was walking with Searle on the Berkeley campus, discussing the notion of background, when an earthquake struck. The visitor realized after the quake that before then he had not held a belief that the earth does not move; he had simply taken this for granted. This convinced him of the hypothesis of the background.

The earth is a mass of dirt I may walk on.
The earth moves around the sun.
The dirt in California is a dry powder in summer.
The earth has existed for a long, long time.
I use both my feet when I walk.
. . .

I believe all of these things. Yet which of these propositions are contents of *bona fide* beliefs in the background of my consciously thinking "the earth does not normally roll beneath me as I walk"?

It is implausible that my conscious thought actively engages all these beliefs. I do not explicitly think these propositions along with the featured proposition. At most I would assent to such propositions if I were to turn my attention somehow to these collateral ideas. But as we list various propositions to which I would assent, or propositions to which I could be expected to reason rather naturally were I to think on-and-on about the earth and my walking – sooner or later, it becomes implausible that all these apparent *belief states* are a proper part of the system of background beliefs on which my thought actually depends. And yet, the force of something like these beliefs seems to be operative as I think "the earth does not normally roll beneath me as I walk". The corresponding background *propositions* seem to be in force for me, implicitly. Not only do I have the practical skills or know-how that does the work (as Searle has argued). But moreover, the relevant background *propositions* themselves seem to form a bedrock for our more mundane experiences, thoughts, and actions.

The preceding line of argument for the background has a form we may summarize as follows. First, assume that an intentional "act" has a content, the content of a propositional attitude being a proposition that prescribes a particular state of affairs. Second, from examples observe that an act presupposes a lot of other things, such as collateral beliefs or knowledge, cognate practices, know-how, etc. Third, from plausibility considerations observe that these items are too much or too inappropriate to be in the content itself. Finally, conclude that they form a background presupposed by the act but not explicitly included in its content.

The background of intentionality, then, includes our fundamental "assumptions" about the world we are dealing with in our intentional activities. But these "assumptions" do not seem always to be *bona fide* background beliefs. For one thing, they outrun the range of beliefs plausibly presupposed by our intentional activities. Furthermore, they often involve practical behavioral skills rather than belief, along with attitudes of evaluation rather than belief, and they may involve sensory imagery, or indeed a sense of the world somehow more fundamental than belief. Moreover, these "assumptions" often reside in cultural formations with a life of their own, extant in my culture rather than in mental formations "in my head". (Here I play on both Husserl's notion of *Lebenswelt* or life-world and Wittgenstein's notion of *Lebensform* or form-of-life.)

4. How the background works

The theory of the *background* of intentionality features four principles bearing on the present discussion:[14]

(1) Our intentional acts or attitudes presuppose a *background* of beliefs, skills, emotions, values, social practices, physical conditions including neural states, and more.
(2) A crucial part of this background is our fundamental, open-ended *background image* of the world around us, indicating how things are as well as how we do things, even how we use our bodies.
(3) This background image consists of *intentional contents* including concepts, propositions, values, rules of practice, and items of know-how presupposed in the activities of people in the relevant community.
(4) This relation of presupposition between an intentional act and its background is a relation of *ontological dependence*.

The background is thus part of the "ground" of intentionality: what makes it possible and enables it to work. More precisely, drawing the notion of dependence out of Husserl's ontology and applying it to the background: intentionality *depends* or is *founded* ontologically on certain background conditions, in that the intentionality could not exist – the experience could not intend what it does – unless those background conditions existed.[15] (This notion of dependence belongs to formal as opposed to material ontology.[16])

For Searle the background consists of practical capacities or know-how, which take over where intentional states like belief leave off. What Searle has christened "Background" (with a capital 'B'), viz. capacities or know-how, is only a part of a wider background of intentionality (we'll drop the capital 'B'). His argument, however, has drawn a bead on the phenomenon of background, which I propose to explicate further and in different ways.

Searle's inspiration was Wittgenstein's last and posthumous work, *On Certainty*.[17] The crucial notion there was that of "fundamental empirical propositions" in our background "world-picture". These "ground propositions" – such as "Here is a hand" (G.E. Moore's example) – form the foundation of our beliefs about the world around us and merge with our rules of practice. To develop a proper conception of the background, we must see that these ground propositions not only are

[14] Here I draw, sometimes verbatim, on D.W. Smith, "Background Ideas", published as "Idee di sfondo" (1999).

[15] Husserl's notion of dependence, or founding (*Fundierung*), was laid out in the Third of his *Logical Investigations* (1900-01). This notion is applied to background conditions that serve as grounds of intentionality, specifically "direct" awareness, in Chapter VI of D.W. Smith, *The Circle of Acquaintance* (1989).

[16] This conception of formal and material ontology was launched by Husserl in his *Logical Investigations* (1900-01) and given a sharp focus in the opening chapter of his *Ideas* I (1913). See D. W. Smith, "Mind and Body" (1995).

[17] See Wittgenstein, *On Certainty* (1972).

part of the *epistemological* foundation for various beliefs (conferring evidence), but along with cognate rules-of-practice are part of the *ontological* foundation of various forms of intentionality. Our everyday propositional attitudes and our ascriptions of them depend on such ground propositions *cum* rules-of-practice.

Wittgenstein's notion of our background world-picture can be developed further in terms of Husserl's earlier notion of the "life-world" or "human world"[18] (a precursor to Heidegger's notion of "world" as in our "being-in-the-world"). Our everyday "sense" of the world forms our background world-picture, which depicts the world as we know it in everyday life, the life-world. In Husserlian terms, this world-picture is a construct of intentional contents or "noemata", embracing concepts, images, propositions, volitions, etc., carried by attitudes of perception, belief, emotion, etc.

Our background world-picture is empirical and highly contingent. It is in many ways a product of human activity, a cultural artifact developed tacitly over thousands of generations. Accordingly, we shall find, the ontological status of the contents in our world-picture is not plausibly that of Platonic or Fregean thoughts and norms in a Platonic heaven. Rather, their status is akin to artworks as characterized by Roman Ingarden following Husserl's account of cultural objects: they are objectively existing abstract entities (so far Platonic), yet they are brought into existence and maintained in existence by acts of consciousness (no longer Platonic).[19]

And if background images or ideas are intentional, cultural artifacts, ultimately so are all intentional contents. This crucial point about the ontology of contents emerges naturally but surprisingly from reflection on the background of intentionality, more naturally than from reflection on the explicit content of a mental act.

5. The role of background

I want to incorporate the notion of background into the classical content theory of intentionality, whose *locus classicus* lies in Husserl, a similar view found today in Searle.[20] According to this theory, an intentional state or act-of-consciousness is experienced by a subject ("I"), has a content, and through its content "intends" or is intentionally related to an object (if such exists). So the structure of an intentional relation is this:

---

[18] Husserl's notion of the "life-world" (*Lebenswelt*) is central in *The Crisis of European Sciences and Transcendental Phenomenology* (1970). Closer detail is found in his account of the "spiritual world" (*geistigen Welt*), also called the "human" (*menschlich*) or "personalistic" world, in *Ideas* II (1952). See Føllesdal, "The *Lebenswelt* in Husserl" (1990), B. Smith, "Common Sense" (1995), and D. W. Smith, "Mind and Body" (1995).

[19] See Ingarden, *The Ontology of the Work of Art* (1961) and *Time and Modes of Being* (1964). Compare Thomasson, *Fiction and Metaphysics* (1999), for a contemporary treatment simplifying and extending the results of Ingarden and Husserl.

[20] See Smith and McIntyre, *Husserl and Intentionality* (1982), and Searle, *Intentionality* (1983).

I — act — content ——> object.

The content is a percept, concept, idea, thought, etc. The content prescribes the object as having certain properties. (The short arrow depicts this part of the intentional relation, the long arrow depicting the whole intentional relation of act by subject to object through content.) In Husserl's version of the story, content mediates the intentional relation much as sense mediates reference in language. In Searle's variation, the content determines the "conditions of satisfaction" of the act/state, the conditions under which the intentional state would be satisfied.

To apply the content theory properly to propositional attitudes, we need to distinguish between states of affairs and propositions. Recent philosophers of language, following Kaplan and alluding to Russell, often collapse this distinction, but we cannot handle propositional attitudes without it. A proposition or "thought" is a content ("sense", *Sinn*) that is propositional in form, and so expressible by a declarative sentence such as 'Wittgenstein was clever'. Its constituents are "ideas", namely, the predicative concept of cleverness and an appropriate nominal concept of Ludwig Wittgenstein. By contrast, a state of affairs is not composed of ideas or concepts at all. The state of affairs that Wittgenstein was clever is composed of Ludwig himself (once flesh and blood) and his intellectual virtuosity (not some concept or idea thereof). What is the conceptual entity that is an idea or "sense" of Wittgenstein and is a constituent of the proposition that Wittgenstein was clever? From Mill to Kripke, we see that this concept is not a descriptive one like "the author of the *Tractatus*". To characterize such a concept is not easy but is a necessary part of the theory of propositional attitudes; I have tried elsewhere,[21] but our focus here is on background.

Now, an intentional act or attitude does not occur in isolation. It is connected, as Husserl and Searle have argued, with a system of beliefs the subject holds about the object or kind of object intended. These beliefs are part of what Husserl called the "horizon" of the act and define what Searle calls the "network".[22] As I would

[21] See the final chapter of Smith and McIntyre, *Husserl and Intentionality* (1982). Recent theories of "direct" reference may seem plausible until we take seriously the theory of intentionality and seek a rich enough notion of content. Then we cannot rest with the attempt to remain neutral about what "propositions" are, eliding them with putative states of affairs whose constituents are individuals and properties rather than *conceptual* entities.

[22] Searle originally distinguished the Network of background beliefs from the Background of practical capacities: see *Intentionality* (1983), Chapter 5. In *The Rediscovery of the Mind* (1992), Chapter 8, he argues that the Network is a special part of the Background, collapsing unconscious beliefs, and hence the Network, into neural dispositions in the Background. In *The Construction of Social Reality* (1995), Chapter 6, Searle again defines the Background as preintentional neural capacities. Husserl's notion of horizon is reconstructed in Smith and McIntyre, *Husserl and Intentionality* (1982), Chapter V. See §3 of Chapter V on the role of background beliefs, ranging from general beliefs (say, about birds) to fundamental ontological beliefs (say, about material objects) to concrete beliefs about a particular individual. Husserl defined the horizon of an act in different ways, none of which coincide with the definition of either network or background as discussed here, but which lead in clear ways into the issues of network and background. Husserl defined the horizon of an act as the range of possibilities

put it, the act presupposes, its intentionality depends on, a system of *background beliefs* whose contents are associated with the content of the act. In a picture:

$$\text{background beliefs} \vdash \langle \text{ I — act — content ——> object } \rangle.$$

(I use the T-bar to depict the relation of ontological dependence: the intentional relationship depends on a network of beliefs.) For instance, when I see yonder bird, I have a visual experience whose content is "that turkey vulture is gliding on a warm air current". This experience presupposes my background beliefs about birds, for instance, that birds have wings. These beliefs are not an occurrent part of my conscious experience of seeing the turkey vulture gliding (tipping this way, then that). Yet my visual experience presupposes these beliefs and could not have the intentional force it has – it could not represent a turkey vulture in flight – unless it rested upon those beliefs.[23]

An intentional act or attitude also rests on further conditions that are not tacit beliefs, but rather a system of *background practical abilities*. Husserl spoke of "habits" and kinesthesis[24]; Searle proposes a background of skills, bodily habits, or dispositions of the nervous system, glossed as "capacities".[25] When I see a turkey vulture overhead (not one of Searle's examples), my visual experience rests on my capacity or ability to turn my head and focus my eyes, my ability to recognize a turkey vulture in flight, my bird-watching know-how. These mind-brain states are not themselves intentional states, but they are an indispensable background of intentionality.

But there is still more to the background. As I watch the bird overhead, my experience of seeing "that bird" and my experience of thinking "That is a turkey vulture" presupposes not only various of my personal beliefs and bodily skills, but also a broad complex of *communal assumptions* about the world in which we live. Wittgenstein called this complex our background "world-picture". Our world-picture, he said, includes our *fundamental empirical propositions* about the world, for instance, that here is a hand, that I have two feet, that the earth has existed for a long time.[26] (Note the indexical, contextual aspects of these propositions.)These are "ground propositions" about the world in which we live, propositions that describe the world as we deal with it in basic ways in everyday life. Such proposi-

left open by the content of the act. These possibilities are empirically "motivated"; they are constrained not only by the explicit content of the act, but also by the "implicit" content, that is, the content of relevant background beliefs.

[23] This kind of presupposition, taken as precondition or "ground" of intentionality, is discussed in D.W. Smith, *The Circle of Acquaintance* (1989), Chapter VI. The kindred notion of logical presupposition, a special form of dependence in Husserl's sense, is noted in Simons, *Parts* (1987): see pp. 290ff.

[24] See Husserl, *Ideas* II (1952). Kinesthesis is awareness of intentional bodily movements. These may be defined by cultural practices (*Geist*). Habits or habitual behaviors may involve both, and may involve very little explicit consciousness of movement. Cf. Dreyfus (1991).

[25] Again see Searle, *Intentionality* (1983), Chapter 5, and *The Rediscovery of the Mind* (1992), Chapter 8.

[26] Wittgenstein, *On Certainty* (1972), remarks 1ff, 94–96, 136, 151ff, 202ff, 308–309, 401, 411.

tions, Wittgenstein observed, shade off into *rules of practice*, governing not only linguistic activity (language-games) but also bodily activity (walking across the room, with my two feet, or sitting in the chair, without checking to see that it has legs). For Wittgenstein, then, the background would consist of fundamental propositions shading into rules of practice. What Searle has done, in effect, is to bring the background rules indoors, from the surrounding community into the individual's nervous system, as internalized norms of behavior: in fact, as neural states that produce behavior in accord with the rules in the community (rule-governed, not rule-following behavior, as Searle rightly stresses).[27] Both beliefs and skills or capacities are mental (in Searle's later scheme, both are neural dispositions). However, I want to insist that our background world-picture consists of propositions and rules that are objectively extant in our culture; they do not reduce to mental (or indeed neural) states, and they perdure outside our minds, with a cultural life of their own. Propositions and rules do not disappear from our ontology on closer look; rather, we cannot explain intentionality – or speech phenomena – without them!

Once the background is brought in, I propose, the ontological structure of intentionality would look like this:

$$\text{background} \vdash \langle \text{I} — \text{act} — \text{content} \longrightarrow \text{object} \rangle.$$

On this model, the *intentionality* of an act or attitude – the relationship binding subject, act, content, and object – depends ontologically on its *background*. This background is a context of beliefs held by the subject, practical capacities the subject has acquired, conditions of the subject's neural system, the subject's psychological motivations, and the subject's cultural environment, which includes extant basic propositions and rules of practice concerning the subject's *Lebenswelt*. So, on the given model, the intentional relationship *cannot exist* unless the background of contextual conditions exist. Accordingly, the act's content can represent or prescribe what it does only against the background of the act.[28]

6. The background of attitudes *and* language *and* attitude reports

Propositional attitudes are inextricably linked with language, and with reports of propositional attitudes. The links among these phenomena are more apparent now in light of our account of the background.

---

[27] See Searle, *The Construction of Social Reality* (1995), pages 139–147.

[28] For the record, Searle (1983) separates the Network from the Background, where Searle (1992) incorporates the Network into the Background, reducing the Background to neural capacities devoid of mentality. I want to keep these separate, in order to keep the ontology as rich as it is. There really are unconscious beliefs in the background (*contra* Searle) of most or all of our attitudes and actions. And behind our attitudes are basic *propositions* while behind our actions are basic *rules* of practice.

Intentional activities – ranging from thought to perception to desire to action to speech – are not restricted to the properly "propositional" attitudes such as thinking that *p*. But let us focus only on the propositional attitudes *per se*, and now only on thinking that *p*.

Many of our thoughts are shaped by our language so that we could not think that "*p*" if we could not say or write '*p*' – use the sentence – in our own language. Indeed, we say we think *in English* (or in Japanese). In light of the theory of background we explain: when I am thinking that Husserl philosophized about intentionality, my so thinking *depends ontologically* on my native language English – in numerous ways. The name 'Husserl' I have acquired from linguistic usage in the philosophical community (the nominee died before I was born). The word 'intentionality' is a term of art used in 20th century philosophy. And the verb 'philosophize' derives from the genre of writing called by the name 'philosophy', which derives from the ancient Greek work. I simply could not have the thought whose content is the proposition "Husserl philosophized about intentionality" unless I were part of a community that writes and speaks not only English but also the idiom of academic philosophy in the 20th century. Accordingly, in my ambient culture – within the background of my thinking, speaking, and writing – there exists not only the *sentence* 'Husserl philosophized about intentionality', a form of speech and writing governed by rules-of-practice (in fact, a form-of-speech and a form-of-writing coordinated by the practice of alphabetic spelling), but also the *proposition* "Husserl philosophized about intentionality", an abstract intentional content. These forms of speaking/writing and thinking – the sentence and the proposition – co-evolved in 20th century culture. And so they are ontologically co-dependent. Here, following the theory of intentionality via content against background, is an account of how thought and language are interdependent: the dependence runs both ways, of course. This dependence is something distinct from the more familiar feature of language where – in the style of Husserl following Aristotle – my saying '*p*' normally serves to express the proposition "*p*" and (in Husserl's idiom) to "intimate" my underlying act of thinking that *p*.

Reports of propositional attitudes are also interlinked with thoughts and the language that shapes them. If Kasia says, 'David thinks that Husserl philosophized about intentionality', that report of my attitude also shares in the relevant background. Kasia's report itself depends ontologically on the presence in its background of the relevant linguistic practices and – according to the account of background adduced above – the proposition that serves as content of the attitude ascribed to me.

In short, intentional activities of thinking, speaking or writing, and reporting someone's thinking – all depend on a common background that includes relevant rules of linguistic practice and relevant propositions or intentional contents. These are the kinds of entities we have divined within the background. The point here is that the same propositions and rules-of-language ground all three of the following activities (described so):

(a) David thinks that Husserl philosophized about intentionality,
(b) David says, 'Husserl philosophized about intentionality',
(c) Kasia says, 'David thinks that Husserl philosophized about intentionality'.
The first is a propositional attitude, the second a speech act, the third a propositional attitude report (or act of reporting).

7. Pragmatics and semantics

Calling on the theory of intentionality, including the notion of background, we can explicate more carefully the philosophical foundation of the distinction between pragmatics and semantics – turning below to implications for propositional attitude reports.

The "meaning" of an expression I utter includes both *what I say*, that is, the content I express and communicate, and *what words I use* in the relevant *context*. A behavioristic analysis would reduce meaning to the physical forms of speech or writing themselves, in context of course. Then "meaning is use". (Although this slogan is widely taken as a gloss on later Wittgenstein, Wittgenstein himself was not a behaviorist and usually said, more subtly: when we know the use of an expression, we know its meaning.) A mentalistic analysis might reduce meaning to the "inner" rather than the "outer", to intentional content or to the speaker's intentions (to express and/or to communicate). But neither such reduction is sustainable when we look at the rich structure of language as an intentional activity of bodily action carrying intentional content and executed in social and physical context. In a proper intentionalistic theory, the meaning of an expression must be fully analyzed as involving speaker's and hearer's activities both mental and behavioral, their commerce with intentional contents as abstract ideas, their shared linguistic practices as defined by rules-of-use (abstract intentional contents, prescriptive rather than descriptive or interrogative), and their context both social and physical. Accordingly, we distinguish the *sense* and *use* of an expression: the sense is an intentional content, for a declarative sentence this being a proposition; the use is the pattern of speech or writing, a pattern of intentional bodily action according to social practice.

Then, whatever else an intentionalist linguistic theory may do, *semantics* will specify the intentional content or proposition normally expressed and conveyed by an expression, while *pragmatics* will specify the rules governing the use of an expression in relevant contexts. Semantics and pragmatics may and should still take the form of schematizing truth-conditions (for declarative sentences), using the algebraic structure of a model-theoretic or possible-worlds semantics/pragmatics – in the tradition of Frege, Tarski, Carnap, Hintikka, Montague, Kaplan, et al. But the *ontology* of intentional contents and indeed rules-of-use must be added to the familiar set-theoretic machinery if we are to truly reflect the structures of *intentionality* present in language. My aim is to bring out those structures of intentionality, notably of content and background, without here trying to formalize truth-conditions in the familiar way.

Still, the pragmatic/semantic distinction – first framed by Charles Morris with reference to Charles Sanders Peirce[29] – must be rethought in light of the semantics of indexicals, along the lines charted in David Kaplan, "Demonstratives" (1989). For Kaplan, a logic of indexicals is still "semantics" because it is systematic in assigning reference, "character" and "content" (in Kaplan's, not Husserl's sense), and truth-conditions: while character (in effect, rule-of-use) does not vary with context, reference and "content" (asserted state-of-affairs) do, but the variation is systematic and tracked by the formal semantics. Now, Montague's formal "pragmatics" was systematic also in this way, so we are deciding how to use the term. For Kaplan, I gather, the term 'pragmatics' should be reserved for the kind of nuanced variation in meaning *cum* use that is not systematic but fluid, and so cannot be written into a semantics, formal or informal.[30] Wittgenstein's discussion of specific "language games" would fall under this conception of pragmatics, and not under semantics. And Wittgenstein's final reflections, in *On Certainty*, serve to bring out features of what I have called the background of both language use and propositional attitudes, and considerations of this background fall under pragmatics, not semantics. Elsewhere I tried to show where intentionality should be worked into a semantics or pragmatics of indexicals[31]; here I want to bring in the notion of background.

There are thus two aspects of the "pragmatic" in our language. The first is the way in which our use of indexicals – 'this', 'I', 'now', 'here' – depends systematically on their context of use. The second is the way in which our language depends on very particular, culturally contingent, and variable features of context – features which cannot and should not be part of linguistic meaning in a narrower sense. Features of the background belong here. Systematic "pragmatics", we might say with Kaplan, is part of semantics; variable pragmatics is not.

Consider: At the dinner table (in modern America) I say to the diner on my left, "That's mine," pointing to the salad plate between our place settings. My meaning depends on the cultural practice that defines the small plate to the left of the large plate as part of that place setting. This rule of setting table is no part of the semantics of 'That's mine', clearly. It is, however, part of the background

---

[29] See the history traced in Tougas, *Context* (1998).

[30] In 1982 I audited a seminar at UCLA that Kaplan taught on philosophy of language, treating Frege, demonstratives, and Kaplan's own ideas. Another auditor asked a question that gave Kaplan pause over its motivation. "Oh," Kaplan exclaimed, "you're interested in *language*!" Indeed, the auditor was not only interested in Wittgensteinian views; she is today a celebrated poet – not a practitioner of formal semantics.

[31] See D.W. Smith, "Indexical Sense and Reference" (1981), and "Husserl on Demonstrative Reference and Perception". The notion of indexical sense, used there, is further elaborated in D.W. Smith, *The Circle of Acquaintance* (1989).

of our conversation at dinner. And this element of background is recounted in the pragmatics of my use of the sentence in that particular context on that occasion.

More unusual is the "deep" background of our language *cum* thought, as discussed above. When I say, 'That is a turkey vulture', pointing to the large bird circling overhead, my meaning depends on a deep background of propositions and rules-of-practice that define our *Lebenswelt.* This background includes, for instance, the propositions "Birds fly", "People walk", "The sky is above the earth", etc., and rules-of-practice about walking and talking. Such deep "assumptions" are no business of semantics, but they are the business of pragmatics – and in that vein I read Wittgenstein's *On Certainty.* Of course, linguists will not attend to these assumptions in the usual course of business, but the point is that dependence on such assumptions lies in the horizon of pragmatics.

8. The pragmatics of propositional attitude reports

Our long story of the background of intentionality in language and thought brings us now to some rather special consequences for the semantics and specifically the pragmatics of propositional attitude reports. One implication concerns propositions and the form of attitude reports; another concerns the "depth" of background ideas on which an attitude report rests. Neither would be evident without delving into the concept of background – far from the madding crowd of linguistics and formal semantics/pragmatics.

First, recall the *ontology* of propositions we elaborated by considering the background of intentionality. While propositions are abstract entities without a proper locus in spacetime, they are nonetheless "ideas" extant in a culture, and somehow brought into being in a culture, a social structure which itself occurs over a period of time and is distributed over a geography. (Similarly for rules of practice in a culture.) What then will the *semantics* of a propositional attitude report specify?

Consider the report cited above:

> Kasia says, 'David thinks that Husserl philosophized about intentionality'.

An intentional semantics will specify that the *sense* of Kasia's uttered sentence is itself a proposition: an intentional content which semantically represents a state of affairs with the structure:

> subject David — thinking — proposition "*p*" —> [state of affairs that *p*].

Such a semantics may be detailed on the model of a possible-worlds semantics incorporating sense as intentional content, along lines charted elsewhere.[32] Here,

[32] The later chapters of Smith and McIntyre, *Husserl and Intentionality* (1982), outline this approach, synthesizing a Husserlian account of intentionality with a Hintikka-style possible-worlds semantics

however, I want to advert to a suggestion extrapolating from a well-known proposal by Donald Davidson: the word 'that' in a propositional attitude report '*a* thinks that *p*' is a kind of demonstrative pronoun.[33] If a proposition is a *bona fide* entity (a view Davidson was exercised to resist), then in the above attitude report Kasia's utterance of 'that' serves to point to something in Kasia's cultural context, namely, a *proposition* which we too would express by the sentence Kasia utters following 'that'. We hearers together with speaker Kasia understand by the sentence 'Husserl philosophized about intentionality' a certain proposition extant in our intentional-linguistic culture. According to the intentional semantics or pragmatics I am suggesting, then, Kasia's attitude report ascribes to David an attitude of thinking whose content is the proposition demonstrated and so designated by Kasia in saying 'that' followed by 'Husserl philosophized about intentionality'. She is referring not to the sentence following 'that', but to the proposition it expresses, an abstract entity extant in her and our culture.

Thus, the semantics/pragmatics of attitude reports is amplified by the enriched ontology of propositions that was wrought by the theory of background. For it was considerations of background that brought out the dependence of thought and language on each other and on propositions extant in the background of our thought and speech. The present interpretation of 'that' in propositional attitude reports joins with Kaplan's understanding of a systematic "pragmatics" which he would prefer to call a semantics. What is novel in the present suggestion is that the demonstrative pronoun 'that' can be used to refer to a proposition, taken as an abstract idea extant in the speaker's culture.

Now for the second implication of the concept of background. Recall our considerations of "deep" background assumptions behind thought and speech. Let us review the cases of Ortcutt and the two Mias, with which we opened our reflections on the pragmatics of attitude reports.

The Ortcutt case is underdescribed. The details concern the speaker's and Ralph's perceptions and beliefs about particular individuals (Ortcutt and a man on the beach in eyesight of Ralph and the speaker). The semantics or systematic pragmatics of the speaker's report, 'Ralph believes of Ortcutt that he is a spy', does not itself specify the background conditions on which the report and the reported belief depend. To interpret this belief report we thus need to specify those background conditions, and this task belongs to what we called variable pragmatics.

---

for propositional attitude reports. Smith, "Indexical Sense and Reference" (1981) applies this type of semantics to indexical pronouns, especially demonstrative pronouns used in contexts of perception, on which see also, with reference to Husserl's work, Smith, "Husserl on Demonstrative Reference and Perception" (1982).

[33] In "On Saying That" (1984), Donald Davidson proposed that the word 'that' in '*a* says that *p*' can be understood on the model of the demonstrative in 'I wish I'd said that' where referring to what was just said. The suggestion might be extended to propositional attitudes, where 'that' in '*a* believes that *p*' is understood on the model of the demonstrative in 'I believe that' where referring to what was just said.

The Mia cases are still trickier. In each case, after Mia says to Edward, 'I am your mother', Edward later says, 'Mia thinks that she is my mother'. The semantics, or systematic pragmatics, must handle the indexical terms: 'I' and 'your' uttered by Mia and then 'she' and 'my' uttered by Edward in reporting Mia's attitude. The content of Mia's thought, expressed by her own statement and attributed to her by Edward's report, is the *indexical proposition* "I am your mother", including the *indexical senses* "I" and "your". Here we need a detailed phenomenology of awareness of self and other, featuring essentially indexical contents which prescribe self and other in the relevant context. (The phenomenology is detailed in my book *The Circle of Acquaintance* (1989).) The semantics of Mia's statement and Edward's report of her attitude must make use of these indexical contents and their dependence on context. But, as the details are worked out, the semantics is a systematic pragmatics.

The differences between the two Mia cases described earlier, however, take pragmatics into the deeper background. In Case 1 the attitude report and the attitude reported depend on Mia's and Edward's background assumptions about parental psychology. In Case 2, however, the attitude and the attitude report depend on Mia's and Edward's background assumptions about reincarnation. In both cases the background "assumptions" may reside not in *bona fide* beliefs held by Mia and Edward, but in propositions and rules-of-practice extant in their cultural communities – say, in the expertise of psychiatrists in Case 1 and of spiritual elders in Case 2. At any rate, these background assumptions have no place in the semantics, or systematic pragmatics, of the sentences 'I am your mother' and 'Mia thinks that she is my mother'. This kind of background can be assessed only in the wide-ranging variable pragmatics that takes us into the "deep" background of language, thought, and culture, into the propositions and rules-of-practice that define our *Lebenswelt*.

The trajectory of this essay is such a study in the variable pragmatics of propositional attitude reports.

References

Block, N., Flanagan, O. and Güzeldere, G. (eds) (1997), *The Nature of Consciousness*, MIT Press, Cambridge.

Davidson, D. (1984), *On saying that*, Davidson, *Inquiries into Truth and Interpretation*, Oxford University Press, Oxford. Reprinted from *Synthese* **19** (1968-69) 130–146.

Dawkins, R. (1968-69), *The Selfish Gene*, Oxford University Press, Oxford.

Dreyfus, H. (1991), *Being-in-the-World*, MIT Press, Cambridge.

Fine, K. (1995), *Ontological dependence*, Meeting of the Aristotelian Society, Birkbeck College, London.

Føllesdal, D. (1990), *The Lebenswelt in Husserl*, Language, Knowledge, and Intentionality: Perspectives on the Philosophy of Jaakko Hintikka (Acta Philosophica Fennica, Vol. 49, Helsinki), L. Haaparanta, M. Kusch and I. Niiniluoto, eds, 123–143.

Hintikka, J. (1969), *Semantics of propositional attitudes*, in his *Models for Modalities*, D. Reidel Publishing Company, Dordrecht.

Hintikka, M.B. and Hintikka, J. (1986), *Investigating Wittgenstein*, Basil Blackwell, London.

Husserl, E. (1990-01), *Logical Investigations*, Vols 1, 2 (transl. by J.N. Findlay, Routledge, 1970; German original published in 1900–01; second edition in 1913).

Husserl, E. (1913), *Ideas I*, i.e., *Ideas pertaining to a Pure Phenomenology and to a Phenomenological Philosophy, First Book: General Introduction to Phenomenology* (transl. by J. Boyce Gibson, 1962; German original published in 1913).

Husserl, E. (1952), *Ideas II*, i.e., *Ideas pertaining to a Pure Phenomenology and to a Phenomenological Philosophy, Second Book: Studies in the Phenomenology of Constitution* (transl. by R. Rojcewicz and A. Schuwer, Kluwer Academic Publishers, Dordrecht and Boston, 1989; original manuscript dating from 1912; posthumously published in German in 1952).

Husserl, E. (1970), *The Crisis of European Sciences and Transcendental Phenomenology* (transl. by D. Carr, Northwestern University Press, Evanston, 1970; German original published in 1954; edited by Walter Biemel from materials written in 1935–38).

Husserl, E. (1973), *Experience and Judgment* (transl. by J.S. Churchill and K. Ameriks, revised and edited by Ludwig Landgrebe; Northwestern University Press, Evanston, 1973).

Ingarden, R. (1961), *The Ontology of the Work of Art* (transl. by R. Meyer with J.T. Goldthwait, Ohio University Press, Athens, 1989; German original published in 1961).

Ingarden, R. (1964), *Time and Modes of Being* (transl. by H.R. Michejda and C.C. Thomas, Publisher, Springfield, IL, 1964; from excerpts of the Polish original titled "The Controversy over the Existence of the World", 1946/47).

Jaszczolt, K.M. (1996), *Reported speech, vehicles of thought, and the horizon*, Lingua et Stile **31** (1), 113–133.

Kaplan, D. (1989), *Demonstratives*, Themes from Kaplan, J. Almog, J. Perry and H. Wettstein, eds, Oxford University Press, New York.

Lowe, E.J. (1994), *Ontological dependency*, Philosophical Papers **23** (1), 31–48.

Quine, W.V.O. (1956), *Quantifiers and propositional attitudes*, Journal of Philosophy **53**.

Searle, J.R. (1969), *Speech Acts*, Cambridge University Press, Cambridge, 1969, 1970.

Searle, J.R. (1983), *Intentionality*, Cambridge University Press, Cambridge.

Searle, J.R. (1990), *Collective intentions and actions*, Intentions in Communication, P.R. Cohen, J. Morgan and M.E. Pollack, eds, MIT Press, Cambridge, 401–415.

Searle, J.R. (1992), *The Rediscovery of the Mind*, MIT Press, Cambridge.

Searle, J.R. (1995), *The Construction of Social Reality*, The Free Press, Simon & Schuster Inc., New York.

Simons, P.M. (1987), *Parts*, Oxford University Press, Oxford.

Smith, B. (ed.) (1982), *Parts and Moments*, Philosophia Verlag, Munich.

Smith, B. (1995), *Common sense*, The Cambridge Companion to Husserl, B. Smith and D.W. Smith, eds, Cambridge University Press, Cambridge, 394–437.

Smith, D.W. (1981a), *Indexical sense and reference*, Synthese **49** (1), 100–127.

Smith, D.W. (1981b), *The Ortcutt connection*, Ambiguities in Intensional Contexts, F. Heny, ed., D. Reidel Publishing Company, 103–131.

Smith, D.W. (1982), *Husserl on demonstrative reference and perception*, Husserl, Intentionality, and Cognitive Science, H.L. Dreyfus, ed., MIT Press/Bradford Books, 193–213.

Smith, D.W. (1989), *The Circle of Acquaintance*, Kluwer Academic Publishers, Dordrecht.

Smith, D.W. (1991), *Thoughts*, Philosophical Papers **19** (3), 163–189.

Smith, D.W. (1992), *Consciousness in action*, Synthese **90**, 119–143.

Smith, D.W. (1995), *Mind and body*, The Cambridge Companion to Husserl, B. Smith and D.W. Smith, eds, Cambridge University Press, Cambridge, 323–393.

Smith, D.W. (1999), *Background ideas* (translation in Italian as Idee di sfondo in *Paradigmi*, XVII, 49, 7–37 (Rome, 1999)).

Smith, D.W. and McIntyre, R. (1982), *Husserl and Intentionality: A Study of Mind, Meaning, and Language*, D. Reidel Publishing Company, Dordrecht.

Thomasson, A. (1994), *Fiction and intentionality*, Philosophy and Phenomenological Research, forthcoming, manuscript of 1994.

Thomasson, A. (1999), *Fiction and Metaphysics*, Cambridge University Press, Cambridge.

Tougas, J.A. (1998), *Context: Its role as an explanatory concept in the philosophy of language and indexicality as a clue to its structure and dynamics*, Doctoral dissertation, University of California, Irvine.

Wittgenstein, L. (1921), *Tractatus Logico-Philosophicus* (transl. by D.F. Pears and B.F. McGuinness, Humanities Press International, Inc., Atlantic Highlands, NJ, 1992; this translation first published in 1961; other editions by Routledge & Kegan Paul; German original first published in 1921).

Wittgenstein, L. (1972), *On Certainty* (edited by G.E.M. Anscombe and G.H. von Wright, transl. by D. Paul and G.E.M. Anscombe, Harper Torchbooks, Harper & Row, New York, 1972; first published by Basil Blackwell, 1969; from notebooks written in German during 1949–1951).

Author Index

Upright numbers refer to pages on which the author (or his/her work) is mentioned in the text of a chapter. Italic numbers refer to reference list pages. (No distinction is made between first and coauthor(s).)

Subject Index